PROSPERITY THROUGH COMPETITION

PROSPERITY *through* COMPETITION

by

LUDWIG ERHARD

Vice-Chancellor and Minister for Economic Affairs of the German Federal Republic

FREDERICK A. PRAEGER

New York

The original German edition

WOHLSTAND FÜR ALLE

was prepared in collaboration with

Dr. Wolfram Langer and published by

Econ Verlag Düsseldorf

ENGLISH VERSION TRANSLATED AND EDITED BY

Edith Temple Roberts and

John B. Wood

Books that matter

PUBLISHED IN THE UNITED STATES OF AMERICA IN 1958 BY

FREDERICK A. PRAEGER, INC., PUBLISHERS, 15 WEST 47 STREET, NEW YORK 36, N.Y.

LIBRARY OF CONGRESS CATALOG CARD NUMBER 58-8185

PRINTED IN GREAT BRITAIN

CONTENTS

KEY TO ABBREVIATIONS

BDL — *Bank Deutscher Länder* (Central Bank)
CDU — *Christlich-demokratische Union* (Christian Democrats)
CSU — *Christlich-soziale Union* (Christian Socialists)
DGB — *Deutscher Gewerkschaftsbund* (German Council of Trade Unions)
DM — *Deutschmark* (after 1948)
ECA — Economic Co-operation Administration
EPU — European Payments Union
GARIOA — Government Appropriations for Relief in Occupied Areas
GATT — General Agreement on Tariffs and Trade
LTP — Long Term Plan
MSA — Mutual Security Administration
NATO — North Atlantic Treaty Organization
OEEC — Organization for European Economic Co-operation
RM — *Reichsmark* (before 1948)
SPD — *Sozialdemokratische Partei Deutschlands* (Social Democrats)

PREFACE

THE PUBLICATION of an English-language edition of *Wohlstand für Alle*, which since its first appearance nine months ago has run through six editions, gives me a welcome opportunity to make a few prefatory remarks.

As readers of the book will readily appreciate, conditions in West Germany were quite abnormal when I took over the direction of its economic affairs at the beginning of 1948. Therefore we must step warily when drawing international comparisons. For the success of one country does not necessarily bear a direct relation to the progress made by its neighbour. I would remind my readers, for example, of the 12 million refugees and stateless persons who poured into a geographically restricted West Germany during the twelve years following the end of hostilities, which means that 23% of its present population did not inhabit this territory prior to the war; of the lessening of output-potential resulting from dismantling and proscriptions applied to production, of the factories and dwellings that had been destroyed, and the dividing up of what was formerly a single economic area.

Nevertheless, as is so often the case in the life of individuals and of all peoples, all these factors have not had merely adverse effects. For example, the countless refugees who during the first post-war years exacerbated the terrible plight of our people, now in a time of full employment have become an asset. Demolitions and dismantlings fostered an urge to build anew, and what is more, it afforded an opportunity to introduce the most up-to-date machines and tools.

Notwithstanding the many differences between nations, which must always be borne in mind, the success which attended German economic policy has a bearing outside German frontiers; this is particularly the case at a time when all progressive politicians are striving to contribute towards breaking down the barriers that still separate the various countries. The principle and application of what I have called 'die soziale Marktwirtschaft'—i.e. a social market economy—was given renewed support by a vast majority of the people at the Bundestag elections of 15th September, 1957. Its success can be traced in every department of the country's economy and in every grade of society. I need only mention that our production today is nearly two and a half times that of the best pre-war year. Our industrial potential has multiplied six times since the currency reform. Our exports, estimated at DM 36 milliard for the current year, put us in third place in world trade. Gold and foreign currency reserves have risen from nil in 1948 to today's total of DM 23 milliard. It is especially gratifying to record that in the same period it was possible to treble the social services, as well as to build more than 4 million houses since 1949, the year when the first Federal Government came into operation.

In outlining these events my sole concern is to demonstrate that we in West Germany have resorted to anything but a secret science. That, in fact, I have merely attempted to apply in practice the principles of modern national economics which all the countries of the West have evolved, with a view to overcoming the age-old antithesis of an unbridled liberalism and a soulless State control, to finding a sound middle way between out-and-out freedom and totalitarianism. It is these endeavours that form the subject of this book.

The appearance of an English edition at this juncture is of particular significance, since it is more necessary than ever to bring the national economies of the free Western world closer together. The suggestion first mooted by the British Government that the Common Market should be supplemented by an extensive free trade zone was immediately welcomed by me. In this I was guided by the conviction that the various national economies had to be orientated farther and farther away from the narrow paths into which the misfortunes of war had led them; nor was this to apply only to small territories. For this reason I emphasized from the outset, and again at the ministerial meeting of O.E.E.C. in Paris on 16th October, 1957, that the transition from a Common Market to a Free Trade zone was an essential element of wise European statesmanship. I believe that such a plan would be in the interests not only of the six countries of the European Common Market, but also of the 11 other members of O.E.E.C. A combination of Free Trade zone and Common Market would give rise to new and beneficial factors. It is not, then, a question of simple addition. Here, as so often, it is a question of the whole being greater than the sum of its parts. Europe will, both in the economic and in the social sphere, benefit incalculably from such a development. The quantitative aspect, that is, the knitting together of Common Market and Free Trade zone, will, I feel absolutely convinced, be converted into a qualitative aspect—a more intensive European collaboration, which will profit all the partners.

If the desire for greater economic integration is today one of the overriding issues, there are other questions and problems that actively concern every government and every people. A generous, international exchange of ideas will therefore be of the greatest benefit all round. Of late, the Federal Government has had to fight, like the governments of other countries, to keep up the value of its currency, to stabilize prices and at the same time to maintain economic progress. There are many echoes in this book of such struggles, and this seems to call for further comment. The Germans are perhaps more concerned about the success of these endeavours than anyone else. Within a single generation they experienced two periods of inflation that were more or less unprecedented in the economic history of the world. So far German economic policy has succeeded on the whole in maintaining the desired stability ever since the currency reform of 1948—a success which is due in equal measure to the implementation of such a policy and the disciplined behaviour of both worker and employer, which fortunately has at the same time been coupled with a continued trade expansion.

If this policy is to continue to be successful, if the slight falling-off in purchasing power that has recently manifested itself is to be remedied, then it will be more than ever necessary to have recourse to unconventional methods. As responsible Minister for Economic Affairs in the Federal Republic, I am therefore determined not to countenance any further price increases without keeping the people fully informed about the causes and effects of such harmful moves. An end must be put to the all-too-familiar and absurd game of wage increases following rises in prices and of price increases following rises in pay. A stage must be reached when individual sections are ashamed to put forward demands that are contrary to the welfare of the community as a whole. My endeavours in this direction are the subject of this book, which also aims to convey to the reader a knowledge of practical economics. But the success of this, perhaps the most important, assignment of every minister of economics in the West depends to a large extent upon whether international co-operation is directed towards these ends.

In my opinion, the historic task of the Federal Republic in the second half of the 20th century that we have just entered upon is to underpin, to strengthen and to defend the free economic order of Europe with the full weight of German trade. The successful rehabilitation of my country must serve as clear documentary evidence to put before the still vacillating and doubting peoples, of the fact that only by firmly rejecting socialist dogmas, of whatever complexion, and by affirming a free economic order can mounting prosperity and genuine security be achieved. In a Europe which allowed the life of the individual to be dragooned into ever more regimented collectives, the intellectual and spiritual powers would atrophy—powers that are vitally necessary in order to combat the infiltration, and also the many enticements, of the East.

LUDWIG ERHARD

Bonn, November 1957

Chapter I

THE THREAD

ON THE OCCASION of the C.D.U. meeting at Recklinghausen in the British zone at the end of August 1948, and some time before I took over the Ministry for Economic Affairs of the first West German Federal Republic, I outlined my attitude to the ideas which were then in the air about the distribution of incomes. I explained my refusal to allow them to take hold again, for I considered them to be false. I wished to remove all doubts about my aim, which was to create an economic structure within which it would be possible to lead ever widening circles of the German people towards prosperity. Determined to overcome the old conservative social structure once and for all, I planned for a broadly based mass-purchasing power.

The old hierarchy was marked on the one hand by a thin upper crust able to afford anything, and on the other by a broad lower stratum with insufficient purchasing power. The reshaping of our economic order had to work towards two things: to bring to an end this division, which hampered progressive development, and to end with it ill-feeling between rich and poor. I do not wish to hide either the material or the moral foundations of my struggle. They determine my actions now as then.

Competition is the most promising means to achieve and to secure prosperity. It alone enables people in their role of consumer to gain from economic progress. It ensures that all advantages which result from higher productivity would eventually be enjoyed.

Along the road of competition, the socialization—in the best sense of the word—of progress and profit is best realized. In addition, personal incentive for higher productivity will remain alive. To allow all working people to receive steadily increasing wages out of higher productivity is a natural part of the belief that through competition prosperity can best be increased. Important assumptions must be made to meet this aim. In considering growing consumption we must not take higher productivity for granted. From the start the emphasis was on an expansion of the economy, especially on an increase in the amount of goods for sale, in order to give an impetus to competition. Above all, the growing number of those seeking work had to be found jobs.

The Trade Cycle Overcome

Circumstances made it vital that the old universally held laws of the cyclical development of the economy should be overthrown. It was widely held that the economy moved forwards in rhythmic waves. Seven years were said to cover the period in which recovery, boom, decline and crisis developed, followed by a convalescence during which healing powers gathered strength to start the next cycle. It is now almost nine years since I became responsible for German economic policy, during which time this rigid rhythm has been broken, thus achieving a steady upward trend of the economy, linked with full employment and a rising volume of goods for sale.

It is against this background that my endeavours and hopes to make economic policy and economic theory successful in finding systematic solutions to these problems should be understood. Such efforts will, however, only be successful as long as competition is not hindered or eliminated through artificial or legal manipulations.

The danger of limitation of competition threatens constantly from many sides. One of the most important tasks in a country based on a free social order is, therefore, to secure free competition. It is no exaggeration when I declare that a law against monopoly is essential as an indispensable 'economic principle'. Should the State fail here, there would be an early end to the 'social market economy'. This principle means that no individual citizen must be powerful enough to suppress individual freedom, or, in the name of false freedom, to be able to limit it. 'Prosperity for all' and 'Prosperity through Competition' are inseparable. The former marks the aim, the latter the path leading to it.

These few remarks already show the fundamental difference between the social market economy and the liberal economy of the old days. Businessmen who believe that because of modern economic developments they can demand cartels are like those Social Democrats who conclude that automation inevitably leads to State control. This reflection should shed light on my theory that it is infinitely more useful to increase prosperity by expansion than to try for a different distribution of the national income by pointless quarrelling.

I do not in any way wish to say that the present division of the national income is the only defensible one or that it should remain as it is for ever. An example may explain briefly what I have in mind: between 1949—when the Federal Republic adopted the social market economy—and 1955, we successfully raised the gross national income from DM 47 Mrd. to DM 85·8 Mrd., while for 1956 another increase of about 7-8% was achieved.

Gross National Income 1936-1955
(expressed in 1936 prices)
in Mrd. DM

1936	1949	1950	1951	1952	1953	1954	1955	1956
47·9	47·1	54·8	62·7	66·7	71·6	77·5	85·8	91·9 (*estimated*)

This measure of the undisputed success of the policy demonstrates how much more sensible it is to concentrate all available energies on increasing the nation's wealth rather than to squabble over the distribution of this wealth, and thus be sidetracked from the fruitful path of increasing the national income. It is considerably easier to allow everyone a larger slice out of a bigger cake than to gain anything by discussing the division of a smaller cake.

I have been scolded repeatedly because I lack all sympathy for this sterile mode of thinking. Success has proved me right. German economic policy has produced a steadily increasing output from which everyone has benefited uninterruptedly year by year. Private consumption rose from 29 to 51 Mrd. DM between 1950 and 1955—expressed in 1936 prices. This striking increase takes first place when compared to that of other countries. According to the O.E.E.C., the index of private consumption per head of population rose in West Germany from 77 in 1949 to 126 in 1955 (at constant prices, 1952=100). During the same period in the U.S. it rose from 96 to 107; in France from 86 to 113; in Britain from 100 to 110, and in Sweden from 96 to 110. If the pre-war period is selected as a basis of comparison West Germany's achievement still easily surpassed the average of all O.E.E.C. countries. Even the most revolutionary reform of our social order could never have provoked such an increase, or part of it, in the private consumption of this or that group compared to what was in fact achieved. Any such attempt would have led to the paralysis and stagnation of our economy.

This scepticism towards the debate about the 'just' division of the national income springs from the belief that wage increases demanded on these lines are like the attempts of some sections of the population to gain advantages at the expense of others. Moreover, it is not easily appreciated that every demand for more presupposes that more is produced. Such an attitude, which can be called almost childish, endangers the basis of our progress. Public support for competition is here the most useful bar to all egoism. As in a healthy competitive economy the individual is not permitted to claim special privileges, so whole groups must not be allowed to benefit themselves in this manner.

My constant endeavour to direct all efforts towards expansion without endangering the healthy basis of our economy or currency rests on the belief that only thus can a suitably decent standard of living be guaranteed to those who, through no fault of their own, but because of age, sickness or as victims of two world wars, can no longer directly participate in production.

The growth of social service payments in recent years has justified this view. The increase in payments by the State from DM 9·6 Mrd. in 1949 to nearly DM 21 Mrd. in 1955, like the pensions reform, was only possible through economic progress. The poor have increasingly shared in prosperity, but only as a result of economic expansion. If, as is stated now, the Federal Republic can afford further and larger increases in social service payments, it can do so only because our economic policy allows us to rely on an increase in our national income in the future.

The Key to Lower Taxes

This belief in a policy of expansion is also essential from other points of view. The political observer will have to accept that the modern State today faces huge tasks. Even if everything possible is done to limit the functions of government—I have contributed by abolishing State planning and ending price controls—it will have to be recognized that midway in the 20th century the functions of the State are unlikely to shrink. Yet the just demands of all citizens and the needs of the economy to cut the tax burden must in the end be acknowledged.

This aim will only be achieved if government expenditure can be kept at its present level, which is not small. If this is done, then, as the national income increases it will bring relief to the citizen and to the economy. It should be recognized how much lower the tax burden could be in ten years, if by then the national income has grown to over DM 250 Mrd. compared to DM 90 Mrd. in 1949 and DM 192 Mrd. in 1956.

The bare facts of the recent past support this view. No one would assert that the individual tax burden has increased relatively since 1949. Yet the State income (Federal, Länder and Municipal) has risen from DM 23·7 Mrd. in 1949 to DM 54·45 Mrd. for the financial year 1955/56. This increase is purely the result of a steep rise in our national income.

If the ceiling to government spending which I have demanded can be imposed, and if the development of the national income continues as in recent times, it is easy to see and calculate the degree of tax reductions that could be undertaken. A true and real solution of this inhibiting tax problem would thus be possible.

Through this increase in general prosperity economic policy contributes something valuable to the democratization of West Germany. In both elections for the Federal Parliament the German voter has shown that he is overwhelmingly opposed to the class war.

The thread, then, is a desire, after years of effort, for increased general prosperity, and, if the only possible path leading to this goal is through increased economic competition, then economic policy is bound at the same time to strengthen the many traditional basic human freedoms.

Fundamental Economic Rights

First consideration must be given to the freedom of every citizen to live his life according to his financial circumstances, personal desires and values. This basic principle of freedom for the consumer must logically be counter-balanced by freedom for the producer to make and sell what he believes to be marketable, that is, what he has found, after studying individual needs, to be essential and likely to succeed. Freedom for the consumer and freedom to work must be explicitly recognized as inviolable basic rights by every citizen. To offend against them should be regarded as an outrage against society. Democracy and a free economy are as logically linked as are dictatorship and State controls.

To achieve increased prosperity, any policy which prefers apparent success to real progress must be abandoned. Whoever is serious in this must be prepared energetically to oppose all attacks on the stability of our currency. The social market economy is unthinkable without a parallel stability of the currency. Only a policy of this kind guarantees that individual sections of the population do not profit at the cost of others.

There have been several such attempts recently. Here, for example, we should mention the agreements of joint management concerns which have led to wage increases overtaking increases in productivity, thus offending against the principle of price stability. Employers who, for these reasons or out of self-interest, have raised prices can be similarly reproached. This could become a real curse if someone wished to introduce a deliberately inflationary policy in order to repay loans more easily. Far be it from me to suggest it, but it would be all the more a curse because even to make such an attempt would lead to a political disaster.

For that reason the trade unions should ask themselves whether their pursuit of higher wages, if it leads to higher prices, does not put them on a par with irresponsible speculators. The German people have reacted sharply in recent times even to the smallest increases in prices by reducing their rate of savings. For instance, the excess of new savings of DM 188·1 million in July 1955 turned into an excess of withdrawals of DM 109 million in July 1956. This serious development was reversed only as a result of energetic measures by the Federal Government.

Such a distorting trend could lead us not only into economic but also into sociological and political dangers. If such reflections are brought to their logical conclusion they should lead us to regard currency stability as one of those basic human rights which every citizen can demand from his Government.

Pyrrhic Victories

These principles can then only be put into practice if public opinion is prepared to give them priority over any selfish sectional interests. No further proof is needed to demonstrate how democracy is threatened than the lobbying and self-assertion of powerful groups. One does not need to be a pessimist to reach the conclusion that many democracies are facing a serious crisis on this score. The problem of organized pressure groups as part of society and the political structure has yet to be solved. This problem has in recent times allowed an increasing number of groups to demand more from the economy than it has been able to afford. Any successes so gained have already clearly proved themselves to be Pyrrhic victories. Every single citizen without exception pays for them every day and every hour through slightly higher prices. It is no consolation, but more a matter for regret, that these questionable successes have been achieved largely at the expense of those sections of the population who for sociological reasons are least able to protect themselves. The most recent price increases are almost exclusively due to the fact that, in spite of requests to be moderate, people have knowingly acted against their better judgment, ignoring all appeals and warnings.

If the future of our young democratic country is to be assured, it is high time it returned to the path of virtue. In this economic and social policy join forces. In the middle of the 20th century a prosperous economy is closely linked with the fate of a country, as, conversely, every Government or country is immediately affected by the failure of its economic policy. This interdependence of politics and economics forbids all narrow thinking. In the same way as the economist must feel a duty towards the democratic State, so must every politician recognize the outstanding importance of the economic well-being of the people and act accordingly.

The social market economy practised in the Federal Republic can claim recognition by politicians as an important and formative factor in the reconstruction of our democratic State. Over a very short period this economic policy has achieved a degree of reconstruction which must be historically unique. It has not only succeeded in providing work and bread for a population which has increased by a quarter, but it has also lifted all these people above the level of prosperity known in the best pre-war years. The social market economy has marched towards reconstruction along a hard but honest path and, by so doing, has regained the confidence of the world.

Chapter II

BIRTH OF THE MARKET ECONOMY

WHAT WAS THE POSITION when I was elected director of economic administration of the bi-zonal economic area on March 2, 1948? Much later—on May 31, 1954, in Antwerp—I described the period before currency reform in the following way:

> 'It was a time when most people did not want to believe that this experiment in currency and economic reform could succeed. It was a time when it was calculated that for every German there would be one plate every five years; a pair of shoes every twelve years; a suit every fifty years; that only every fifth infant would lie in its own napkins; and that only every third German would have a chance of being buried in his own coffin. That seemed to be the only life before us. This demonstrated the boundless delusion of planners that, on the basis of raw material stocks and other statistical data, the fate of a people could be determined for a long period in advance. These mechanists and *dirigistes* had absolutely no conception that, if a people were allowed once more to become aware of the value and worth of freedom, dynamic forces would be released.'

The reader's temper would be tried if I attempted to reconstruct here a complete picture of the days of currency reform, but a few of its aspects may not come amiss.

The first industrial plan, based on the Potsdam decisions of August 2, 1945, intended to limit German industrial capacity to 50-55% of the level of 1938 or to approximately 65% of that of 1936. In judging this plan it must be remembered that the population had been greatly increased by the stream of refugees. The attempt to carry out the plan foundered, above all because it was impossible to reunite Germany economically.

The second industrial plan, which was published by the Anglo-American military government for their zone on August 29, 1947, in principle allowed production up to the level achieved in 1936, with a number of limitations. In the meantime productive capacity was only 60% of that of 1936.

Suppressed Inflation Paralyses the Economy

Actual production of the bi-zone in 1947 amounted to only 39% of production in 1936. This sombre picture covered all parts of the economy. Textile production was barely one-seventh of present output.

Industrial Production in the Bi-zone
1936 = 100

	1946	*1947*
All Industry	33	39
Coal	51	65
Iron and Steel	21	25
Non-ferrous Metals	18	24
Chemicals	43	43
Mining and Quarrying	31	33
Vehicle Building	17	19
Electrical Engineering	36	65
Precision and Optical Instruments	30	30
Textiles	20	28
Leather and Shoes	26	27
Rubber Products	34	40
Woodpulp and Paper	20	21

To attempt in those post-war years to halt the inflation (the result of the questionable manner in which rearmament was financed between 1933 and 1939, and above all the cost of the war, amounting to about RM 560 milliard) by fixing prices and controls was more and more likely to fail. We endured the phenomenon of a 'price-frozen inflation'. The vast sum of money in circulation prevented any central economic planning. Turnover no longer went through regular wholesale and retail channels, or did so only in small part. Increasingly goods remained in the warehouses, except where they could be used in compensatory transactions and so sustain business on a small scale. We had returned to a state of primitive barter. The general index of production during the first half of 1948 moved around 50% of that of 1936. Dr. Wilhelm Röpke declared at the beginning of 1948 that Germany had been annihilated to such an extent, and plunged into such chaos, that no one who had not seen it with his own eyes could possibly imagine it.

This collapse naturally led to heated discussions about the best methods for recovery. Those who wanted a planned economy challenged those who wanted a market economy—a battle which animated not only the Germans but also the Allies. The next chapter—'Market Economy conquers the Planned Economy'—will give an account of these discussions. The German planners tended to collaborate closely with the occupying powers of the British zone who were acting on the instructions and following the ideas of the Labour Government which at that time was at the peak of its economic experiments. Liberal forces in West Germany, however, felt themselves more strongly attracted towards the Americans. It was no accident that as a result Victor Agartz headed the Central Office for Economic Affairs in Minden (British zone), while at the express wish of the U.S. occupying power I took over the Ministry for Economic Affairs of the Bavarian Government as from October 1945.

The Big Chance

The big chance for Germany came in 1948: it depended on linking the currency reform with an equally resolute economic reform, so as to end once and for all the whole complex of State controls of the economy—from production to the final consumer—which, following in the wake of the people's nonsensical demands, had lost all touch with reality. Today few can realize how much courage and sense of responsibility were needed for such a step. Some time later two Frenchmen, Jacques Rueff and André Piettre, summed up the combination of economic and currency reform thus:

> 'The black market suddenly disappeared. Shop windows were full of goods; factory chimneys were smoking; and the streets swarmed with lorries. Everywhere the noise of new buildings going up replaced the deathly silence of the ruins. If the state of recovery was a surprise, its swiftness was even more so. In all sectors of economic life it began as the clocks struck on the day of currency reform. Only an eye-witness can give an account of the sudden effect which currency reform had on the size of stocks and the wealth of goods on display. Shops filled up with goods from one day to the next; the factories began to work. On the eve of currency reform the Germans were aimlessly wandering about their towns in search of a few additional items of food. A day later they thought of nothing but producing them. One day apathy was mirrored on their faces while on the next a whole nation looked hopefully into the future.'[1]

The market economy was in fact introduced by a few decrees and by a determination not to compromise. The decision to create something quite new was expressed in the 'Gesetzes- und Verordnungsblatt des Wirtschaftsrates des Vereinigten Wirtschaftsgebietes' of July 7, 1948. On bad (pre-currency-reform) paper the law governing the principles of planning and price policy after currency reform was announced ('Gesetz über Leitsätze für die Bewirschaftung und Preispolitik nach der Geldreform'). This law gave the Director for Economic Administration the right to throw into the waste paper basket in one swoop hundreds of decrees promulgating controls and prices. Within the framework of these governing principles he was 'to take all necessary measures in the field of controls and to determine in detail which goods and production should be freed from price controls'. I was concerned to remove as quickly as possible as many measures of general control and price regulation as could be.

Next day the order 'concerning price fixing and price supervision after currency reform' was published, which abolished dozens of price regulations. We took the only possible path: we disposed of all that was invalid, and specifically named only what we wished to retain. We took an enormous step towards the final aim of removing the direct bureaucratic influence on the economy. At the C.D.U. meeting in the British zone in Recklinghausen on August 22, 1948, I explained these steps:

> 'It isn't as if we had had any choice. What we had to do in this situation was to loosen the shackles. We had to be prepared to restore basic moral principles and to start with a purge of the economy of our society.
>
> 'We have done more, by turning from a State-controlled economy to a market economy, than merely introduce economic measures. We have laid new foundations for our social and economic life. We had to abjure all intolerance which, from a spiritual lack of freedom, leads to tyranny and totalitarianism. We had to strive for an order which by voluntary regrouping and a sense of responsibility would lead to a sensible organic whole.'

The general public never realized what went on behind the scenes during this transition to a market economy. To give one example: It was strictly laid down by the British and American control authorities that permission had to be obtained before any definite price changes could be made. The Allies never seemed to have thought it possible that someone could have the idea, not to alter price controls, but simply to remove them. To assume such courage in a German so soon after the end of the war did not fit into the administration's way of thinking just after an overwhelming victory.

I was helped by General Clay, probably the strongest personality in the High Commission, who stood behind me, endorsing my orders. Price control over German consumer goods and the most important foodstuffs was now no longer subject to Allied supervision. This first success, however, did not mean that in the coming months and years the Allies refrained from trying to influence German reconstruction according to their ideas. In the period which followed, one discussion led only to another. First it was a question of dismantling, then of lower taxes, then trade union freedom, the control of prices, the setting up of technical offices, the reorganization of our foreign trade policy, etc.

These criticisms are not meant, indeed must not, impair the feeling of gratitude which the Federal Government and the whole German people owe to the United States and its citizens for the Marshall Plan. This generous, even magnanimous help, together with its successor plans, amounted to 1·5 milliard dollars between April 1948 and the end of 1954. In addition there were the considerable deliveries by GARIOA[2] which had started before the Marshall Plan began, amounting to 1·62 milliard dollars from 1946 to 1950.

General Strike v. Market Economy

The year 1948, especially the second half, became one of the most dramatic periods in the history of the German economy. The idea of freeing the markets was a challenge to the remaining forces of State control. There were many developments and circumstances which made it difficult to move steadily and without reservation towards greater freedom. In those first months after reform the price index rose considerably. It was little use to point out either that on June 18, 1948, with prices officially fixed at a relatively low level, no goods were available, or that every price expressed in DM represented only a fraction of the RM black market price during the months before currency reform.

It was essential not to let oneself be side-tracked during these difficulties, not even when the trade unions called for a general strike for November 12, 1948, in order to finish the market economy at a single blow. In the Economic Council the barometer registered storm. In practically all desk drawers of the department for the administration of the economy, headed by a man who was battling energetically against all controls and fixed prices, there lay ready secret fresh drafts of decrees which had only just been abolished. The office itself had begun to doubt the soundness of its chief's thesis.

I declared at the end of August 1948:

> 'I maintain, and events will prove me right, that even if the price pendulum has passed the frontiers of what is permissible or moral as a result both of one-sided pressure making for higher prices and of psychological pressures, we shall soon enter upon a phase when, as a result of competition, prices will be reduced to their appropriate level. This level will secure the best relationship between wages and prices, between nominal incomes and the price level.'

This statement, which did not seem to fit in with existing facts, earned me the reputation of being an incurable optimist. When, several months later, facts proved me right I was 'elevated' to the role of a modern economy prophet.

Have developments borne out the prognosis?

The economy immediately after reform seemed to be facing an apparently insatiable demand from consumers, representing an endless amount of arrears. The need for making good and refurbishing was equally strong in all branches of the economy. An overwhelming demand had accumulated in the building sector because of war damage and the need to house eight million refugees. Though in the first few days after reform supply and demand appeared generally balanced, the picture soon changed. The hoarding of goods, so much discussed and morally to be condemned, became a thing of the past. For the producer as much as for the consumer, money returned to its former important role. To have kept investment in industrial undertakings at a low level proved to be right. Industry was forced to offer for sale what it was making currently and to get rid of stocks.

Keeping One's Head

At the time, the amount of hoarding, which had now become conspicuous, though it had been known before, aroused very great anger. Considerable courage was needed to say what made economic sense:

> 'You know that I am accused of being the Patron Saint of hoarders. I remain untouched by such calumnies. Much as I deplore hoarding, I nevertheless feel obliged to point out that a radical emptying of our storehouses would necessarily have meant that the purchasing power freed by currency reform would have found nothing to buy. Currency reform would then either have been condemned to founder from the first day, or else the country would have had to be constrained by means of State controls and fixed prices. It should be remembered that hoarding regarded as such was simply an unavoidable manifestation of currency reform; it was a phenomenon taken into account when making the reform. It is dishonest to protest, if it is clearly realized that, had this cushion not been available, currency reform might have foundered.'

The difficulties sprang from easily identified causes. Current incomes and the change-over of the RM savings accounts—amounting to DM 3·5 Milliard—flowed immediately and exclusively into consumption. My close collaborator, Leonhard Miksch (who died all too early in 1950), drew attention in October 1948 to the great increase of money in circulation since currency reform, which could not be influenced by the German authorities. He wrote:

> 'It is time to ask the public to face these facts, which contradict the expectation that a radical reform can be achieved as the result of great sacrifices by savers alone. While during the first months after the stabilization of 1923 the total money in circulation increased from 1,488 million on November 30 to 2,824 million on March 31, 1924, i.e. by 90%, in 1948 it

rose within three and a half months from 2,174 million on June 30 to 5,560 million on October 15—an increase of 156%.'

By December 31, 1948, currency in circulation (including Berlin) had risen to DM 6,641 Milliard. This watering down of money meant that demand irresistibly rose faster than supply, particularly as the latter was at first inhibited by a shortage of imports. In addition, the urgency to reduce stocks became less pressing with increasing liquidity. Even the fact that by freeing the economy production was increased by 50% from the middle to the end of 1948—surely a remarkable success for the market economy—could not prevent an even more marked rise in prices in those autumn months. For that reason many were inclined to throw overboard their newly recovered freedom. To such attempts I could only reply:

> 'If we lose our nerve and give in to spiteful demagogic criticism, we shall return to the state of slavery. Then the German will lose anew the freedom which we have now happily returned to him. We shall once more return to the planned economy which will lead us step by step via State control and bureaucratic interference to totalitarianism.'

In fact the course of prices was upsetting. Compared with June 1948, all prices had greatly increased by the end of the year.

	Index of wholesale prices of industrial products (1949=100)	*Cost of living (1938=100)*			
1948		*Foodstuffs*	*Clothes*	*Household Goods*	*Heating and Lighting*
June	91	142	201	189	105
September	101	147	244	202	115
December	104	168	271	211	119

But, as so often in economic life, what is unpopular and socially unpleasant has one aspect which is economically good. Price changes may have been greatly in excess of the adjustment required to meet a changed cost structure, so that appreciable profits were made. This, in turn made people angry, leading to disagreeable reactions. Such profits, however, were utilized only in small part for private consumption by industrialists. Rather they took the place of fresh savings which could not otherwise be mobilized at this stage. The old savings had been wiped out by currency reform.[3] This manner of capital formation may be criticized, but at the time it formed the basis for the reconstruction of destroyed capacity.

The Wrong Way for Tax Policy

The impetus behind this movement nevertheless promoted greater production immediately after reform, and increased incomes could only be satisfied by more goods. The need to invest, which was enforced in this way through prices, was also expressed in taxation policy. The Military Government decree No. 61 of June 20, 1948, laid down relatively generous allowances for depreciation and a series of other privileges instead of effectively lowering taxation.

Taxation policy was carried on in this way even when it was returned into German hands. New stimuli for investment were continually being offered, and extra effort was encouraged because overtime payments remained tax-free. The joy of working, so recently regained, now meant so much more since wages at last had purchasing power again, while one was able to live one's life freely.

The effect of these changes is clearly shown by the statistics of hours worked per week by industrial workers. The re-found joy in work led to longer hours, and only recently have there been signs of any slackening. Industrial productivity, which has risen by over 60% since 1949, now permits shorter working hours. This is certainly socially desirable, but it must take place gradually, if it is not to endanger the whole of the national economy and the stability of the currency.

Weekly Hours Worked

Year	*Male*	*Female*	*All industrial workers*
1947	39·8	36·1	39·1
1948	43·0	40·0	42·4
1949	47·3	43·8	46·5
1950	49·1	45·5	48·2
1950	49·0	45·2	48·0
1952	48·5	44·7	47·5
1954	49·5	45·9	48·6
1956 (end)	49·0	45·5	48·0

(Up to the first figures for 1950, for the bi-zonal economic area; after the second set of figures for 1950, the federal area.)

At first, taxation decrees proved an aid to reconstruction, but later taxation policy began to conflict frequently with economic policy. Taxation became the means whereby the State gave concessions and so sometimes had undesirable consequences.

As far as price increases are concerned, the danger of a crescendo must be borne in mind. The stock of money was permanently fed by the steady creation of new money under the West German Currency Reform. From August 8, 1948, the prohibition against allowing credits on current account was lifted, with the result that short-term bank credits grew.

This reference is not meant to be critical, since economic necessity made it unavoidable. The volume of credits rose from DM 1·4 Milliard at the end of July 1948, to DM 3·8 Milliard at the end of October and to DM 4·7 Milliard at the end of the year. During the following year short-term loans rose by another DM 5·1 Milliard. The renewal of the credit facilities necessarily encouraged an increase in stocks, since this seemed worth while to the private manufacturer while prices were rising. That was the situation in the autumn of 1948; it was not cheerful.

Prices Drop

Optimism, derided at first, proved nevertheless to be well founded. In the first half of 1950 retail prices fell 10·6% below the level of the first six months of 1949. West Germany thus left the clique of countries which seemed to have surrendered to inflationary policies. International comparison of the further course of the cost of living shows that even in the Korean crisis, and during the boom from 1954 to 1956, this 'hard' policy could be continued.

Cost of Living Price Index
(1950 = 100)

	June-Dec. 1952	*Sept. 1956*	*June 1957*
Federal Republic	110	113	115
Norway	126	142	145
Sweden	125	138	144
Great Britain	119	137	142
France	131	133	134
Italy	114	130	131
U.S.A.	110	114	117
Switzerland	108	111	112
Netherlands	101	109	120

Clearly a revolution in economic policy had taken place. Even today it is evident, for besides yielding overwhelmingly beneficial results it was in part responsible for the balance of payments surplus which has emerged in the meantime. How did this change, the origin and direction of which can be traced back to the policy initiated at the end of the year 1948, take place?

An important element of stabilization was the wages policy which in the beginning—at a time of considerable unemployment—did not follow price increases. The wages freeze was still in force, though this could not be reconciled with a market economy. Therefore it was a natural step that on November 3, 1948, a decree for lifting the wage freeze should be introduced. Only thus did the trade unions receive back their freedom of movement; an event which would have been unthinkable without the accompanying decline of State control of the economy.

The relative moderation of the trade union wages policy was surely due to the failure of the attempt to stop the new economic policy by the general strike of November 12, 1948. On this day public opinion made it clear to the leadership of the trade unions that it was following the wrong path in its obdurate battle against the market economy.

Even in that time of confusion the working man understood how the developments then taking place would eventually lead to his advantage, despite several unpleasant events.

Financial Measures

The trade unions were not the only critics, as a glimpse at the newspapers of those days proves. Pessimism reigned everywhere. 'Prices are running away', 'Erhard at the end of his tether', 'Chaotic picture of prices', 'Economists in favour of a return to planning', were some of the headlines. Even worse, perhaps, was that within the economy one side began to insult the other. Everyone was ready to ascribe the fault to someone else—industry to trade, trade to industry, the urban dweller to the peasants and vice versa.

Gross hourly wages of all workers had risen from DM 0·99 in June 1948, to DM 1·13 in December 1948; a noteworthy increase, which nevertheless had been matched by better productivity. Surely in no other figure is success better expressed than in productivity per working hour. This rose from 62·8% in June 1948, to 72·8% in December and to 80·6% in June 1949 (basis 1936 = 100) (cf. table on page 26).

The graph on page 25 shows the development of gross weekly earnings and the cost of living. In the late autumn of 1948 the Bank Deutscher Länder (BDL) for the first time resorted to traditional Central Bank measures. In one move it increased the minimum reserve ratios of the commercial banks from 10 to 15% and confined the rediscount facility to

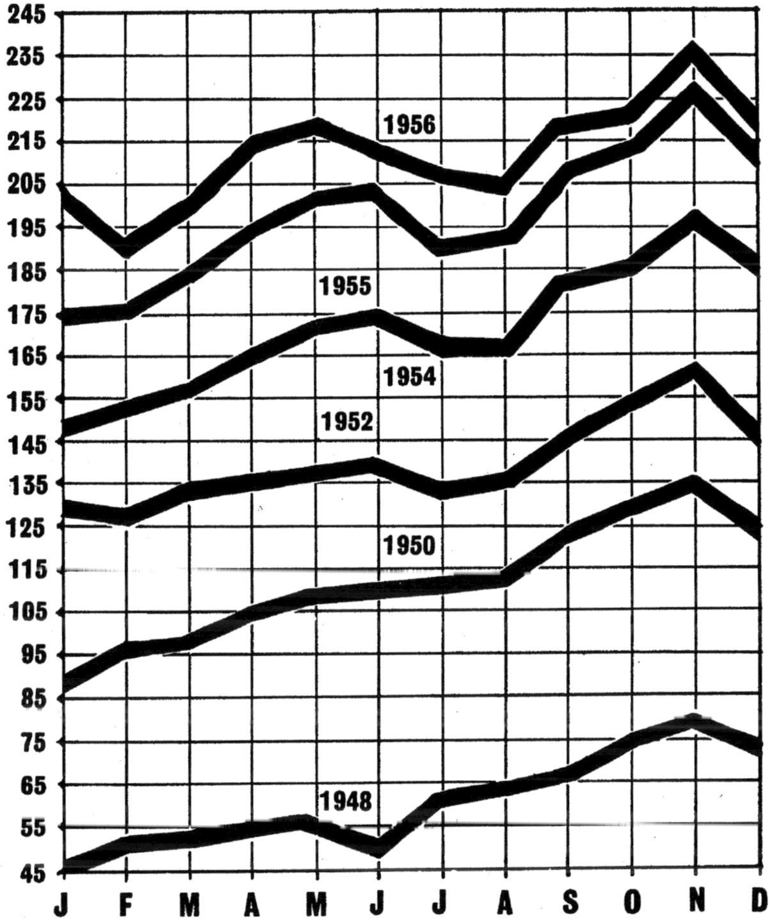

THE DEVELOPMENT OF INDUSTRIAL OUTPUT

The production index for industry as a whole (1936 = 100) has risen year by year since 1948. The pre-war level was achieved again in 1950. Meanwhile the output for industry as a whole has more than doubled (1956 = 213).

cases in which bank acceptances served foreign trade or purchases of raw materials, or were unavoidable as part of the Government's food policy. On December 1, 1948, loan institutes were asked, as a result of these measures, to restrict their credits to the amount outstanding at the end of October 1948.

As well as these measures by the Bank Deutscher Länder other factors began to work restrictively: the creation of money under West German currency reform stopped at the end of September 1948, with the distribution of the second per capita.[4] The switch-over of the RM accounts had been completed by the end of the year. A new phenomenon, which is still with us, appeared on the horizon to help us: the budget in the last quarter of 1948 for the first time showed a surplus, with anti-inflationary consequences.

Out of this freedom-loving spirit, which showed itself in the dismantling of the planned economy, grew the desire to regulate the budget through a systematic limitation of spending. On June 28, 1948, the decree to stabilize the currency and public finances was issued. Recruitment for the administration was limited, rises forbidden and official travel abroad limited to a minimum. This decree certainly mirrored good intentions, if they could be implemented in the extensive administrative machinery. When I moved into the Ministry of Economic Affairs at Hoechst, I found 2,500 people working there. By 1949 they had been reduced to 1,647.

The Price Mirror and the Programme for All

The attempts of the economic administration to stabilize prices were expressed in the regular publication of a price mirror, based on information supplied by industry, the retail trade and the unions. This was meant to show what price, calculated carefully, could be regarded as appropriate for individual articles. The first price mirror of September 11, 1948, gave a price of between DM 24·50-30·00 for men's shoes. At that time the Programme for All was started, under which 700,000 pairs of shoes were produced in August at closely calculated prices.

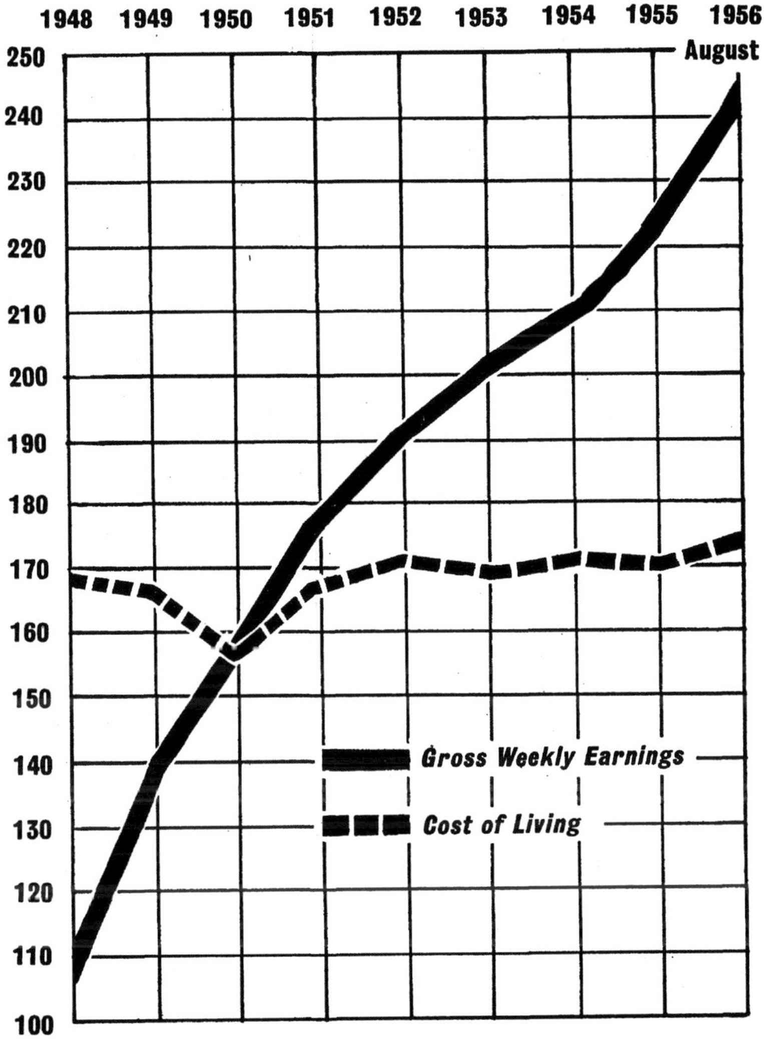

COST OF LIVING FIGURES AND WEEKLY EARNINGS

The above chart shows how the gross weekly earnings of all industrial workers rose (1938 = 100) from 109 in 1948 to nearly 250 at the end of 1956. Only a very small proportion of this wage increase was absorbed by higher prices (Index 1938 = 100; second half-year of 1948 = 168; end of 1956 = 178).

Finally, mention should be made of the 'law against driving prices up' which was promulgated on October 7, 1948, and which until the present time has provoked ardent parliamentary debate. But it does not reflect historical truth—no, it really contradicts it—if this law is cited as one of those which later caused the reversal in prices.

This happy change was reached as a result of economic equilibrium, which was helped by falling world-market prices from the end of 1948. Further, it was important that, thanks to the Marshall Plan, the supply of raw materials improved. With the turn of the year companies began to invest more in machinery and raw materials. For example, while during the first half of 1948 commercial and non-commercial imports barely reached DM 1·2 milliard, they rose in the same period of 1949 to DM 3 milliard. These factors helped appreciably to further the success of our aims. Thus the first phase of German reconstruction was marked by turbulent prices, accompanied by a rise in real wages and a marked increase in productivity.

Rapid Increase in Production after Currency Reform
(1936 = 100)

	2nd quarter 1948	*4th quarter* 1948
All industry	52·1	75·4
Production goods	46·4	68·3
Investment goods	46·6	75·7
Consumer goods	43·4	66·6
Foodstuffs industry	55·0	78·8

This correction in prices—whereby I mean the bringing about of an equilibrium at a changed nominal level—proved essential, even compulsory. Now the scissors of prices and consumer purchasing power began to shut, but in favour of the consumer. In a few weeks the picture changed radically. No longer was every price paid; the cancellation of orders increased as a result of shortage of money. One read headlines such as 'warning signal in the sector of consumer goods', and pessimists, typically, were tending to turn to the other side.

The Second Phase

While in the first phase after currency reform many believed that higher prices might remain, a drastic fall was as passionately feared, for it was thought that it would not permit the economy to cover its costs. Falling prices, until the outbreak of the Korean crisis at least, revealed to the consumer the outstanding advantage of the market economy over any forms of State planning. This knowledge would have been more convincing if the man in the street had been in a position to compare prices internationally, for while prices in West Germany were still dropping, appreciable increases were taking place elsewhere.

Cost of Living Index

	1949	*1950*
Federal Republic	107	100
France	90	100
Australia	91	100
Netherlands	92	100
Great Britain	97	100
Canada	97	100
U.S.A.	99	100
Italy	101	100
Sweden	101	100

By the middle of 1950 and this is typical of this period of steadiness as far as prices are concerned—most representative indices had sunk back to the level of the middle of 1948. The cost of living index of a working class family of four people in the combined economic area fell from 166 in the last quarter of 1948 to 160 for the average of 1949 and to 149 for July 1950 (1936 = 100). This incidence of falling prices was all the more impressive as during this period wages were rising.

The movement had already begun in the second half of 1948, but it was the year of 1949 that was remarkable for the strong increase in real wages. Unlike later periods of sharper increases in wages, the increases in 1949 were combined with price falls, and consequently led to particularly strong real wage improvements. In this lay the special characteristic of the second phase after reform from the middle of 1948.

The gross hourly earnings of male industrial workers grew from DM 1·22 in December 1948, to DM 1·33 in December of the following year. In June 1950, they were DM 1·36. At the same time the cost of living index sank to 168 in January 1949, and to 151 in June 1950 (1938 = 100). The real wages of industrial workers (i.e. the relationship between gross weekly earnings and the cost of living index) rose by 20·5% in 1949.

These opposing trends of wages and prices brought home the facts about the social market economy. In those months I repeatedly drew the attention of the public to these developments, in order to demonstrate in a practical manner the inner laws of market economy, which finds its best expression in rising incomes while prices are falling. But this phase, too, did not pass without tensions. The factors making for this development were briefly: an adjustment of the price level to the amount of purchasing power in the hands of the public while production of goods rises; at the same time, a damping down of the economy through a budget surplus, and in addition the belated effects of the American recession. Further, the liberalization of imports begun in the autumn of 1948 forced more adjustments.

These deliberate measures led, for the first time in one and a half decades, to heavy international competition hitting the German home market. Industry was forced to re-examine its production programmes which had been drawn up when its economy was cut off from abroad, and thus revealed the marks of an autarchic ideology. It was then necessary for industry to look to its markets.

The Customer is Right

The pressure of falling prices led to a state of affairs which the German public could barely remember. The customer became king again; a buyers' market began. How clumsy were the consumers' first attempts to walk in this new land which German economic policy had opened up! In the understandable hope of buying even more cheaply tomorrow or the day after, the consumer held back; he learned to judge more carefully. This comprehension by the public was absolutely essential for our further development, since without this hard lesson the deeply rooted attitude of a sellers' market—one utterly foreign to the market economy—could never have been eradicated.

The newly created buyers' market in the nature of things led to certain consequences. Insofar as the eagerness for capital investment aimed only to increase capacity, some holding back was noticeable. It was no longer a question merely of producing, but increasingly it was one of producing for the market. First place was given to investment for increased efficiency. Many plans, based on a sellers' market, turned out to be wrong and unworkable.

Statistics of the trend of production clearly reflected this phase. From December 1948, to June 1950, the output per hour in the Federal Republic rose from 70·3 to 89·0% of that of 1936. The most thorough increase in efficiency took place in those sectors where pressure of competition was especially strong. If, for example, productivity in the first and second half of 1949 is compared, it is seen that in this short time the textile industry showed an increase from 82·2 to 95·7; the shoe industry from 69·0 to 75·8; building of vehicles from 49·1 to 65·7, while—characteristically—mining, which at the time was outside the sphere of the market economy, showed only an increase from 61·3 to 62·5 (1936=100 for output per working hour). It needs no stressing that only these great successes in greater efficiency made possible these marked wage increases without endangering price stability.

The Inheritance of False Full Employment

It was inevitable that unemployment should develop into a serious problem. This undoubtedly unpleasant result afforded many opportunities to damn the new economic policy.

Such a reaction is typical of the impatience shown by people when faced with essentially long-term developments. I repeatedly explained that neither the German worker nor the German people would be well served by providing them with mere employment—it was necessary to create certain, that is, real jobs.

Currency and Economic Reform Increases Productivity
Production per Working Hour (1936 = 100)

		Annual growth
*1948**		
June = 62·8	1949 = 83	
Sept. = 72·4	1950 = 93	+12%
Dec. = 72·8	1951 = 103	+10·8%
1949	1952 = 108	+ 4·9%
March = 78·5	1953 = 114	+ 5·6%
June = 80·6	1954 = 121	+ 6·1%
Sept. = 82·1	1955 = 130	+ 7·4%
Dec. = 82·7	1956 = 134	+ 3·4%
1950		
March = 87·7		
June = 90·0		
Sept. = 98·0		
Dec. = 93·6		
1951		
March = 100·2		

*British and U.S. zone only.

Unemployment then grew from the unreal full employment of the days before currency reform to 760,000 at the end of 1948. During the whole of 1949 unemployment mounted, even during the summer months. Month by month the number of the unemployed increased, from 962,000 in January to 1·56 millions at the end of the year. A hard time for a responsible economist! Once more the collapse of my economic policy was being predicted.

The increase in unemployment would not have been so large if all the time more people—not least from the stream of refugees—had not demanded work. The sharpness of the criticism made many forget that, for party political reasons, the same people who were now confidently expressing their scorn, had before currency reform predicted an army of unemployed of between four and five million. But statistics of employment showed most clearly how the unemployment resulted almost completely from the search for work by newly available workers. From the end of 1948 to the end of 1949 there was a decline in employment of only 150,000, while the peak of unemployment during the winter, i.e. in February 1950, was only 1·2 million more than at the end of 1948. This enormous stream persuaded the knowledgeable in favour rather than against the free economic system, since it proved how many people in West Germany thought work once more worth while, and also necessary.

At this time another event took place, which is hardly less important than the reforms of the middle of 1948. This was the transition to a fundamentally different foreign trade policy, which deliberately exposed the German economy to international competition. In this connection the devaluation by 20% of the DM on September 19, 1949, must be mentioned. A new level of dollar parity of DM 4·20 against DM 3·33 hitherto, was established. This devaluation was reflected in the development of foreign trade.

Foreign Trade and DM Devaluation

	Monthly Average	Export *DM*	Export *$*	Import *DM*	Import *$*
1949	3rd quarter	326·4	93·2	579·8	177·9
	4th „	399·3	94·6	875·8	211·7
1950	1st „	502·3	118·8	823·3	197·9
	2nd „	596·3	140·6	737·8	175·5
	3rd „	727·3	171·3	939·7	223·3
	4th „	963·5	229·4	1,280·5	304·4

Finally it should be mentioned as a specially important factor that the Federal Republic—when, following the British example, most European currencies were devalued—devalued less than Britain and France, thus losing some competitive power.

How fundamentally, then, the situation changed during the first fifteen months of the first Federal Government administration! Between October 1949 and December 1950, exports trebled. As expected, the liberalization of foreign trade also led to rapidly increasing imports, so that the balance of payments, in spite of the rise in exports, worsened. Imports not only fed rising consumption, but in the form of raw materials were essential for eventual exports of high quality products. This process needed time—and nerves. Added to the troubles of unemployment were worries about the worsening foreign trade balance, which on private account alone in 1949 ended with an over-all deficit of $158 million and in 1950 of $243 million. The total adverse trade balance in 1949 came to $1,114 milliard and in 1950 to $723 milliard.

Freer Credit as Cure for All?

In this situation the Minister for Economic Affairs could not just stand idle. His diagnosis of the situation was: the internal economy is inhibited, the existing productive facilities are not being fully used. But the index of industrial production had risen from 75·2 in December 1948 to 96·1 in December 1949 (136 = 100). In view of the unemployment it seemed possible that the internal economic situation might benefit from a generous credit policy, helped by other measures of expansion. In fact, my so-called deflationary policy was being criticized and increased credits demanded, but it became increasingly clear that these critics were deliberately glossing over the importance of currency stability.

Thus, from the Opposition to the Allies, a chorus of criticism grew up. The latter, in a heated 'war of memoranda', preferred full employment more than the stability of our currency. This quarrel, begun in December 1949, on the occasion of the memorandum from the Federal Government discussing the basis for further Marshall aid, dominated the following weeks.

The disciples of the English full employment thesis, the followers of 'cheap money' and of 'austerity' surprisingly made a pact with American officials of the High Commission. The latter, alarmed by the large import surplus, worried about the approaching end of Marshall aid. Thus nearly all forces joined for a general attack on the market economy, forgetting that only through greater productivity and free competition, on the basis of the stability of our money, could we secure our position in the world market. Only thus was it possible to find a way to care for the greatly increased number of people in West Germany.

I firmly opposed forced artificial expansion. I had to put up with being scolded for inactivity, which was all the more grotesque since hitherto I had always been criticized for too much vitality. I was in no doubt at all that such a frivolous policy of expansion would not only have endangered the stability of the currency, but also our balance of payments for a considerable time. Thus we would have become dishonest at the beginning of the path which aimed at making us an honest partner in world trade. In view of the decisive importance of our foreign trade, such a disaster had to be avoided.

How much this growing interest in exports in the period before the Korean conflict became conscious can be proved by my speeches of the time. To give just one of many examples, at the annual meeting of the Union of German Dockyards on September 20, 1950, I declared:

'The foreign trade policy which we are pursuing, in spite of much criticism over the past nine months, is based on the conviction that our economic task—the employment and maintenance of over 12 million more people than before the war—cannot be carried through, but must founder in a cul de sac unless we create more air in this manner . . .

'Above all we must not try to achieve an apparent success

through increasingly watering down our money, which has at last become stable, and thus move towards inflation. In that way we would steal imperceptibly the money of those who have saved. That would be the most damnable method which could be conceived.'

Thus, against all advice, West German economic policy was carefully directed; on the one hand, to limit the damage of mass unemployment, on the other to avoid endangering the advances already made, particularly towards the security of our currency, which would enable Germany to return to the world markets. In those difficult days it was important to remain firm, and not to do what was advised by real and false friends. I even found it necessary to employ some stratagems to meet strong political pressure in favour of dangerous and unnecessary measures.

Medicine against Recession

In these ways I tried to keep to the narrow path between inflation and deflation. The catalogue of the various measures used by the Ministry for Economic Affairs and the Central Bank confirms that a modern market economy is without doubt in a position to meet a recession effectively without endangering the stability of the currency.

The economic measures taken were carefully thought out. At the end of March 1949 the Bank Deutscher Länder loosened up the credit squeeze which had begun at the end of October 1948 with the limitation of credits. On June 1, 1949, the minimum reserve requirements were lowered from 15 to 12%, or from 10 to 9%. On May 27, 1949, and on July 14, 1949, the rediscount rate was cut by one half per cent on each occasion, bringing it down from 5 to 4%. In the late summer, credit institutions were allowed special help to provide monies for long-term production and investment to the tune of DM 300 milliard. On September 1 a further reduction of the minimum reserves of the banks as well as rates for loans and sight drafts took place.

The pressure of mass unemployment forced a further strengthening of the expansionist economic policy in the winter. Financial help for the creation of public works programmes as well as help for building was granted. Within the framework of this special action DM 3·4 milliard was made available. Short-term credits, which at the end of 1948 stood at DM 4·7 milliard, rose in 1949 by a further DM 5·1 milliard and in the first half-year of 1950 rose again by 2·3 milliard. The volume of medium and long-term credits of the banks, including the Bank for Reconstruction, reached the sum of 2·6 milliard; in the first half-year of 1950 it rose by a further 2 milliard.

In April 1950 the Federal Government decided to lower taxes and to remit others in order to step up consumption and lighten the burden on the economy. It was truly contradictory that in spite of the demands of the Allies in their many memoranda, in which they condemned German inactivity, they at first refused permission for this tax reform. It should be remembered how much energy had to be spent on discussions with the Allies, whether on questions of a steel quota or on the sensible development of dismantling and decartelization, or over the use of the so-called counterpart funds, or about the best methods of bridging the dollar gap or even about the further slackening of controls. It need hardly be mentioned that this phase of the buyers' market came at a convenient moment for me to throw overboard the meaningless remains of controls and price regulations.

In this situation I declared in an annual survey over the Bavarian Radio on December 27, 1949:

> 'The passing year 1949 was one of consolidation, yet, at the same time, of recovery and expansion. If in the past year I promised that we should be successful in handling the social problem, no one can deny that, partly through raising nominal incomes, but particularly through raising a supply of better quality goods at lower prices, the standard of living of the German people has improved.'

Even without Korea . . .

It would not be historically accurate to ascribe to the Korean boom the solution of difficulties which here had been carefully studied, analysed and overcome. Our resistance to all attempts to weaken our policy of stable money had already borne fruit. The index of production climbed from 90·9 in January 1950 to 107·6 in June of that year, a rise of nearly 20%, and appreciably more than in the same period of the previous year.

The steady pressure on prices and the growing buyers' market at home made exports doubly attractive. As a result, exports increased from DM 485·5 million in December 1949 to DM 651·9 million in June 1950. In these six months the import surplus declined from DM 532·7 million in January 1950 to DM 138·6 in June of that year. Unemployment dropped during this period by 360,000; the number of employed increased even more.

Today, with all relevant statistics available, we know that it would not have needed the Korean conflict to continue the advance of the economy, or to increase its speed. The contrary is true: the Korean boom brought more difficulty than help to German economic policy.

It should be remembered that for the consumer a favourable trend was interrupted. The cost of living index had dropped from 168 in January 1949 to 148 in September 1950 (1936 = 100), while simultaneously earnings registered a rising trend. With the outbreak of the Korean conflict in September 1950 the world received its most serious shock since 1939. German economic policy had just paved the way for further expansion, and a further healthy and natural development was thus deeply disturbed.

Chapter III

OVERCOMING THE KOREAN CRISIS

THE UNREST AND UNCERTAINTY which the Korean war brought in its train led to a considerable increase in demand. A slight hope that the consumer would react quietly proved false. On the other hand on the positive side it should be mentioned that since currency reform a great deal had been invested; though, lacking an adequate capital market, the greater part of these investments were too expensive. Here moral evaluation and sober economic judgment may differ. In the first five months of the Korean conflict the increase in demand led to an increase in the volume of production from a point in the index of 107·6 in June to 133·3 in November 1950. At the same time the price index of basic industrial materials rose from 218 to 265, and that of industrial products from 178 to 195 (1938 = 100). In spite of the increases in prices caused by these unsettling events, they were less marked in Western Germany, due to her astonishing elasticity of production, than elsewhere in the West.

Unhappily the consumer had also to suffer this rise. The cost of living index climbed from its lowest point, 148 in September 1950, to 151 at the end of the year, and to 179 at the end of 1951 (1938 = 100). Rising prices in the world market and the nervousness of the consumers and buyers in all parts of the economy are reflected in these indices.

Few believed that the freedom of the consumer, which represented for me one of the essential basic human freedoms, would survive the crisis. This is what I said on February 6, 1952, in Zurich:

'It was self-evident that a people as experienced in inflation as the Germans should have reacted to an event such as Korea in so sensitive a manner. In other words, everyone went off the rails a little. Some wanted raw materials under all circumstances and at any price, which is understandable in a country such as Germany, which is so poor in raw materials. On the other hand we had to reckon with the consumer who, experienced in tragic events, wondered whether on the morrow his needs would be met, or whether we should have to return to a system of planning or rationing. So the German consumer was ready to buy bad goods today at a high price rather than to get perhaps nothing tomorrow. And all that in a situation which was restricted from a monetary and a foreign currency point of view.'

Troubles in Bonn

There were then troubles indeed in Germany. The situation in many respects was similar to that at the end of 1948. The foes of the market economy made pacts with the ever-prevaricating. Even those with experience of economics regarded a return to planning as unavoidable. That the Social Democrats, in opposition, should do all within their power to destroy the economic policy they disliked was not surprising. But it was serious and dangerous that the policy of a market economy found only partial support within the Government and coalition, and sometimes had to meet open and covert opposition.

Within the Government and the coalition the year 1951 produced a depressing picture of disunity and thus a growing inability to take action. It was only thanks to the strength of the social market economy that the free economic system was preserved through the difficulties of this time. To recall here the details of the discussions which then took place would be tedious. But it should be remembered how action was paralysed, some difficulties made unnecessarily more difficult, and their solution retarded by these discussions themselves.

How many different points of view confronted the Minister

for Economic Affairs! The Ministry of Finance wished to copy the English purchase tax; suggestions were made to appoint a special commissar for foreign currencies, in order to limit the functions of the Minister for Economic Affairs. A special economic cabinet under the guidance of Dr. Ernst was devised, and by the end of 1951 a proposal was put forward for the creation of a special overlord ministry, which would have reduced the Federal Minister for Economic Affairs to a mere cipher.

In such circumstances it became increasingly difficult to put sensible ideas into effect. Thus my plan to break through the bottlenecks in the supply of basic materials by straightening out prices foundered. Another idea to help the basic material industries by building up stocks with 'savings for reconstruction', in order eventually to qualify under the Law of Investment Assistance by industry was held up for months. The law was finally passed in the Federal parliament on December 31, 1951. Added to these difficulties were interventions from the Americans, which curtailed Marshall aid, opposed a suitable initial position for Germany at the foundation of the E.P.U., and held up the much needed freeing of counterpart funds. Extraordinary declarations were made—the head of the E.C.A. mission in Germany described the German tax system as the most 'anti-social in the world'. In addition there was constant pressure from the U.S.A. to introduce controls, in order to qualify for the acquisition of scarce materials.

Battles with the International Ruhr Authority about the most important material in short supply—coal—took place daily. Sharp discussions with the D.G.B. (trade unions) had to be endured. Its Federal committee, after months of hesitation, decided to stop collaboration in all economic policy discussions.

This list could be continued almost indefinitely; similar occurrences persisted until the beginning of 1952—when the necessity of continuing with the market economy became obvious even to the most ignorant. This change became clear in two particular events. At the end of 1951, Germany was no longer in danger of exceeding her credit limit with the E.P.U.;

on the contrary, for the first time Western Germany became a creditor country within the E.P.U. At the same time, prices steadied.

These eventful weeks were reflected in all my speeches:

> 'Because in Germany I kept to the rules of economic order and healthy commonsense, I was asked: freeze prices now or resign. I neither resigned nor ordered a price freeze. That my socialist opponents should have looked at things from a party political point of view I cannot grudge them. It was worse that even good friends should have gone so wrong as to think that my economic policy would land Germany in disaster. I argued that one should just remain quiet for a time, and this proved itself worth while.'

This brief survey of the events of those days shows how necessary it was to keep one's nerve. An indication has already been given of the spending spree which began in the last half of 1950, and which in the spring of 1951 led to 'grotesque increases in turnover'. Purchases of shoes, for example, rose by 90 per cent within a year. How immense was the performance of the German economy, and how the system of market economy proved itself, is shown by the trend of business in the retail trade. Taking clothing and household linen as an example, the value of retail sales rose as follows:

Increase in Turnover during Korean Boom

First half year 1949	86	Second half year 1949	114
,, ,, ,, 1950	109	,, ,, ,, 1950	152
,, ,, ,, 1951	136	,, ,, ,, 1951	157

Many factors stimulated this psychosis. Falling prices in the month before the Korean conflict had led producers and the public to be careful in their policy of stocking. Then the stormy movements of prices in the world markets set in.

West German industry, which was still in process of reconstruction, soon reached the limits of its capacity. A considerable part in this process was played by the spending of hoarded money, which had been accumulated for different motives and from different sources since the time of currency reform. On top of all this, the once urgently needed measures to stimulate the economy began to work just at this particular time. The Income Tax Law of April 23, 1950, aimed at cutting taxes—welcome in itself—was finally sanctioned by the Allies, but in a completely different economic and political climate. To fill the cup to the brim it should be added that the purchasing boom by the consumer did not come only from current income, but at least in part from savings accounts, which had been built up in the past few years, and were now used almost exclusively for consumption. For several months the increase in savings accounts almost ceased.

Increase in Production leads to Bottlenecks

Production figures reflect this hectic development: the over-all index rose from 107·6 in June 1950 to 130·9 within a year, and even to 147·8 at the peak of the year in November 1951 (1936 = 100). The capital goods sector benefited especially from this Korean boom, as is shown by the index of capital goods, which rose from 108·4 to 164·1. The consumer goods sector suffered in the first six months of 1950 from buyers' resistance; a real stagnation took place. The index measuring this production, however, jumped steeply between June 1950 and November 1951 from 101·9 to 148·4.

It naturally followed that this stormy development brought with it bottlenecks which the general nervousness intensified. These bottlenecks were felt particularly where natural or structural limits were set to a rapid growth in capacity.

As a result of much effort since the collapse in 1945, West German coal production was increased appreciably; the general industrial index on the day of currency reform stood at 51% of the 1936 figure; coal production, because it had been favoured, stood at 76·4%. Already in June 1950, however, coal mining had fallen behind in relation to general production. Even if by the end of 1950 it was possible to make a further increase of 15%, the difference between the two sectors was bound to widen still further. A similar state of affairs reigned in the iron and steel sector.

Was this really a fault of the market economy? Did this justify abandoning our free economic system? I tried to give a clear answer to this question in the *Handelsblatt* of December 31, 1951:

> 'In any reckoning of failures the market economy is always debited with just those sins that belong to the account of planning and State control, the remains of which the market economy has so far been forced to carry with it. The bottlenecks in the basic industries are discussed, but there is silence about the fact that it is in these sectors that bureaucracy has celebrated its triumphs. It is there that the function of the market, particularly the free adjustment of prices, has been completely eliminated.

Naturally these bottlenecks did not allow us to remain idle. It has already been mentioned that a thorough purge of prices foundered in the face of many-sided resistance. Among the many obstacles, the formulation of the Law for Investment Assistance by Industry of January 7, 1952, must be remembered. After months of discussion this had been passed by the Federal Parliament on December 13, 1951. This Law of Investment Assistance was later much criticized. But in fact it represented a remarkable attempt to master the sudden difficulties through self-help. Historically speaking, it will one day find a just appreciation. In implementing the decree, the hard-pressed basic industry sector received not less than DM one milliard of credits, divided thus:

DM	296	million	for the iron and steel industry
,,	228	,,	for coal mining
,,	242	,,	for electricity
,,	77	,,	for water
,,	50	,,	for the Federal railways

This aid enabled investment plans to be pushed through to a total of DM 4,745 milliard. Added to these credits from the Investment Assistance Law were DM 2,227 milliard of retained earnings from the individual industries, and DM 1,518 milliard of other credits.

The Trade Balance Worsens

Rising prices in world markets, as much as the unavoidable pressure to meet growing production, led to considerable increases in imports. Moreover, on September 1, 1950, the liberalization agreement between the O.E.E.C. countries raised quotas to 60%. The commercial trade balance worsened steadily; in the second half of 1950 it showed a deficit of DM 535 milliard. The balance of payments looked even more unfavourable. Already within four months of the start of E.P.U. the German quota of credits of $320 million was exhausted.

Nevertheless this increase in imports was sensible as a defence of the market economy, because in this situation it was important to stretch as far as possible the supply of goods. It is fair to say, then, that the fight against the planners in Germany, i.e. against those who wished to throw overboard the freedom of the economy, became at one and the same time a battle with the E.P.U., in order to get it to accept for the time being the German foreign trade deficit, confident that later it would change completely.

Among the measures which my Ministry took or supported at this time should be mentioned first of all the means of reducing imports to a politically possible limit. Licences were regulated, and above all cash deposits were demanded up to 50% of the German equivalent of the foreign currency needed for the imports. The issue of import licences in the hands of the private foreign trade banks was transferred to the Central Banks of the Länder. On February 21, 1951, steps had to be taken to halt temporarily the liberalization of E.P.U. imports, after the difficulties of the Korean conflict had brought further big increases in demand. In addition monetary measures were taken: thus the minimum reserves ratios were increased by an average of 50% on October 1, 1950. Simultaneously, facilities to rediscount bank acceptances were limited to certain institutions (October 31, 1950). The discount rate and the rate for secured overdrafts were raised from 4 to 6% and from 5 to 7% respectively (on November 27, 1950)—also against the wishes of the politicians. On November 1, 1950, the Länder Central Banks were asked to cut the discount credits which they had granted to commercial banks by 10%.

All the same, the foreign currency situation remained critical. Even the grant of a special credit of $120 million from E.P.U. could not immediately exorcize the evil of a balance of payments deficit. By suspending liberalization, the danger of acute balance of payments difficulties was successfully averted—but at the price of a tight administrative limitation of imports. The Bank Deutscher Länder, with the full agreement of the Federal Ministry for Economic Affairs, continued its restrictive line. At the beginning of 1951 regulations in regard to credits were further tightened. In January 1951 all commercial banks were asked forthwith to avoid all increases in short-term credit, and on February 28, 1951, there followed the request to reduce the volume of short-term credits by about DM 1 milliard.

Other measures went hand in hand with these efforts. In the Federal Ministry for Economic Affairs a special raw material board was set up. At the beginning of 1951 the so-called economic security law (Wirtschaftssicherungs Gesetz) was passed, which allowed the Government to intervene in production and in the distribution of goods. The interventions that followed as a result of this law were kept within modest limits. These measures were taken principally as a result of pressure by the Americans, who only wished to allot raw materials against authorization by the State. I must confess that I never took these rules particularly seriously, and above all I did not greatly value their economic importance.

Rearmament Without Inflation?

The Korean war allowed for the first time the idea of German rearmament to appear. This is an important date and one must recall first reactions. I constantly and earnestly urged from the first that we should avoid inflation. Thus I opposed the widely held view that everything to do with armaments would necessarily mean inflation. On September 15, 1950, I said:

> 'Possibly as a result it will be necessary to use certain measures of direction, but these need not disturb or endanger the system of the market economy. The great danger which is now threatening, and which I anticipate with certainty, comes from another direction. If the State will have to spend considerable sums on West German participation in the defence of Europe, then some people and even some parties will consider that this money cannot be found out of the budget, but that the central bank credit would have to be mobilized in some way. Though it is unlikely that the form of the "mefo" bills of exchange[5] (mefowechsel) or the limitless prolongation of treasury bills will be copied, basically all manipulation of this kind comes to the same thing, namely the beginning of an inflation.'

The C.D.U. meeting in Goslar on October 22, 1950, at the height of the Korean boom, offered me a welcome opportunity to speak openly about the problems of the day. It was at a time when opinion seemed resigned to the ruin of West Germany. Thus the chairman of O.E.E.C., the Dutch Foreign Minister, Dr. Stricker, said: 'Europe is facing the bankruptcy of West Germany.' The Federal Government, through 'reckless imports within four months', had used up the E.P.U. credit of $320 million. West Germany's future was thus very doubtful; an inflation similar to that following the first world war was imminent.

Opposition at home joined with international criticism—the

one hoping for my fall, the other expecting bankruptcy. Here is my view as submitted to the C.D.U.:

> 'The economy, and economic progress, know no absolute law. It is thus quite wrong for the socialists to demand, as they have recently done, that every price increase must be compensated by a corresponding increase in wages. We believe that with increasing productivity reductions in prices can well go parallel with increases in wages to support the case of market economy. To defend the market economy is not a dogma but, for the sake of the German people, an important commandment. And it is for this reason that the Federal Government has brought in the generous programme of anticipating imports, which, in expectation of supplies of foreign currency in the next three or four months, guarantees the foodstuffs and raw materials which we require to secure German nutrition and the maintenance of employment and production. The Federal Government was fully conscious of the fact that for this programme all available means had to be brought to bear. But only a courageous policy promises success in this situation.'

Calmness—but no Crisis

With prices rising day by day, and the foreign trade balance becoming ever more unfavourable, to speak of such things was only possible through a deep conviction that the market economy was right. It still took months before the change became apparent, but this turn towards salvation was, as a result, all the more positive and lasting.

While the monthly average of 1950 showed an adverse foreign trade balance of about DM 250 million, and even during the first quarter of 1951 no noteworthy improvement took place, the trend changed in the second quarter, leading to a favourable balance of nearly DM 350 million. This was the turning point, which initiated the period of a permanent foreign trade surplus.

Thus the year 1950 became the most exciting in the young story of the market economy. In the following months of 1951 it became even clearer that all the difficulties were being successfully overcome. The skilful political economist knew that we were 'out of the wood'. The battles over the market economy and over the position of the Federal Minister for Economic Affairs, however, only reached their peak in 1951.

This year brought the decline and end of the Korean boom, and with it the first answer to the significant question as to whether the see-saw of economic trends was unavoidable, or whether the modern market economy was in a position to overcome this cycle.

Supply and demand in many sectors became better balanced without a slowing down of economic progress. The rise of prices, conspicuous since the autumn of 1950, slackened visibly in the second half of 1951. First of all this decline affected raw materials; later, at the turn of the year 1951/52, it also affected the cost of living. The cost of living index for clothing, for example, dropped from 212 in May 1951 to 205 by the end of the year (1938 = 100).

This change also made itself apparent in the sector of production. The consumer goods industry in the second half of 1950 had to deal with an increase of roughly 40%. The usual decline in December, too, proved itself to be a turning point. The index dropped from its peak of 141·0 in November 1950 to 112·6 in July 1951. Yet production was still 15% higher than in the comparable period of the previous year. One could no longer speak of a crisis unless one wished to regard the hysterical increases of the Korean boom as normal.

There was even less cause for worry when at the end of 1951 a lively recovery pushed the index of production up to 150, higher than the previous peak. Then again followed months of a slight slackening of the economy until the middle of 1952. Yet the figures generally prove that the Korean boom in the consumer goods sector already ended with the turn of the year 1950/51—quite contrary to the opinions current in those days.

At this time a remarkable new trend began in our economy.

Until the end of 1950 the restoration of investment and consumer goods production ran in a merrily parallel line. In the future there was to be a distinct contrast. The readiness to engage in capital expenditure remained; the index within this sector rose from 141·3 in November 1950 to 164·1 in November of the following year, and in 1952 retained almost uninterruptedly its upward trend. The result of this development was that industrial production rose 30 points above the index of output of the consumer goods industry.

This differential development—apart from a short interruption at the end of 1953—continued also during the following year. How little it was possible to speak of a crisis, in spite of many fears, is best shown by the general production figures. The index of total production moved in this time as follows:

Index of Total Industrial Production (1936 = 100)

1950 1st half year	99·7	1951 2nd half year	134·3
1950 2nd half year	121·7	1952 1st half year	133·4
1951 1st half year	127·7	1952 2nd half year	145·3

While, as already mentioned, in the consumer goods sector the Korean boom had already ended by the end of 1950, in the investment goods sector, the hangover of unfulfilled orders continued somewhat longer. This prolongation of the Korean boom thus led to a continuation of bottlenecks in coal and steel. In consequence of these changed structural conditions the import of American coal became an increasingly important problem.

The bottleneck in coal supplies, imposed by the traditional West German export obligations, but also by the particularly intractable stand of the International Ruhr Authority during the Korean conflict, became steadily more apparent. Coal imports of all kinds (pit, brown and bituminous coal, coke and briquettes) thus rose from 5·3 million tons in 1950 to 10·4 million tons in the following year, with the result that in the same period the export surplus shrank from 20·1 million tons to 14·4 million tons.

The lively economic activity at this time is reflected in the employment figures. For the average of the year the numbers of employed rose from 13·83 million in 1950 to 14·56 million in 1951 and 15·0 million in 1952. This increase of 1·2 million over a short period expresses more pointedly than statistics of unemployment the upward economic trend. This was continuously swollen by new recruits to the labour force, who—apart from the immediate problem—represented a most unusual enrichment of the West German production potential. In the later years of the boom particularly, it was proved how little my wish for greater expansion could have been realized but for this welcome help. Within this period of three years the number of unemployed fell from 1·58 million in 1950 to 1·38 million for the average of 1952.

Return to Liberalization

In spite of the noticeable cooling of the economic climate, the restrictive monetary and credit measures were for some time retained. No change in favour of an economic policy of expansion was called for so far, as prices generally did not show any very clear signs of falling. Lower prices in some sectors were insufficient to neutralize increases left over from the time of the boom.

Some of the measures of economic policy should be mentioned here:

1. As regards financial policy tax brakes were applied at the end of 1951 through an increase in company and turnover taxes, as well as in the abolition of important concessions regarding income tax. The change in the income tax law alone added an extra burden of about DM 1 milliard.

2. In monetary policy there was at first only a limited relaxation of the credit squeeze. The decisive loosening did not take place until October 1951. The compulsory cash deposit of 50% against imports, which was reduced to 25% at the end of December 1950, effectively lost most of its importance: it was completely abolished at the end of 1951.

3. Of much greater importance was the fact that the liberalization of imports from the O.E.E.C. countries was again put into force step by step from January 1952. The first free list in the beginning of January 1952 covered 57% of imports from the O.E.E.C. area (measured by the value of imports in the relevant year of 1949). Already from April 1, 1952, it was increased to 77% of imports.

4. The minimum reserve requirements of the banks were first lowered on May 29, 1952, by 1% and later lowered again. The Bank Deutscher Länder during this time made its measures of credit policy more selective. For example, rediscount quotas for some banks were introduced, and the lines of credit policy more definitely outlined, in order to restore open market operations from the autumn of 1951.

Parallel with these complex and dynamic events there went developments in production and turnover, and a strong increase in wages and salaries. The year 1951—similar to that of 1949—is marked by a sharp increase in wage rates.

The gross hourly earnings of industrial workers rose in this year by 14·8%; the gross weekly earnings by 13·3%. In contrast to 1949 a part of the increase in wages was offset by price increases, so that real wages in 1951 effectively rose only by 5·4%, while the increase in 1949 was 20·5%. These two figures clearly demonstrate the truth of the thesis that increases of wages in excess of increases in productivity are nonsensical and damaging and, thus, that the mass of consumers are best served by the maintenance of price stability.

The Ideal Trinity

The Korean boom finally ended with the turn of the year 1951/52. This was the finish of the third phase of the social market economy—the phase of testing and safeguarding this system of economic policy. But the march of events allowed us to detect the weak spots of our economy. The next period covers the years 1952, 1953 and part of 1954, to be followed by a powerful boom.

What characterized this fourth phase? Here that trinity, which for every modern market economist must be the ideal picture, came to life. Rising production and productivity accompanied by rising nominal wages, and the increase in prosperity, thanks to stable or lower prices, brought all-round benefits. It may be accepted that the social harmony of this happy trinity was decisive for the overwhelming electoral success of the party of the Federal Minister for Economic Affairs on September 6, 1953. In this situation I said:

> 'Our economic policy serves the consumer; he alone is the yardstick and judge of all our economic activities. This policy of the social market economy has proved to the whole world that the principles of free competition in production, of free consumer choice, as well as the free development of the personality, guarantee economic and social successes better than any form of State direction or State control.

Industrial production during 1952 and 1953—apart from the usual seasonal changes—was marked by a steady increase. Starting with the trough in February 1952, at 128·6%, November registered a peak of 160·8 (1936 = 100). The seasonal low in January 1953, at 134·0, could not halt developments. Production in November 1953 stood at 175·6. The year 1954 is marked by a particularly rapid rise, so that in November of that year production was double that of 1936, and that of the spring of 1950.

This enormous increase is irrefutable proof of the inner force of the German economy, and also a vindication of that dynamic economic policy which was realized in Germany, and of the indefatigable efforts of all sections of the population. To state this is all the more justified since the increase in the volume of production did not end with the doubling of the pre-war performance. In spite of all the difficulties of international comparisons of industrial production it cannot be denied that the rate of progress of the German economy overtook almost all those of other countries. This is still true if, instead of starting comparisons when the German economy was shattered, the year 1950 is chosen. Even in West Germany, by 1950 the pre-war level was well surpassed. (Index of 1950 = 110·9 per cent of 1936.)

International Comparisons of Total Industrial Output (1950 = 100)

	1938	*1949*	*1950*	*1951*	*1952*	*1953*	*1954*	*1955*	*1956*
Federal Republic	107	80	100	119	126	139	155	178	192
France	81	99	100	113	118	115	125	137	159
Norway	65	88	100	107	108	114	125	129	140
Canada	48	94	100	107	110	117	116	126	134
U.S.A.	43	87	100	107	111	120	112	124	128
Great Britain	75	93	100	104	101	107	114	121	120
Denmark	—	89	100	102	98	102	108	113	113

Hidden behind this general development was a change of emphasis in favour of the consumer goods industries—a change which rightly permitted one to call 1953 the 'year of the consumer'.

It has already been shown how the course of the investment and consumer goods industries differed in past years. The drop in output of the consumer goods industries to 111·5 in July 1952 (investment goods 155·6) troubled consumers and economists alike. But the trough also indicated a change—as a result not of chance, but of deliberate intention. A big increase in consumer goods pushed the index of consumer goods production up to 164·5 in November 1952 and to 180·4 in November 1953, thus reaching the level of production of investment goods again.

Mass Purchasing Power Grows

A 60% rise in output within a period of only eighteen months was rewarded through an improvement in mass incomes. Salary and wage increases for civil servants and employees were accompanied by increases in wages and pensions through the Law for Payments for the Equalization of Burdens. Further, the limited tax reform of June 24, 1953, brought about on average a lowering of payments by 15%.

With prices going down, the market proved itself particularly absorbent. For the first time in two decades the break-through to an all-out expansion of business was successful. The eagerness of the public to consume was marked not only by increasing purchases of traditional consumer goods, but above all by a rising demand for durable goods. The demand for a higher standard of living, which amongst other things was expressed by an increasing amount of travel, was firmly established.

How did the balance sheet for the West German people look after Korea?

Between the end of 1951 and the middle of 1954 almost two million more people found secure employment. Simultaneously the number of unemployed dropped from the seasonal low in October 1951, with 1,214 million, to 820,900 in the seasonal low of 1954. Gross weekly earnings of all industrial workers rose from DM 68·52 for the average of 1951 to DM 74·00 in the following year and to DM 80·99 in 1954.

Though as a result of the Korean conflict the cost of living index in 1951 rose by 7·7% compared with the previous year, a welcome calm followed. In 1952 the index rose again by 1·8%, but in 1953 it dropped by 1·8%. These averages hide various cross-currents. Thus the index for clothing dropped from 111 for 1951 to 98 for 1953 and to 97 the following year.

As already mentioned, the tendency to invest more slowly was due to the fact that the determination to increase capacity had given way to the wish to modernize. Industrial initiative appeared to be held back by the unstable political situation, the uncertainty of the plans of the Messina powers and the fate of the European Defence Community. The capital goods industries, however, were much helped by the Law of Investment Assistance, and self-finance by the basic industries was facilitated by higher prices. Prices of coal at the pit rose from DM 32·92 to DM 52·08 per ton between 1950 and 1953; the basic prices of steel rods (Thomasguete Oberhausen) from DM 227·35 to DM 400·62 per ton.

These price increases reflected the need to free the basic industries from the fetters of State control and to allow them to charge the market price.

Building also contributed appreciably to the general economic growth in 1952/53. Here the first part of the Housebuilding Law, with its cheaper finance, was effective. The number of completed flats rose in the period 1952/53 from 443,000 to 518,000 units. At the middle of 1953 it should be noted that 10% of the labour force was employed in building.

During these years the building industry faced up to its task of providing proper accommodation for the millions of refugees and bombed-out persons. The annual construction of flats since 1953 has added more than half a million flats. In the past three years more than 540,000 new flats annually have been built. In 1929, by contrast, 197,000 new flats were built. The annual financial expenditure since 1954 moved between DM 9 and 11 milliard, the public authorities financing about 30%, while the capital market helped with 40 to 50%.

This picture of a growing economy was also reflected in the foreign trade figures. While the import-export balance in 1949 and 1950 seemed to be 'incurably' in deficit to the tune of DM 3 milliard, by 1951 the deficit had fallen to DM 1·49 million.

The phase of long-term improvement in the balance of payments had begun, after months of thoughtful discussion. In 1953 the favourable balance amounted to DM 2·5 milliard. And this was in no way due to a restriction of imports. Imports increased considerably from DM 11·37 milliard in 1950 to more than DM 14·7 milliard in 1951 and DM 16·2 milliard in 1952. Only in 1953 did the level of imports become stabilized. In 1954 imports grew to 19·3 and in 1955 to 24·47 milliard DM and by 1956 came to DM 27·96 milliard.

From this situation grew an increasingly serious problem,

which occupied the political economists: the result of these surpluses was to make the economy more liquid. That has not in the meantime been fully appreciated, purely because of the neutralizing effect of the sterilization of money through record budget surpluses.

The Mistake of the Planners

The Marshall Plan, which, in its fourth year, still brought in 106 million dollars, ended on June 30, 1952. It was superseded by M.S.A., which, during the next two years, until June 30, 1954, granted us a payment of 98·6 million dollars. I have already mentioned my scepticism regarding all projection of trends and about the belief that these economic trends can always be tied down into plans.

The end of the Marshall Plan is a suitable occasion to review the so-called Long Term Plan (LTP). This initial plan (LTP), which played a big role in the discussion of economic policy at the beginning of 1949, formed the basis of the economic and financial developments until 1952. The targets, worked out in painful collaboration between the German and American authorities, were then regarded by those German experts who believed in planning as too high. How much this pessimism was refuted by events may be illustrated by some examples.

1. For 1952/53 LTP aimed at an industrial production of 110% of 1936. In fact 145·5% was achieved.

2. The target for the standard of living in 1952/53 was fixed at 20% below that of 1936. In fact, private consumption per head of population in 1936 equalled DM 768 and, in 1952/53, DM 827 (expressed in 1936 prices).

3. The LTP forecast that the German export trade would be about 2,818 million dollars when Marshall aid ended. In fact, exports in 1952 came to 4·04 million and in 1953 to 4·42 million dollars.

4. Typical of the limitations of such plans are the following points: it was said that an increase in coal production must be achieved by all possible means, since the increase of general

production was closely linked with the supply of coal. From this point of view a daily production of 425,000 tons for 1952/53 was regarded as absolutely essential. In spite of considerably exceeding the LTP targets in all other economic sectors, the daily production of coal mining remained considerably below 408,000 tons.

The balanced economic situation later allowed a further slackening of the restrictions which had been introduced during the Korean crisis. After the high discount rate of 6% was reduced by 1% on May 29, 1952, there followed four further reductions, so that on May 20, 1954, the level of 3% was reached—a low one for German economic conditions.

The Development of Discount and Bill Rates

Valid from		*Discount rate*	*Bill rate*
1948	1 July	5	6
	1 Sept.	—	—
	15 Dec.	—	—
1949	27 May	4½	5½
	14 July	4	5
1950	27 Oct.	6	7
1952	29 May	5	6
	21 Aug.	4½	5½
1953	8 Jan.	4	5
	11 June	3½	4½
1954	20 May	3	4
	1 July	—	—
1955	4 Aug.	3½	4½
1956	8 March	4½	5½
	19 May	5½	6½
	19 Sept.	4	5
1957	11 Jan.	4½	5½

Step by step the minimum reserve requirements were lowered during these months from the high levels they had reached during the Korean war.

The Break-through

It was important to point out that the state of the market was one in which there was a rising volume of goods for sale, in order to sustain the advance. Here is what I said on the occasion of the opening of the technical fair in Hanover at the end of April 1953.

> 'I do not wish to reply to the gossip which says that the arrears are made up and consumption satisfied. That is blasphemy. But it is easy to sense something else. I have felt it when, during the past quarter, I said that we must go beyond merely satisfying the people's basic needs and their day-to-day demands. We must see to it that in German households, and particularly in working-class households, durable goods, such as refrigerators, washing machines, vacuum cleaners amongst others, will be used.'

In reply I was told how much a pensioner earns, and that such people were not in a position even to think of such purchases. Naturally it is not the pensioner who can start increasing consumption. In the U.S. it was surely not the poorest who drove the first motor cars. But it is always true that the luxury of today is in general demand tomorrow and in general consumption the day after.

If we lack the courage to fight social resentment, if we cannot bear it that without being especially deserving some become consumers of the new product before others, then we shall have to continue living in an artificially preserved poverty.

If we do not begin to try to improve the life of our people, we are undermining the basis of technical progress. Then we shall leave the circle of civilized nations. We can only participate in a further happy and healthy development if we have the courage to consume.

Was this pure theory or a sensible glimpse of the future? Some statistical data here may prove the point:

Production of Refrigerators

	No.	Value in DM Million
1949	not available	28
1950		40
1951		75
1952	214,000	108
1953	363,000	158
1954	521,500	323
1955	588,700	241
1956*	691,500	248

*1st—3rd quarter

At the second international exhibition of bicycles and motor-bicycles in Frankfurt/Main on October 17, 1953, I took the opportunity to counter a frequently heard argument, which was to fight the overcrowding of the roads by restricting motoring:

> 'I believe that it is no concern of the State how the individual citizen wants to spend his money—it should not in this sense do any moral teaching. Every individual shall be happy according to his own lights. . . . What is more, I believe that the traffic problem can only be solved through expansion; with further motorization the necessary will have to be done concerning road building and the opening up of new communications.'

When I said this the figure of production of motor-bicycles and *mopeds* had gone up from 143,800 in 1949 to 290,800 for 1951 and 524,400 for 1953. The expansion which we had expected from this economic sector can be even better illustrated by the production of motor cars. Already the break-through of self-interest had taken place on the part of employers and workers, as purchasers of motor cars. Production here increased even more markedly, from 104,055 in 1949 to the current yearly figure of 850,000.

Pessimism at Work

When at the turn of the year 1953/54 the feeling that the boom was ending began to spread—it was even said and feared that the power and ability of the German economy to expand was slowing down—I found it essential to contradict this:

'The German economy leads the other European national economies in any comparison of the rate of development. This dynamic must not slow down; it is thus necessary to re-enliven the driving forces of the economy, which are the will to invest and to modernize and to keep fresh the joys of consumption.

'There is no logically compelling reason which must lead to a slackening of the tendency to improve, since the average standard of living, in spite of all progress, still remains at a level which contradicts all indications that arrears have been made up and that the consumer is satiated.

'Everything depends on keeping production going and increasing it, because as a result of production of goods—and only with it—the national income, i.e. the purchasing power, is created which ensures sales.'

And on another occasion, reviewing the year of 1954:

'If—as stated—the proper relationship between investible funds, the demands for capital, and the requirements of consumption cannot, for a number of reasons, be worked out in advance, then I consider it more advantageous in the present situation to maintain high consumption, and to allow strains to arise in the capital market rather than reduce consumption to adjust savings to a satisfactory level but at the price of causing anxiety about sales.'

Chapter IV

HARNESSING THE BOOM

IN 1954 the transition to the next, the fifth chapter, of the young history of market economy, that is, the transition to the boom, was already clear to those looking into the future. The new task which presented itself was again not easy to solve. Above all it was a question of effectively countering the danger of an inflationary over-taxing of the boom.

The implementation of this task proved so difficult that many tended to take a one-sided view of the problem, forgetting what tremendous progress had already been made in all sectors of the economic and social life of the people. Since the middle of 1956 the threat of collapse has been easier to control. With the slowing down of economic progress the transition to a calmer and steadier development may be regarded as assured.

The second part of the task, which was to control a slight inflation of costs, will be discussed later. At present it is a matter of dealing with certain newly-created sources of income which, introduced in this fifth period, will not be fully effective before 1957. These must be absorbed without endangering price stability.

The full transition to the boom in 1954 is clearly recognizable in the index of industrial production shown on page 61.

These figures demonstrate how the years 1954 and 1955 were ripe for investment returns. Progress was uneven in the investment and consumer goods industries during this period.

This particular boom was at first welcome, since at the time there were still unused reserves of human labour—in the second quarter of 1954, 1·15 million were unemployed. Realizing the connection between an economic policy of expansion and the raising of the standard of living, I approved this growth:

'That economic success is at the same time the basis and cause of all social progress, and alone can offer a large measure of economic security, cannot be denied—because where nothing exists even the trade unions lose their rights. A national income can only be divided if, first of all, a national income has been created.'

Production During the Boom

	1953		*1954*		*1955*		*1956*
	1st half year	*2nd half year*	*1st half year*	*2nd half year*	*1st half year*	*2nd half year*	*1st half year*
All industry	145·6	161·5	162·1	181·2	187·9	206·9	207·3
Investment goods	167·6	178·4	193·6	215·1	242·2	261·1	274·5
Basic Industries	132·3	141·2	147·6	164·5	174·3	186·9	188·9
Consumer goods	142·2	161·5	157·6	173·2	174·2	193·8	191·3

(1936=100)

The graph on page 23 shows production trends for the whole of industry since currency reform, Table 1 in the Appendix that of the most important economic sectors.

The conflicting rhythm between the consumer and the investment goods sector in the first phase of the boom I described thus:

'In view of the coming shortage of labour, which has been evident to the intelligent for some years, naturally the pressure in the past two years for greater productivity and for modernization has been particularly strong. But consumption must not lag behind. Much more is it the task of a good economic policy to see that all individual sectors of the economy benefit in turn from the boom. But it will not be the same for both sectors: always one or the other will be ahead by the length of a nose.'

The statistics of the increase in production over the same period of the previous year are impressive.

Rate of Growth of Industrial Production
Percentage Increase Over Twelve Months

	1953	*1954*	*1955*	*1956*
January	+ 4·0	+ 11·0	+ 17·4	+ 13·2
February	+ 7·3	+ 10·2	+ 16·7	+ 8·1
March	+ 10·7	+ 8·4	+ 15·8	+ 10·1
April	+ 12·0	+ 9·7	+ 14·9	+ 12·4
May	+ 11·1	+ 13·8	+ 15·8	+ 11·0
June	+ 10·9	+ 12·1	+ 16·2	+ 6·0
July	+ 14·7	+ 9·3	+ 15·2	+ 8·6
August	+ 10·9	+ 11·1	+ 15·4	+ 7·4
September	+ 11·1	+ 11·7	+ 14·8	+ 6·2
October	+ 9·3	+ 12·0	+ 13·7	+ 3·9
November	+ 9·2	+ 12·5	+ 14·5	+ 4·5
December	+ 13·8	+ 13·3	+ 12·2	+ 4·5

During the middle of 1954 it became evident that we were approaching a prolonged boom. This forecast was mainly based on the trend of orders. The order book for all industry during the first six months of 1954 exceeded that for the same period of 1953 by 23·6%. In the basic industries it was even more, 33·3%. In the capital goods industries the rise was 27·8%, while in the consumer goods sector an increase of only 6·6% took place.

In the second half of 1954 we were approaching full employment, which, since the crisis of the thirties, politicians as well as theorists in economics had come to regard as the most desirable aim. During the five months of June to November 1954, unemployment for the first time fell below the million mark; a year later, on September 30, 1955, with 18 million employed, the figure of unemployed had sunk to less than

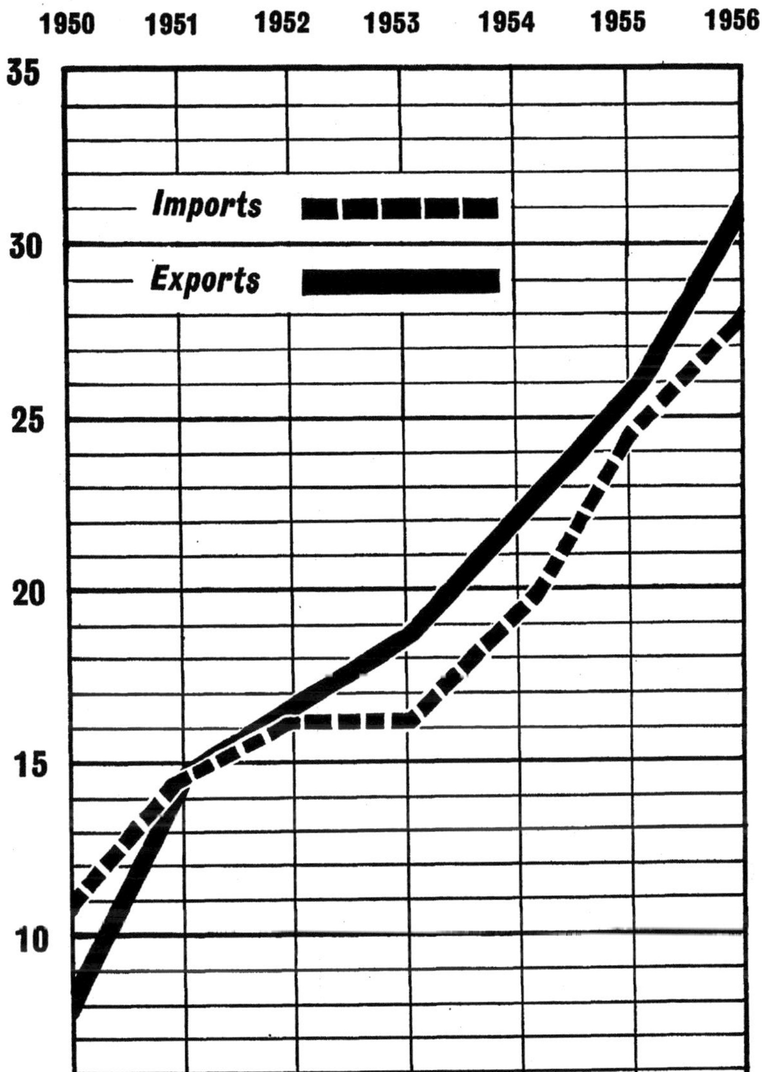

FOREIGN TRADE OF THE FEDERAL REPUBLIC IN DM MILLIARDS

The above chart shows the impressive development of the export trade, whereby an excess of imports over exports of DM 3 Milliard in 1950 was transformed into an excess of exports over imports of a like amount in 1956.

500,000. In many trades and areas full employment had been reached.

These facts are further confirmed by data for 1956. In September the unemployment figure had dropped to 411,100 while the figure of employed had risen to 18·1 million. Within a year about 800,000 people had found new jobs, and only a tenth of them had come from the fortunately shrinking reserve of the unemployed. One would have thought that this success would have found some acknowledgment even in the camp of my opponents.

Employment and Unemployment

	Employed	*Unemployed* *(in thousands)*	*Total*
30.6.48	13,468	451	13,919
30.9.48	13,463	784	14,247
30.9.49	13,604	1,314	14,918
30.9.50	14,296	1,272	15,567
30.9.51	14,885	1,235	16,120
30.9.52	15,456	1,051	16,507
30.9.53	16,044	941	16,986
30.9.54	16,831	823	17,653
30.9.55	17,807	495	18,302
30.9.56	18,610	411	19,021
30.9.57	19,400	367	19,767

This trend in the labour market shows that far more people than there were unemployed according to the statistics have found employment. In the past seven years the unemployment figure dropped by 900,000, while the figure of employed rose by 5 million. In the autumn of 1956 the unemployment figure was 2·2% of the potential of employment (men 1·4%; women 3·6%).

Headhunters at Work

This unusual problem for Germany, which grew out of so-called full employment, obscured what had been achieved. I therefore thought it necessary to stress on September 8, 1955:

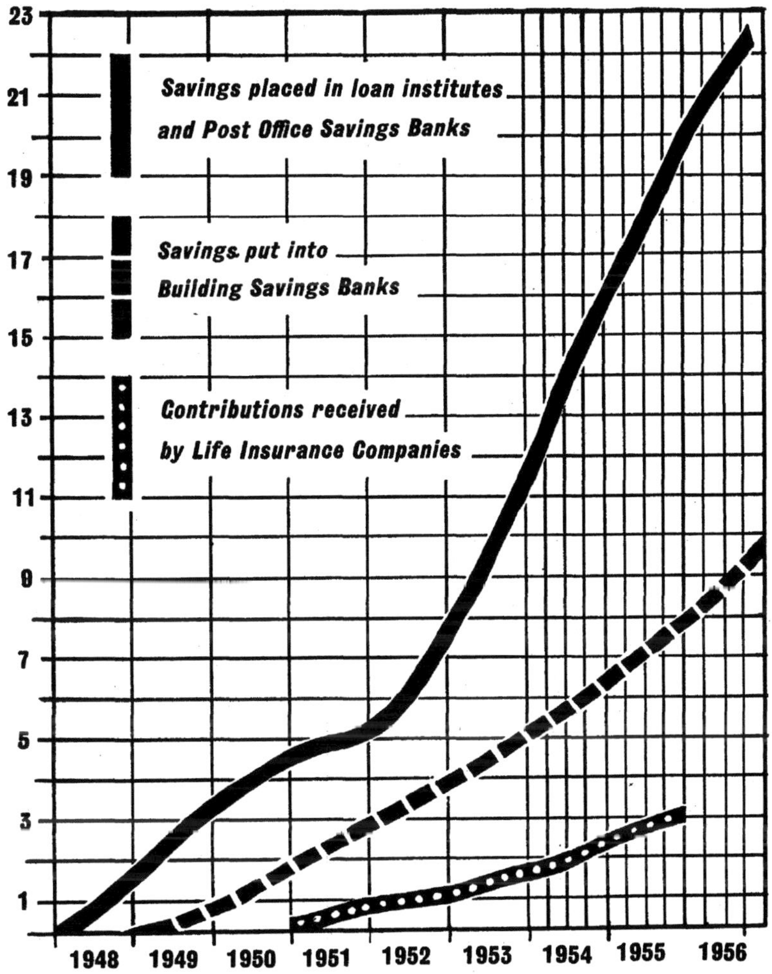

DEVELOPMENT OF SAVINGS

Despite the disturbing effects of two currency devaluations a savings total of DM 35 Milliard was reached by the end of 1956; the increase in savings during the last four years is particularly noticeable.

'Whoever keeps his ears open might sometimes assume that with full employment, a high level of production, and with growing consumption, a disaster had befallen us, and special efforts would have to be made to subdue our economic performance. Commonsense spurns such views. It will not accept that what has been to the advantage of each individual can be dangerous or damaging from a general economic point of view.'

These new events were met by an awkwardness which eventually led to a clarification of the real issues. Some believed that they could fight the consequences of the changed situation of the labour market by trying to entice workers. This unhappy practice threatened to ruin any sane wage policy. Plain speaking was needed:

'I have been told by the trade unions: "Look what is happening in the labour market, and ask yourself whether we of the unions can still pursue a responsible wage policy, when recruiting officers from one industry are going through the country taking labour from other industries." I am not against a free choice of jobs or against the freedom of the worker to choose his own place of work; but what is happening now I can only describe as the work of headhunters, who are trading in human lives.

'These happenings are not only to be condemned economically; they should be morally and socially condemned. No argument exists which could justify the use of such means.'

This shortage of labour increasingly proved to be the most serious problem facing the economy:

'The best solution, which would simultaneously have favourable social and economic consequences, is to be found in an increase in the productivity of our economy. We must therefore do everything we can to modernize. We must use every means to increase productivity, to compensate what we lack in quantity, i.e. through a higher standard of efficiency.'

As Minister for Economic Affairs I had to see that no difficulties would develop in the wake of the quick upward surge on the investment goods side, and at the same time I was trying to emphasize the necessity to increase effort, and, through modernization, to arrive at a better output and thus raise the efficiency of human labour. I stressed several times that, with full employment, it was indisputable that the enterprising investment of today would be the gain of the worker tomorrow.

If, in these months, I felt that I had to express some scepticism about the boom in the investment sector, it was because the signs of mistakes and misunderstandings in respect of the capabilities of the economy were increasing there. Therefore, I said on November 12, 1955:

> 'The present level of investment of 27% of the gross national income proves clearly enough that our economy has recognized in time the approaching problem of a shortage of labour. But it must now also be ready to appreciate that a further increase in investment, which strains the capacity of the relevant branches of industry, and therefore leads to an over-taxing of the boom, cannot be an acceptable means of economic policy. Consumption, as well as investment, should be guided by the budget.'

In fact investment in 1955 was appreciable, as can be recognized in the figures of production and also in the share of investment in the national income.

Use of National Income by Percentage

	1936	*1949*	*1950*	*1952*	*1954*	*1955*
Private consumption	60·5	65·2	63·8	56·1	56·1	56·1
Government consumption	20·8	18·3	16·3	17·9	16·5	15·4
Investment and Foreign Aid	18·7	16·5	19·9	26·0	27·4	28·5
Gross National Income	100	100	100	100	100	100

Use of National Income by Percentage (cont.)

Expressed in 1936 Prices

	1936	*1949*	*1950*	*1952*	*1954*	*1955*
Private consumption	60·5	61·7	60·6	58·1	59·2	59·4
Government consumption	20·8	22·0	19·1	19·3	17·4	16·2
Investment and Foreign Aid	18·7	16·3	20·3	22·6	23·4	24·4
Gross National Income	100	100	100	100	100	100

In 1956 in the private sector—according to these estimates—an increase of approximately 8% took place, with a gross investment of barely 6%, while Government consumption remained unchanged. The total gross national income in 1956 increased by 7·1% (these calculations are made by eliminating all price changes).

Insofar as one can abstract the investment in plant and equipment from the total sum of investment, the past years showed the following trend:

In Million DM

	1952	*1953*	*1954*	*1955*
In actual prices	24,680	27,735	30,630	38,100
In 1936 prices	10,942	12,566	14,078	16,791

Increases in Wages and Salaries

The clear picture of a boom shown here finds its reflection in the trend of incomes of the employed population, and even other sectors of the population. The gross hourly wages of the industrial worker, which in relation to 1953 had increased by 4·6%, and to 1954 by 2·9%, rose considerably in 1955 (by 6·8%). The trend continued even faster in 1956, and in the first three-quarters of that year rose by 8·5, 8·9 and 8·4%

respectively over the same periods of the previous year, though the increase in productivity did not keep pace.

The strong impetus of this movement in the wages section meant, according to statistics of the BDL, that net wages and salaries had grown from DM 54·1 milliard in 1954 to DM 60·9 milliard in 1955.

This increase by nearly 7 milliard far exceeded that of any previous year. According to the provisional calculations of the BDL, 1956 shows an increase of just under 12% and a rise to DM 67·9 milliard. Pensions (after tax deductions) also increased, pensions and maintenance payments rising from DM 17·7 milliard in 1954 to DM 19·6 milliard the next year. Here, too, appreciable increases of 12% can be seen for 1956 compared with the previous year, the total of these payments thus rising to DM 22 milliard. Total incomes thus rose altogether from DM 71·8 milliard in 1954 to DM 80·6 milliard in 1955. These figures certainly highlight the enormous strides made in social advancement. In 1956—again according to the preliminary figures of the BDL—total incomes reached DM 89·9 milliard, and were thus double those of 1950.

Date	*Gross Wages and Salaries total DM Mrd.*	*Per employed DM*	*Deductions*	*Net Wages and Salaries DM Mrd.*	*Pensions etc.*	*Total Incomes*
1950	39·3	2,839	5·3	34·0	11·4	45·4
1952	53·5	3,560	8·4	45·1	15·0	60·1
1954	63·8	3,922	9·7	54·1	17·7	71·8
1955	72·2	4,193	11·2	60·9	19·6	80·6
1956	80·8	4,473	12·9	67·9	22·0	89·9

This favourable trend, and the intention of the Federal Government further to increase social service payments, can naturally only exist in a flourishing economy. The general increase in prosperity may be seen by making a comparison of the national income per head of the present population, after allowing for price increases, with the figures for 1936.

Comparison of National Income per Head

	1936	*1949*	*1950*	*1952*	*1954*	*1955*
In RM/DM	992	836	939	1,086	1,230	1,350
1936=100	100	84	95	109	124	136
1949=100	—	100	112	130	147	161

We not only succeeded in overcoming the ravages of the war, but output in 1956 was 45% higher than that of the last year of peace, and, compared with 1949, was up by 70%. These are figures which speak to the unbiased observer more clearly than long commentaries about the success of the social market economy.

Rapid Reaction of the Saver

Among the economic factors responsible for the boom, but which were also influenced in turn by the prevailing economic situation, the rate of saving must be mentioned. The beginning of the boom coincided with an intensive period of saving. It is therefore justifiable to describe 1954 not only as a year of investment but also as a year of savings. This identity, which predominated again in the following year, 1955, only broke up in 1956. The total amount of savings had risen from the beginning of 1954 to the beginning of 1955 from DM 11·24 milliard and, until the same time in 1956, had grown by nearly another DM 4 milliard to DM 20·67 milliard. The building societies' deposits also showed a similarly favourable trend, though naturally on a smaller scale.

This remarkable willingness to save was at the time a strong stabilizing factor, while the later slowing down of savings gave some cause for worry. The total amount of savings was DM 20·67 milliard in January 1956, but by November had grown to only DM 22·495 milliard. That, without a doubt, indicates a relatively lower rate of growth. Happily, a change for the better has taken place more recently.

The increase of voluntary savings since currency reform proves how much can be done when the population has confidence in the stability of the currency; this in spite of unfavourable conditions, for, after all, savings have twice been wiped out in Germany (cf. graph on page 65).

The opening phase of the boom was finally marked by another important event. With the ending of the so-called Law for the Encouragement of the Capital Market the way was clear to help the capital market to return to a role appropriate to a market economy. From this date (December 31, 1954) the rates of interest and yields on the various securities worked together again according to the rules of a market economy. The tendency towards lower rates of interest thus brought about was interrupted because credit restriction had become necessary in the economic circumstances of the boom. At the same time it can be assumed that this good start was not wasted. The recovery of the capital market, together with the revival of savings accounts and insurance premiums went ahead together to satisfy the heavy demand for investment in respect of the capital market (cf. Table 2 in Appendix).

This view of the value of the capital market encouraged the hope that a renaissance of the stock market might soon be brought about.

The repercussions of the boom could also be clearly seen in the development of foreign trade. Both 1954 and 1955 were marked by a very strong rise in the volume of foreign trade, whilst a burst of imports in 1955 halved the surplus of the trade balance of 1954. The year 1956 showed an unexpectedly strong rise in both imports and exports, as well as a return to a surplus in the trade balance. The impetus behind this rise in exports followed some slackening in the capital goods industries at home, which freed capacity for deliveries overseas. Without a doubt this trend would have gone further if the Federal Ministry for Economic Affairs had not at this time adopted a policy of easing imports. Germany's position in the world market had become stronger. Its export performance came third, after the U.S.A. and Great Britain.

These facts, stamped out by economic success, could be taken as proof that at the same time price stability could have been maintained. This idea, however, as all experience shows, is very difficult, if not impossible, to realize in this phase of the economy. But it has to be acknowledged that the stormy upward trend of export and internal demand was accompanied by only relatively small price increases. There was, and is, no need for dramatization. A strong upward trend of prices might have been feared all the more, as during the boom orders always surpassed deliveries. So far as exports are concerned, this is still the case today.

Prices which had remained stable until the second half of 1954 now rose slightly. In the previous two years prices of manufactured products tended to fall. They dropped from a level of 121 to 116, and this lower level was maintained until September 1954 (1950 = 100). From that moment a slow but steady increase took place. In February 1956, the level of 1952 was again reached and moved until September of that year between 120 and 121. Not until the autumn of 1956 were there further increases, so that in November the price level compared with the same months of the previous year rose by 2·9% and compared with November 1954 by 5·1%.

In view of these price movements during the past two or three years the trend of the cost of living index must be regarded as relatively stable. For 1954 as a whole it remained at the 1953 level (i.e. at 108% of 1950), then rose in 1955 to 110% and has moved since January 1956 between 112 and 114%. For 1955, it is calculated that a rise of the total cost of living (of the medium consumer group) of 1·8% took place compared with the previous year. In the late autumn of 1956 the total index had gone up by 1·8% compared with the same period of the previous year; it rose above the level of 1954 by 3·7%. A comprehensive view of the development of these economically important prices is given in Table 3 in the Appendix.

Compared internationally, the Federal Republic, as is shown in the following table, can be proud of its record.

Cost of Living Index (1949/51 = 100)

	1953	1954	1955	9 months of 1956
West Germany	103	103	105	108
Belgium	106	108	107	110
U.S.A.	109	109	109	111
France	126	126	127	129
Denmark*	115	116	121	128*
Sweden	120	122	125	132
Great Britain	120	122	128	132
Norway*	129	135	136	142*

*1950 = 100

Price Stability is Imperative

The slight drop in the level of consumption which took place shows the disadvantages of the boom. I have again and again pointed out that, in the long run, no amount of economic progress can be big enough to offset even the most apparently harmless softening of the currency. I warned repeatedly:

'The economic question is not whether prices should be kept stable, or whether in certain conditions they may be allowed to rise. The level of prices must in all circumstances be maintained. The only question is how we can secure this.'

I absolutely deny that a strong expansion must be naturally or lawfully combined with a general rise in prices. In the interest of all those drawing incomes and all savers, the aim must be a rising and more embracing prosperity while keeping prices stable.

'Perhaps the experience of the past has often been interpreted differently; however I see no reason to relax my efforts, through responsible monetary, credit and financial policies, to prove that an expansion can continue while prices remain stable.'

Finally in the crucial weeks and months I had frequently to

oppose those who thought that only by a steady, although slight, weakening of the currency could those impulses grow which in the long run would secure economic expansion. I said at the time: 'After the past ten years many false ideologies and dogmas have been practically discredited; in real life it seems to me to be time also to destroy this last and perhaps most dangerous illusion.'

All measures taken to restrain economic development were based on the wish to safeguard the stability of the currency, but I could never have abandoned the principle and the aim of an expanding economy. Because it is so important to find the right measures to make further steady progress, one of many of my sayings on the subject deserves to be reproduced here:

'I really cannot be accused of wishing to propagate a restrictive policy for selfish reasons, nor is it true that I could suppose that to depress this boom forcibly is a worthwhile aim. No—certainly not—because the secret of the success of our economy lies in the fact that we have never retreated from the difficulties, but have always found the solutions through moving forward dynamically and by expanding. And thus it shall remain, though naturally it should not be overlooked—and not only today—that some difficulties are becoming increasingly obvious.'

Unpopular Truths

Out of this basic conception several measures to curb and direct the boom have been taken. These attempted to influence those factors which caused disturbances or set off new dangers. For example, in this connection, the many psychological influences should be remembered. These were based on the conviction that the actual dangers were not a necessary part of life but rather had their roots in the disregard of economic limitations. My original thesis here naturally was always the stability of the currency. A special chapter has therefore been devoted in this book to that campaign.

In those months I never tired of declaring the unpopular

truth: that wages and prices, in spite of all denials and tactical manoeuvres, remained indissolubly linked.

> 'When wages, even if only on one sector of the economy, get out of control, then they cannot remain stable elsewhere. This means that it is not possible (and thus must not happen) that in any branch of the economy wage demands to the size of X can be met, while other industries are only able at the best to grant half X or only a quarter X, unless price increases are to gain ground.
>
> 'It is irresponsible to allow a price simply to get out of hand or to believe falsely in exploiting to the last such favourable boom conditions. Such behaviour in a situation like this creates naturally a precedent which it is a temptation to follow. But that means inflationary trends, which must be stopped at the start.'

Such thoughts then caused me, in spite of much opposition and shaking of heads in those turbulent months, to fight against all avoidable price increases, whether in industry or agriculture. I tried to oppose all wage increases which were not justified by progress in productivity. On the other hand there was considerable scope for higher wages, since the trend of productivity was showing good results.

Higher wages were balanced by progress in productivity during 1955. But the discrepancy between progress in productivity and the increase in total incomes for 1956 cannot be denied. Gross wages and salaries per worker rose—according to preliminary estimates of the BDL—by about 7%, total incomes by almost 12%, compared with 1955, while the increase in productivity in 1956 was 3·4% per hour worked in industry and 2·4% elsewhere. No one can say that he acted without knowledge of the consequences, for I had literally run up and down the country to explain this simple truth to even the most limited mind.

No Doubt About Price Responsibility

The connection between price increases and the growth of personal incomes in excess of the progress of productivity, i.e. above what the economy can produce, must not be overlooked in this phase of economic development. The inevitable consequences can be measured to within 1%. The responsibility for these price increases, for the slight watering down of purchasing power, shall and must be ascribed to those responsible. That is true as much for the joint management concerns[6] as for the Government and members of Parliament. It should be stated once more that there is nothing against changes which are made within what is economically possible. Such improvements are even desirable, since they absolutely meet the requirements of the market economy.

The psychological campaign which I initiated was meant to be accompanied by other plans, which only partly succeeded. My suggestions were aimed at slowing down the effects of the growing surplus of foreign trade by making the financial system more liquid. Above all, this was to be achieved through increasing imports to make more goods available at home, and thus exercise a pressure on prices. After months of discussion in the Government and Parliament, cuts in customs duties were proclaimed on April 1, 1955, but not to the extent that I had wished, or regarded as desirable. The degree of liberalization with the O.E.E.C. countries was increased step by step, and the free list for imports from the dollar area considerably widened.

Special measures aimed at achieving a remedial effect where the difficulties appeared greatest. A limitation of public funds for investment went side by side with a retrenchment of public investment in building.

Because my proposals were often accepted only in part and often too late, I increasingly supported the BDL, and even encouraged it to depart from the very liberal monetary and credit policy which had been introduced after the end of the Korean boom.

The Federal Ministry for Economic Affairs and the BDL both judged the economic situation alike. On August 4, 1955, the low discount rate of 3% which had been valid since May 20, 1954, was altered to 3½%. This step was followed on March 8, 1956, by a further increase in the discount rate of 1%, and on May 20 a new tightening of the reins lifted the discount rate to 5½%. This logical policy was reinforced with other measures by the BDL. Thus, on September 1, 1955, the minimum reserve requirements were raised and rediscount facilities limited. The most remarkable fact of the economic situation of those months was that my close collaboration—or rather agreement—with the Central Bank was by no means generally approved.

These many-sided developments were not without success. During the middle of 1956 the return to a healthy and realistic production rate took place. The tempo of expansion adapted itself to the potential growth of the economy. The annual increase in production which, in 1955, was over 15%, dropped to 8% or less, but remained at a level which could not be termed a stagnation or crisis. The lowering of the bank rate on September 6, 1956, from 5½% to 5%, and the further cut by ½% of January 1, 1957, can be regarded as evidence of consolidation.

Success is Achieved

There are many reasons for this better balance. I believe that the psychological campaign, together with the measures taken by the BDL, played an important role. The increase in imports in those sectors which were particularly endangered by rising prices, was also effective. Even the imports of foodstuffs rose from DM 2·14 milliard in the fourth quarter of 1955 to DM 2·82 milliard in the same period of 1956.

All statistical data indicate that the phase in which the threat of a boiling over of the boom became a real danger could be considered as past, to make room for a period of steady upward development. Nevertheless it should not be overlooked that a heavy mortgage remains from this period, with which economic policy will have to come to terms. In particular, this is true of those wage increases which exceeded the increase in production. The socially necessary increase in pensions and assistance payments from public funds, and the increase in the social security payments during social reform must be mentioned here, particularly since only a part of this expenditure could be financed from increased contributions. In any case here are sums amounting annually to milliards which will reach the market simply as spending power. Insofar as the cut in taxes becomes effective the same is true. These changes in the structure of incomes have naturally forced us also to improve the earnings in the public service, so that even in this quarter incomes have received a renewed impetus. Finally, one must consider the widening of consumer purchasing power in relation to the will to save.

Much Depends on the Will to Save

Whether those potentially expansionist tendencies will cause trouble will depend on savings. In the third quarter of 1956 the growth of savings came to only DM 90·7 million—one-eighth of that for the same period of 1955. Fortunately it appears that the most recent measures of the Federal Government have renewed the will to save. It is to be hoped further that satisfaction with the Government will increase social confidence, and thus increase saving.

This development can be taken as evidence of how much the saver reacts to a real or assumed deterioration of the value of money. Reminders that a debasement of the currency is not taking place and that worries are groundless will therefore not be successful psychologically. To clarify what has already been stated, the fate of a one hundred mark note paid in on the day of currency reform is sketched out here. The trend of the price index at the time clearly shows that only a small part of the rise in interest rates and compound interest rates on monies paid into a savings bank has been eliminated by higher prices.

Price Index of the Cost of Living

		2nd half of 1948=100
In payments on 21 June 1948	=DM 100	
Total Deposit on 31 December 1948	=DM 101·22	—
Total Deposit on 31 December 1949	=DM 103·75	1949= 99
Total Deposit on 31 December 1950	=DM 106·39	1950= 92
Total Deposit on 31 December 1951	=DM 109·58	1951=100
Total Deposit on 31 December 1952	=DM 112·87	1952=102
Total Deposit on 31 December 1953	=DM 116·26	1953=100
Total Deposit on 31 December 1954	=DM 119·75	1954=100
Total Deposit on 31 December 1955	=DM 123·34	1955=102
Total Deposit on 30 December 1956	=DM 127·45	30 Dec. 1956=105

To counter all possible misunderstandings at the outset, it should be noted that the comparison of savings and the cost of living index in no way constitutes a special appeal for a stabilization of the index of savings.

The future shape of our foreign trade will also be of great importance. Expansionist tendencies to which it might give rise could in the future be even more important, since the neutralizing effect of budget surpluses is not likely to be as marked as in past years.

In the final phase of the boom, in spite of a noticeable slowing down in the rate of increase of production, a higher level of costs, wages and prices has been established. It is possible to point to several factors which will further provoke higher prices in those economic sectors nearest to the consumer, unless my repeated appeal that wages should only be allowed to rise in step with higher productivity is obeyed.

The central problem of economic policy is therefore to keep the further growth of the economy free from inflationary tendencies. To maintain the stability of money is the basic condition for a balanced economic growth, and for true and certain social progress. The economic policy of the Federal Government must thus in future be increasingly directed towards maintaining financial stability. Whether restrictive measures will finally be needed will depend on the readiness of all sections of our population to deny themselves those special advantages which are gained at the expense of all.

Chapter V

THE MARKET ECONOMY CONQUERS PLANNING

'The economic policy began with the slogans of "Free Market Economy" and of "Liberalization". It ended in the spring with import controls, which demonstrates the failure of the whole policy, above all as regards foreign trade . . . In the meantime nearly all principles and theories which the Federal Minister for Economic Affairs has repeatedly put forward here . . . have completely failed. . . . You will agree with me that the Federal Minister for Economic Affairs, who campaigned for a removal of State controls, is now about to re-introduce controls which will work ineffectively . . . after the whole economic policy has gone wrong.'

It is not so long ago—on October 11, 1951, during the Korean crisis—that the speaker of the largest opposition party of the German Federal Parliament put forward these hypotheses which today seem unrealistic. In the meantime the sovereignty of the consumer in West Germany, and the free formation of prices in almost all sectors of the economy, have become a reality. Every businessman can and may produce and sell freely what the market demands. Furthermore, he is free to manage, to modernize, and to invest his money against other businessmen in the competitive market.

The opening quotation brings to mind how passionately the quarrel over the principles of the market economy raged only a few years ago. Hostility to the free market among the opposition was almost unanimous—if from different motives. Some tended to deny the validity of these principles, while others believed it impossible to realize them in a post-war Germany with its productive capacity destroyed and with its millions of refugees.

Today this lively and vital battle has become a thing of the past. Records of the discussion which then took place read today like pages of a thrilling novel. It is worth while to leaf through these pages of recent German history. The first post-war German Parliament, the Economic Council in Frankfurt, and later the Federal Parliament of the first period of the legislature, lived through exciting days of passionate parliamentary debate.

In the days of currency reform the largest opposition party, the S.P.D., made it clear that it did not want freedom from controls for the German people. I intended to remove, in the course of currency reform, all controls affecting production, trade, and, above all, the consumer. We read in the records of the memorable Meeting of the 18th Economic Council of the combined British and American Zones, which took place immediately before currency reform of June 17 and 18, 1948, the argument of the economics spokesman of the S.P.D., Dr. Kreyssig. His view was that since Germany had not had a normal economy for years, currency reform would be unable to work any miracles. He called for Government controls over the economy and, in particular, stressed the need for directing the most essential consumer goods where they would be most needed. Prophesying a catastrophe if prices were decontrolled, he believed that German industrialists would promote a Morgenthau policy which would be even more disastrous than the one put forward by Morgenthau himself. The S.P.D. was firmly convinced that only through systematic planning and a systematic guidance of the economy could it return to a healthy state.

Thus Dr. Kreyssig clarified what the S.P.D. had said at earlier meetings of the 14th Economic Council on April 21 and 22, 1948. At this meeting I had outlined my plans for currency reform:

'Naturally, in these discussions, my aim is not only to achieve merely a substantial closing of the gap between the supply of goods and the demand for them, but to attack the evil at its root. Any solution which would force us, in spite of slight easements, to continue with the present form of government controls, including the price freeze, in our future economic system would be disastrous. Any solution which does not lay the ghost of the price frozen inflation, but on the contrary further increases surplus purchasing power, would necessarily require further action in respect of currency. . . .

'In decisively opposing this economic principle I am by no means advocating a return to the liberal economic policies of the past and the irresponsible free-booting methods that prevailed.

'That today's system will either have to adopt freer market economic methods, or else sink to absolute totalitarianism, everyone who is conscious of the overbearing character of our economic situation will have to acknowledge. . . .'

Different Conceptions

Dr. Kreyssig, of the S.P.D., made it clear that his conception was fundamentally different. But it is only fair to remember that some who did not support the S.P.D. thought along the same lines—which is perhaps not surprising, as industrial production then amounted to 50% of that of 1936, while the population had increased by millions.

Dr. Kreyssig maintained that only through a carefully developed plan could Germany once again find her feet, and attacked those in favour of free enterprise. Another S.P.D. deputy, Herr Schoettle, today the chairman of the budgetary committee of the Federal Parliament, supported Dr. Kreyssig in his view that the economic situation could not improve through individual enterprise. He wanted over-all political decisions from the top, from which would stem definite plans and guiding principles to encourage this or that section of the economy.

In opposition to Dr. Kreyssig's pessimistic views I said at the memorable meeting of the Economic Council a few hours before currency reform:

> 'I believe that there is full agreement that the lesson has been learnt about the system of State control, after a period of chaotic and criminal financial, economic and currency policy. Not only has the collapse of this kind of order or apparent order taken place, but it has also brought about the collapse of the idea of all State controls. . . .
>
> 'Every segment of our population is longing to be freed from this straitjacket. The path must lead back to freer market economic systems, and towards the removal of the controls which have daily plagued every individual, consumer as well as producer.'

In view of the many demands for Government control over prices, I believed it right to speak openly in the Economic Council, and before any currency reform, of my basic beliefs that State controls and lack of freedom in price establishment cannot be separated from each other. Who demands the one must understand that the other will follow:

> 'Let us make it quite clear—and the German people are well aware of it—that controls on the one hand and the price freeze and the fixing of prices on the other were the obvious signs of a maladministration under which the people groaned for fifteen years. If we are not resolved to end these classical symptoms of mismanagement, then the people will never believe that currency reform will lead to a return to prosperity. . . .
>
> 'It is impossible to try to drive the economy from two sides. It is not possible on the one hand by means of some magic key to control trade, and on the other to order things differently as a result of natural demand freely exercised by each individual citizen on the basis of a free choice of goods. I completely refute the principle of planning and controlling if it will plague the consumer or producer from morning to night.'

The Plunge into Cold Water

Dr. Kreyssig believed differently. He thought it wrong to throw the sick man into cold water and expect him to swim. The seriousness and extent of the disease of the German economy would be exposed to all on the day of currency reform. His party could not follow Dr. Erhard, because after currency reform, even if wages increased slightly, each worker would have to limit himself to the purchase of one pair of socks or a shirt.

The S.P.D. was ready to condemn immediately the social market economy, perhaps in anticipation that this criticism would soon no longer prove acceptable. Barely three weeks after currency reform Dr. Seuffert, speaking for the S.P.D. (then, as now, their specialist on financial political questions) declared at the 19th meeting of the Economic Council on July 8 and 9, 1948, that he did not believe that the people were glad to look into shop windows that were full, and that this development could only lead to further tensions. Possibly some were glad that this or that was once more available, but an improvement in the general position had not taken place.

In view of the developments during those first weeks and months after currency reform, the S.P.D. involved itself in ever-growing contradictions, due perhaps to its inability to change from its basic position of hostility. At the 20th meeting of the Economic Council on August 17-20, 1948, Dr. Arndt of the S.P.D. said that if any improvement had taken place it had come about as a result of the currency reform.

The S.P.D. made it clear that it intended to overthrow the initiator of the market economy. Increasingly, it realized how much the consequences of this economic policy would react on its own party. At the 20th meeting of the Economic Council it demanded that the Director for Economic Administration be removed—a demand which failed, after passionate discussion, by 47 to 35 votes.

Was the forecast of the S.P.D. that shortages would continue for years justified? Here are a few statistics taken at random:

	1949	*1951*	*1953*	*1956*
Leather shoes per million pairs	41·34	48·16	56·11	71·72
Spinning wool per ton	43·393	65·106	68·069	72·016
Spinning cotton per ton	144·729	216·944	238·285	277·049
Ladies' stockings per million pairs	23·0*	46·7	79·2	151·8
Household and other china per ton	38·154	49·194	59·810	76·399
Cigarettes in milliards	22·09	26·64	34·76	48·86
Coffee (kilogramme per inhabitant consumption)	0·48	0·71	1·37	1·82

*1950 figure, as 1949 figure not available

Between 1955 and 1956 production of consumer goods rose by another 8·3%

The remarkable declaration of Dr. Schoettle of the S.P.D., that millions of people would be unable to compete for years in a free market if money were the only criterion, forced one to the logical conclusion that the S.P.D. intended to introduce something other than money which would finally determine purchasing power. It is clear here that the S.P.D. felt that its continued hostility to the free movement of prices would lead to a system of rationing.

Dr. Schoettle predicted that my policy would expose large sections of the population to infiltration from the East.

Into the Arms of Communism?

What about this 'despair' which was to throw the people into the arms of Communism? At the elections for the first Federal German Parliament on August 14, 1949, the Communist Party received, with 1·362 million votes, 5·7% of the total. In the next Federal Parliamentary elections on September 6, 1953, it only got 2·2%, of 607,860 votes. In view of this fact it seemed a suitable moment to repeat my belief in the free market economy:

> 'I can imagine what would have happened if we had not taken this path, but had worked more carefully, i.e. if we had slipped into currency reform half with coupons and half with freely determined prices. What authority would have been in a position, without knowing the market, to give out coupons or the right to procure even in the most general form?
>
> 'It has been suggested that State control and free price establishment could be separated, as if it were conceivable that one could have the one and leave the other. Upon closer inspection this proves to be a complete illusion. Economic control and price policy belong together like Siamese twins, but, like them, they are no more than a monster.'

The same meeting of the Economic Council performed another historic task: it abandoned the wage freeze, that typical product of the war years and State controls. The introduction of this law, which had been of the greatest consequence, took only a few minutes.

The Senseless General Strike

The meeting of the Economic Council had taken place immediately before the date of the general strike, which for the first, and so far for the last, time in German history attempted to 'sweep away' the free market economy through industrial action. My views in regard to these intentions were:

> 'I believe that in fact this strike is unjustified. If it is meant to draw my attention to the fact that things are not yet quite in order, that much remains to be done, and that all of us carry a social obligation to create a more favourable relation between wages and prices, then I can tell you that this strike

is as unnecessary as a hole in the head. You must believe me when I say that I know what lies before us.'

At the 27th meeting, December 2-3, 1948, Dr. Kreyssig (S.P.D.) described my policy as catastrophic. The battle continued in the following weeks. The Opposition demanded an independent price bureau, which would have taken over price policy from me. To this I replied at the 28th meeting:

'. . . If the demand for an independent price bureau had any sense at all, then it could only be that an independent office would be in a position to remove faster and more effectively the economic tensions from which we suffer. I have often indicated here that it is quite wrong to regard much of the political play with prices as a result of economic policy. It has become clear in the meantime that this price adjustment and the new level of prices were the necessary result of currency reform.

'Now it is a question of adjusting the level of prices to the volume of money as altered through currency reform and also to international price levels. . . .

'An independent price bureau would either pursue the same price policy . . . or, if it were to follow another kind of policy, it would be a reactionary policy, which would result in goods vanishing once more from the market, and would bring back all the circumstances of a price frozen inflation.'

With the currency reform, the veil which had made all calculation impossible had been torn off the economy; behind lay pseudo-employment. Even before currency reform I pointed to the necessary process of change, coupled with a temporary increase in unemployment, which would have to be part of the bargain. The increase of unemployment was a worry. It was a question of keeping one's nerve. At the 37th meeting of the Economic Council of May 23-25 I declared:

'We must do everything to solve this serious social problem.

But do not forget what I have been saying for some time: we must follow a moderate credit policy. We must not take the pressure off the economy, because the inner structural fault of the German economy shown up by the past fifteen years must be corrected. We must not give up the idea of modernizing the economy as much as possible and of removing everything without a real social or economic function.

'The fall in prices since January has indirectly led to an improvement of the position and a rise in real purchasing power. On that credit policy is based. If we now altered course radically, if we allowed a generous loosening up to take place, then it is to be feared that this socially healthy process would come to a stop sooner than the social condition of our people warrants in the circumstances.'

The S.P.D. took the opportunity of this difficult situation to speak of 'the latent crisis of the market economy', to which I replied:

'I believe that we must not be dogmatic in our views. The last three-quarters of the year showed us how problematic the workings of a planned economy are. Figures can be made to prove anything, but figures are washed away by reality.

'That is true for all schemes, notably for those which will have to be thought up to meet the danger of increasing unemployment; for the investment plans which we have carried out, and for the efforts we are making to find capital to finance these plans.

'Personally, I strongly oppose arbitrary measures for capital investment. All will depend on the investment of capital in an organic manner. I am convinced—whether you believe me or not, and much I have said in the building has not been believed—that we can overcome the present stagnation through the market economy, while the rigidity of planning would certainly lead us deeply into trouble. . . .'

Did an easy optimism lie behind this statement or was this realism to be confirmed by events? Let us take a few of the important economic data of the next two years:

	30.6.49	*31.12.49*	*30.6.50*	*31.12.50*	*30.6.51*
Employed	13·49	13·56	13·85	14·16	14·72
Unemployed (in millions)	1·283	1·559	1·538	1·690	1·326
Index of Industrial Production (1936=100)	87·4	96	107·6	126·3	130·9

Unemployment Worries

Troubled by a level of unemployment of more than 1½ million at the end of 1949, but forgetting the increase in the number of employed and the steep increase in industrial production, the S.P.D. renewed its offensive on the market economy at the 36th plenary session of the Federal Parliament on February 9, 1950. Here the Minister for Economic Affairs of North Rhine Westphalia, Dr. Noelting (who has since died), declared for the Opposition that the situation in the labour market had never been more alarming since the end of the war. The stabilization of economic conditions was not even in sight, while the German economy seemed to be stagnant at a level of about 95% of 1936, while population had increased by 20%.

Certainly, Dr. Noelting seemed to be right, but only for a little while. The index of industrial production had dropped from 102·2 in November 1949, to 90·9 in January 1950, but within the year—by November 1950—it had shot up to 133·3 and increased further to 147·8 by November 1951.

Dr. Noelting continued that, for the Social Democrats, the development of employment and unemployment figures was the decisive economic barometer. One wonders whether this statement is still valid for the S.P.D. today, when it is the best proof of the soundness of the market economy. What are the figures?

	Yearly Average 1949	Yearly Average 1956
Employed	15·543 million	18·06 million
Unemployed	1·230 „	0·761 „

Away from the Path of Righteousness?

In view of the unemployment then prevailing Noelting demanded that an anti-deflationary economic policy should be pursued to break the spiral of unemployment, lack of purchasing power, and slackening turnover. I could not fail to reply to this advice.

> 'A deflationary crisis is a condition marked by a reluctance to invest; it is a condition leading to a continuing hoarding of money and disinvestment. I declare that just the contrary is true of our present economy. There is a noticeable demand for capital for investment. . . .
>
> 'You can say what you will: the moment you set about creating milliards in order to attain the goal of full employment from one day to the next, you are in fact introducing price increases. If your dogma does not allow this, you must again establish comprehensive Government institutions to prevent such price increases artificially, a situation that will lead us back to the forms of State controls which we have happily overcome.'

Dr. Kurt Schumacher, the chairman of the S.P.D., also went into attack. In stressing that a liberal economic policy must not be pursued for its own ends, but must protect the country from the possibility of a return to earlier conditions of unfulfilled demand, rationing, and the annihilation of the capital market which might lead to a return of State controls, I underlined that our economic policy was based on a Christian conception. Replying to Dr. Schumacher's question as to what I knew of a Christian conception, I said: 'That economic policy is Christian which helps people, each individual human being—and that is the economic policy which we are pursuing.'

The S.P.D. continued to demand credit expansion to overcome unemployment, but such an expansion of credit would have resulted in rising prices during this phase of developments and thus would have endangered the stability of the currency. On July 1, 1950, the S.P.D. Deputy, Kurlbaum, a well-known German economist and member of important German economic undertakings, said that a sufficient expansion of credit was only possible if some restraints were kept in being to counteract an undesirable trend of prices. On July 28 the S.P.D. again went into battle with a demand for the 'removal of the Federal Minister for Economic Affairs from his office', which was defeated by 187 votes to 142, with 28 abstentions. I then declared:

> 'No, ladies and gentlemen, you want to remove a man who has successfully resisted you. Finally I only wish to say one thing in reply to your demand—how well that would suit you!'

Patent Recipes are Useless

The passionate parliamentary debates about the preservation, and even more about the approval, of the market economy during the Korean crisis and the resulting boom began with the 102nd meeting. They were critical weeks during which many other deputies of the Federal Parliament began to doubt whether it was possible or justified to continue the market economy. During this meeting, on November 15, 1950, one of the S.P.D. speakers, in connection with the new difficulties appearing in the basic materials sections, asked whether the Federal Government, and particularly the Minister for Economic Affairs, would draw the necessary conclusions from the collapse of economic policy.

At the meeting of the Federal Parliament on November 14,

1950, I tried to get approval for a rational view in respect of coal supplies:

> 'It is easy after the event to say that developments could have been foreseen in the spring. No country could have done this. The whole world has experienced the same trends as we have in Germany. I can disclose that more and more European countries have been approaching us to ask how we have managed to keep prices more stable than elsewhere in Europe. . . .'

Certainly, it could not be denied, the coal situation had become difficult. But mining belonged to those spheres where the principles of market economy were most difficult to practise. Was the admittedly difficult position which seemed to give the Opposition the right to criticize really so catastrophic? The supply of pit coal at this time (including coking coal and briquettes) gives some idea:

The Coal Position (in million tons)

	Production	*Imports*	*Exports*	*Available*
1950	103·0	4·3	24·1	83·2
1951	109·9	9·8	23·6	96·2
1952	113·6	12·2	23·3	102·5

At the height of the Korean conflict the S.P.D. renewed its attempt to destroy the social market economy. Even today the parliamentary records of those months reproduce something of the passions of this quarrel. Dr. Noelting, at the 126th meeting of March 14, 1951, formulated his sharp attack on the Chancellor and on his Minister for Economic Affairs by pointing to a steep rise in prices. He believed that much more could have been done to soften the impact of this price rise. Is it really true that this rise in prices attacked the German consumer with full force? What does an international comparison show?

Cost of Living Price Index (1950 = 100)

	June 1950	*Sept. 1950*	*Dec. 1950*	*March 1951*	*June 1951*
U.S.A.	99	102	104	107	108
Great Britain	100	100	102	104	109
Belgium	98	104	102	109	110
France	96	102	106	115	112
Sweden	99	100	104	113	117
W. Germany	99	100	101	106	108

Dilettantism and Facts

In the same speech Minister Noelting said that it was the wrong price policy, begun in the summer of 1948 with the removal of price regulations, which had led to the present critical state. If everyone could invest as they wished, then everyone would need more coal, steel, electricity and gas, all in short supply. Increases in production and capacity should, in part at least, be directed to open up bottlenecks. These bottlenecks were the cause of the decline in exports, thus increasing indebtedness abroad.

Liberalization could not be undertaken without a timetable; Dr. Erhard's view that, if Germany bought from abroad, then other countries in turn would buy from Germany, had proved erroneous, with the result of increasing debts. Germany, being the weakest link in the chain of European countries, should not try to be a pace setter. A frivolous dilettantism, a doubtful megalomania had reigned, and all of the S.P.D.'s warnings had been thrown to the wind.

Is this judgment of 'dilettantism' and 'doubtful megalomania' confirmed by sober facts? When Minister Noelting painted this sombre picture in March 1951, our trade balance with the E.P.U. was in deficit by DM 25·5 milliard, but already the next months brought an appreciable improvement in this trade balance. The statistics of the BDL show the facts:

Trade Balance in DM million

	April	*June*	*Aug.*	*Oct.*	*Dec.*	*Total 1951*
Imports	621·1	575·5	690·7	677·6	782·7	8872·5
Exports	848·2	889·1	949·6	939·7	1152·1	10627·6
Balance	+227·1	+313·6	+258·9	+262·1	+369·4	+1755·1

In view of these facts it was right to reject the advice of Noelting that we should be satisfied with the role of 'fellow-traveller'. Noelting continued his speech, in which he demanded a reduction of the salary of the Federal Minister for Economic Affairs, by saying that more luxury had been allowed than had been warranted with the index of production at 117.

Was this emotional accusation, which affected many listeners, based on fact? Britain, which had been cited as an example, had in 1951 the largest trade deficit in postwar times, £1,197 million. The Labour Government resigned in October 1951, after one and a half years, to make room for a Conservative Government.

Noelting pointed to the impossibility of an economic policy which in its dogmatic rigidity had moved into a vacuum. State controls, he continued, were never desirable, but sometimes essential. The Minister for Economic Affairs had held that a little planning was as impossible as a little pregnancy. That was why the S.P.D. believed that only a little Erhard would remain in the future. In the name of the S.P.D., he asked the Federal Parliament to decide to reduce the salary of the Federal Minister for Economic Affairs.

Economic developments furnished the best reply to Noelting's speech. Here are a few of my remarks at the same meeting:

'I should like to establish that our economic policy has managed to re-create a purpose in the lives of our German people; that the important basic democratic rights—free choice of job and free choice for the consumer—have been won; that only as a result of this economic policy the German people have been able to believe in their work; that this economic policy has resulted in safeguarding the currency; and that we have been successful in rebuilding foreign trade from nothing. . . .

'The basis of our economic policy remains. . . . Though we persist in our principles, we are prepared (because of the developments provoked by the Korean conflict) to change methods and procedure. We wish to maintain the function of the market. But we realize that some freedom of movement and some lack of restrictions will have to be replaced by well-planned and logical rules.'

This discussion put me in a very difficult position. The general state of nerves in the world concerning the control of raw materials led to conditions where only by accepting such controls were we able to receive certain raw materials. The International Materials Conference began its activities. Personally I regarded these methods as ineffectual, and in fact we protected ourselves rather cunningly by giving only some statistics. That in the main was what 'controls' consisted of, and later I received the satisfaction of being proved right internationally in my belief.

The development of the Korean boom in the meantime was not only a cause for worry for the Opposition. A few months later—at the 167th meeting of the Federal Parliament on October 11, 1951—the S.P.D. thought that the end of market economy was about to come.

Was the S.P.D. right in its judgment of popular opinion? In North Rhine Westphalia the last general elections for the Länder Parliament had taken place on August 16, 1950, with 2·29 million votes for the C.D.U. In the next election, for the Federal Parliament on September 6, 1953, 3·92 million voted for the C.D.U. In Hesse at the Länder election of November 19, 1950, 348,148 votes went to the C.D.U., and on September 6, 1953, 849,125. These figures speak for themselves.

During the period of passionate parliamentary debate the Federal Minister for Economic Affairs had no doubts that the few controls arising from the Korean crisis, which had served mostly to impress opinion abroad, would soon be abandoned.

A New Conciliatory Tone

Thus ended the last large-scale discussions in the German Parliament about the 'to be or not to be' of the market economy. In the Federal Parliamentary elections of September 6, 1953, the electors replied with such conviction that the Opposition felt that it was pursuing the wrong path in its criticism. Although in later years further discussions took place, according to the records of the Federal Parliament, there is not a single one which can in any way be compared in violence or emotion with the discussions in the period of the Economic Council and the first legislature.

What a different, more conciliatory tone reigned later, when the economic situation was discussed at the 106th meeting of the Federal Parliament which took place in Berlin on October 19, 1955. Here Dr. Heinrich Deist, a leading member of the iron and steel industry, and highly regarded by the S.P.D., declared in the name of his party that they were proud of the fact that they had based their political, economic and social order on fundamental freedom. Such a development would have been impossible without the participation of all sections of the population, or without the interplay of power of the different political groups which was part of the important basic elements of political democracy.

Securing the stability of the currency had been one of the most important tasks, and everything would have been in vain, had not full attention been given to this task. All efforts to secure the stability of the currency would be supported by the S.P.D. They were living in a time of intensive economic activity, but it was wrong to speak of an overheating of economic developments. The economic system of the free world would in future depend on a high degree of employment coupled with stable prices and a stable currency.

This basically conciliatory position—leaving on one side some differences of opinion—also governed the second major economic debate at the 153rd meeting on June 26, 1956. Turning towards the Opposition I declared:

> 'I am glad to be able to establish that we do not differ greatly in our diagnosis of the economy. Everything mentioned by you as regards the importance of prices, the utilization of capacity, the lengthening of delivery dates as a sign of a dangerous trend of which we should beware, I fully agree with.
>
> 'I also agree with you that the critical sector is to be found on the investment side. . . .
>
> 'Even the analysis of the situation in foreign trade with its creation of large surpluses I regard as right, and I believe that the whole House agrees with me. But I should like to establish that, if in this connection the impetus to reduce customs duties has come from the Ministry for Economic Affairs, this has not been due to a complaint from O.E.E.C., but, on the contrary, the momentum we have developed and the wish to lower duties which we have proclaimed, has probably smoothed many paths for the O.E.E.C. in Paris.'

And at the conclusion of extensive discussions with S.P.D. spokesmen:

> 'On the whole I should like to state that I consider this discussion fruitful, and it is without irony, but sincerely felt, when I say that I am glad that in the course of many years I have been able to battle with the Opposition in the realm of economic policy.'

It must nevertheless be doubted whether this conciliatory tone in the economic policy field led to a closer relationship between Government and Opposition. A few weeks after this debate the Parliamentary group of the S.P.D. once again spoke of the 'questionability of the economic policy of the Federal Government', and of 'the dishonesty and irresponsibility of the economic propaganda of the Government and coalition parties during the past seven years'.

This also reflects the conflict between the liberal economic forces within the S.P.D. and those unable to detach themselves from the socialist doctrines of the old school.

Chapter VI

MINISTER FOR ECONOMIC AFFAIRS NOT THE REPRESENTATIVE OF PRIVATE INTERESTS

I HAVE IN FRONT OF ME newspaper clippings from those first years of my work as Director of Economic Administration in Frankfurt and as Minister for Economic Affairs in Bonn. I was then called 'Minister for Economic Affairs—Enemy of the Consumer', 'Erhard—Minister for Heavy Industry', 'The Patron Saint of Hoarders and Profiteers', and variations of similar titles were given to me.

The accusations have, of course, long since vanished from all serious discussion, and even the most malevolent of my opponents have ceased calling me such names. After my long efforts, and many battles with the representatives of important interests in the German economy, they have had to recognize the unworthiness of their views.

However that may be, the theme of the relationship of the Minister for Economic Affairs to the citizen, the link between Government leadership of the economy and the economy itself, and, above all, the question of the place of the economy within the whole life of the State and the social order, create such interesting and important problems that they should be examined more closely. This is all the more so because the fundamental principle of market economy shares those same maxims which should be followed by a modern social and freedom-loving democracy.

I should like to put at the beginning of these reflections a sentence which I have often repeated: the yardstick and criterion of what is good or bad in economic policy are not dogmas or the points of view of pressure groups, but exclusively the human being, the consumer, the people. Economic policy can only be regarded as good if and as long as it is regarded simply as useful and welcomed by the individual.

Whoever takes these reflections to their logical conclusion must agree with me that in every national economy vested interests exist. But these must not be allowed to determine economic policy, and no useful synthesis can be derived from a conflict between these interests. Any fragmentation of the national economy into vested interests cannot therefore be allowed. We must not take the path of dissolution; we must not withdraw from that real comprehensive order of economic society which alone can guarantee the social harmony of the nation. Our most serious purpose must be to meet this danger.

Employers Must be Responsible

I have never allowed any doubts to arise about my fundamental beliefs. At the C.D.U. Party meeting at Recklinghausen on August 29, 1948, I explained:

> 'I do not regard myself as the representative of special interests, and certainly not as the representative of the interests of industry or trade. It would be quite wrong to assume that. To be responsible for economic policy means to be responsible to the people as a whole. I am deeply convinced that the difficult problems facing us can only be solved if in using the market economy we manage not to favour groups, but rather to secure a decent standard of living for all our people and continually increase it through hard work and higher output. It is quite wrong to brand me as a man who is only interested in defending certain interests. The contrary is true. In the last analysis I demand not only great sacrifices from those responsible businessmen who have power over the production and distribution network of the economy, but also their understanding and sense of responsibility as well.'

I cite these examples from the early stages of the market economy to document once more that all those who later believed themselves able to assert their special interests and were then disappointed could not justify their actions by reference to my fundamental moral beliefs. I have always insisted that any sectional interest can only justify itself if it serves the interests of the whole community.

No group within the economy can demand special rights. That statement, however, does not contradict the fact that, when looked at by individuals, the economy is essentially made of parts. It is a question of striking a balance between those interests which brings about a general well-being.

In this connection I have on a former occasion pointed to the role of the State as supreme judge. I should like here to use the perhaps somewhat banal picture of a game of football, if I may. I believe that, as the referee is not allowed to take part in the game, so the State must not participate. In a good game of football it is to be noted that the game follows definite rules; these are decided in advance. What I am aiming at with a market economy policy is—to continue with the same illustration—to lay down the order and the rules of the game.

Freedom as the Main Aim

In a football eleven, for example, it is not customary to put all eleven men at the goal. If that were done, the spectators would rightly begin to whistle, since they would regard this as unfair and contrary to the rules. We demand from 'forwards' that they should go forward. If they believed that they should 'pack the goal' or even stand in it, we should consider this inappropriate and disturbing, and would not tolerate it. The economic order has to take into account similar functions. I believe that it is thanks to this economic model of our economic order which is behind all my actions that we have been successful. This model remains valid even if on occasion we have had to be prepared, and shall have to be prepared, to abandon it.

The spectators of a game of football would deeply resent the players coming to an agreement about the number of goals this or that side was to be credited with, and then not playing a fair and interesting game as expected and paid for with gate money. In the same manner I conceive it to be the basis of any market economy to retain freedom of competition. This can only exist where nothing is permitted to suppress freedom, but where freedom is guaranteed by statute and is one of the most prized things in the community.

It is my firm conviction that we shall retain a free enterprise economy only for as long as the State protects freedom. If, on the other hand, free enterprise complains that that would be an unfair limitation of freedom by the State, then I can only reply that this is to misunderstand freedom, if in the name of freedom and with the dogma of freedom it is believed that freedom itself can be suppressed.

As there is in the State, that is, in the political social structure, an order based on basic constitutional law which regulates the life of man and his relations with others, so there is for the economy. Here responsibilities are clearly divided. The businessman is responsible for his own business; there he can rightly demand that his activities should remain free from all State intervention, in fact, that he may enjoy and exercise real freedom of enterprise and freedom of manoeuvre. I am at the head of those supporting the businessman in this demand. But the State alone must carry responsibility for economic policy. We know where it leads to if these two functions are confused.

These short explanations are meant to clarify how, according to my conception, the basis of market economic policy should be formed, and where I should like the dividing lines to be drawn between the individual and the State.

It has to be explained why I consider these questions of such decisive importance, and why I consider the economy to have such vital importance. But I do not in any way wish to give the impression of believing that a patent medicine can be found in the economy for all our social troubles. Far from it! As the individual needs his physical life to be a human being in the transcendent sense, to be able to unfold his soul and spirit, so does a people. The economy is perhaps the most primitive aspect, but it is also the most essential; only on the basis of a healthy economy can society fulfil its true and final aims.

This basis must be sound, if tensions and splits are not to be fostered. To give a spiritual and material direction is in the final instance the task of politics. If my views allow suspicions to arise that I overvalue the material side, I wish to declare that I believe, on the contrary, that, except perhaps for the genius, man can only become conscious of his personality and dignity if he is not plagued by material worries, and by the petty troubles of everyday life. That is, when, thanks to circumstance, the material side no longer plays a dominating role.

Division of Work Between the State and the Economy

It is, I repeat, not the task of the State to intervene directly in the economy, in any case not before the economy asks for such intervention. It does not fit into the picture of an economy based on the spirit of adventure if the State takes a hand in production. Such a position in the nature of things means that the economy must not call upon the State to represent its interests. It is essential that this be made clear.

It is impossible to ask the State on the one hand that it should refrain from economic activity, and then, at a given moment, to call on it for help. A division of work already exists between business undertakings in the sphere of operations and economic policy as the task of the State, and particularly of the Ministry for Economic Affairs. Sometimes I get the impression that, in view of these functions, mistakes are made or some uncertainties exist. I repeat that the State is exclusively responsible for economic policy within the framework of its democratic parliamentary competence and rights. Although the interest of the businessman in economic policy is legitimate, as is his demand to be heard, he and his associates must not practise economic policy.

If it is established that for the Federal Republic the liberal economy of former days, as well as the directed economy, are things of the past, then it is clearly a duty to clarify what is new in our economic policy. What is new is that the State these days no longer wishes to deal with the individual, and among other things the Minister for Economic Affairs no longer issues orders to businessmen; he has freed them from rubber stamps, permits, concessions and licences. This principle is applied: the businessman, as well as the worker and every other citizen, must be free in his personal activities.

This naturally does not imply uninhibited behaviour or licentiousness. Instead of the State's direct command or—and this second is as important as the first—instead of renouncing all intervention, modern economic policy aims to utilize all available instruments granted by economic policy in order to free new energies continuously and open up new possibilities, but also to block all ineffectual paths. In other words, it aims, through a choice and combination of means, to urge the economy forward to progress and further expansion.

The Register of Sins

It must be admitted that much is still lacking in the conception mentioned here. In this connection I have once spoken of the extensive register of sins which are the signs of the erroneous wants and demands of the German economy and the shortcomings of economic policy in general. I then added that, regrettably, we had little reason to be particularly proud of the progress of the market economy so far.

I discuss elsewhere the tendency of German industry towards monopolies. High in the register of sins, too, is the demand to extend collective compulsory insurance. To all this belongs the false idea that the economic fate of individual economic or professional groups can be reduced to equality or improved. I am thinking of the demand for special adjustable tariffs which would eliminate competition from abroad. Added to it are certain attempts to liberalize our foreign trade with care, or, as it is customary to put it, to act responsibly (meaning to move as slowly and timidly as possible). The German public knows about the strong resistance to lower tariffs and of the objections to a complete return to free convertibility. All these examples demonstrate the flaws that still disfigure the free market economic system.

These points may suffice to show how little we have succeeded in disciplining vested interests within the State. We have not so far found a final solution, and it may be asked whether it will ever be possible to complete such a task.

The various attempts of these groups to influence parliamentary and Government views must be admitted. This is true not only of Germany, but of other parts of the world. But it is high time to agree that this problem is a real ill, or, at least, a critical problem of our time.

As a rule this all-in wrestling takes place between groups representing certain interests on the one hand and the State entities on the other. The final decision naturally can only rest with the latter. But the dividing line between the two is not definite enough to allow me to speak with a good conscience of any such thing as a socio-economic or Government political order.

Arising from the economic-political conception which I have outlined above, I believe it to be our duty during a time of reconstruction to oppose everything looking remotely like protection or favouritism for certain groups. We must act as a unit, and thus keep different interests in the background. A suspicious and destructive tendency which has recently been noted is to think in terms of group interests and to obtain special privileges for them. This is an evil which I want kept within bounds.

Dangerous Special Interests

My opposition to the demands of these groups is based on my conviction that, from the economic and political points of view, it is simply impossible for the State to dole out a little more or less here or there in the way of gifts or favours. Such actions would lead to an untenable situation for the State and especially for the Ministry of Economic Affairs. Where would be the yardstick by which it could be decided that this or that branch, this group or that profession shall be favoured by the State, while others, for some reason, must stand back? Such action is fundamentally wrong.

The solution can never, or only rarely, be found by striving for single targets, but lies in controlling the entire economic system, from which eventually all will profit. If the national economy as such flourishes—and here it should be understood that I consider the economy as an indivisible whole of our socio-economic life—then all the branches and sections of the economy will also flourish.

My scepticism as regards all special demands has been reinforced by experience. For example, it is generally known that I have supported the law concerning skilled craftsmen,[7] but in the years since it was passed I have had to fight attempts aimed at an imitation of this special regulation, where conditions differed radically, both materially and sociologically. Sometimes I gained the impression that we were moving towards a co-operative State based on the old guilds. No one can resent my energetic opposition of such tendencies. It would be absolutely disastrous for West Germany to take this path. What has brought us world-wide praise is the dynamic which we have developed, the will to expand, the courage to produce competitively and to carry responsibility.

To take into account special interests, to give in to individual demands of certain economic circles is impossible because of the inter-dependence of all economic activity. Every single economic measure reacts even on those sectors which are not directly included in the action, and which, seen superficially, appear unlikely to be affected.

The Fairy Tale of Classification

Human, all too human, factors play their part. What is sauce for the goose is sauce for the gander. Envy, which particularly afflicts us Germans, plays its important part. An advantage granted to one does not allow his neighbour to rest quietly. It must be remembered here what a big part officials play in our social life. The 'success' of one group quickly animates the members of another group to goad their official, their spokesman or their leader to similar 'achievements'. But it is precisely this which leads to fragmentation and forces us off the path leading to the welfare of all. If I remain sceptical as regards these efforts, I do so because I like to look further than this particular phase. If the background is brought into the light, then as a rule little more remains than a desire to be a bit more comfortable, to attempt to escape from tough competition and to acquire for the group concerned an undeservedly large part of the economic cake.

No one is prepared to accept that in the nature of things a lesser performance is essentially expressed in a lower return. All sorts of demands can be made, but certainly not one which expects that, with a lower performance, less effort and paralysing restraints, more can be done, and that every individual will be better off.

Enterprising economic undertakings should certainly show that kind of pride which is expressed by the urgent desire to be saved and freed from too much State interference.

From Citizen to Subject

I have written earlier of the 'register of sins' against the market economy. Here I want to discuss some other events which are relevant. Side by side with the demands of certain industrial circles for monopolies are requests of certain trades to be protected by special laws. I shall start with the simplest—the attempt to have trade designations[8] legally protected. As regards these attempts I can only ask: is it the title and rank which is the sign of an individual's ability, or is this not apparent from his work, his performance, his personality? Is it really essential to have trade designations to exercise a trade? I do not wish to dramatize the possible damage which might result from such rules. Nevertheless I consider such demands to be dangerous, for, after such a first step, a second would surely follow. It can be argued that someone with a definite trade designation would then have to fulfil definite fixed duties. He would not only have to offer proofs of qualification but also a moral guarantee to exercise that protected trade. Then there would be new categories of trades requiring combined abilities, and slowly the free citizen would return to the status of a subject who has to be servile in order to maintain himself.

It is, in fact, just as I once said: The privileged, who are inside, want to make life difficult for all those who want to join them. If I look for the spirit animating these efforts then I am forced to declare the ugly truth: it is pure egoism and nothing else which tries to combine such demands with sociological ideals and ethical principles. In fact protection is demanded, fences are requested to be built around trades, defences are sought to retain positions artificially.

Discussions with the Retail Trade

This seeking for titles or protection has found a clear expression in the requests made by several branches of the economy for its own trading laws. Here a discussion of the demands of retail trade is unavoidable. The battle for a trade law has gone on for some considerable time. It is fair to say that in these discussions there has been much coming and going, and some believe that my Ministry has not steered a clear course. Such an attitude overlooks the fact that there are two sides to this problem: one of principle and one of tactics. From the point of view of tactics I welcomed every month that went by without the passing of this freedom-limiting trade law. Up to the time of writing, in spite of pressure from other quarters, a trade law of this kind has not gone through.

If my Ministry had not bitterly opposed it, we would long ago have had a trade law which would have broken up trade into dozens of branches, and the entrance to any single one of these branches, as also the passage from one to the other, would have been protected by a hurdle of special knowledge. After all I have said on these pages I need hardly stress further that such a law would have constituted the absolute denial of all my conceptions of a free economic order.

This is a suitable moment for a short historical review. The law for the protection of the retail trade, which, it should be noted, came into force in 1933, the year Hitler came to power, provided first of all for the complete control of retail trade. When this embargo proved impossible to enforce, the law was in practice changed into a law to restrict entry. After the second World War the fate of this law differed greatly in the different zones and Länder of West Germany. According to the American directive of March 29, 1949, complete freedom of trade was introduced into the U.S. zone, while in the British and French zones the licence to trade under the 1933 law continued to be valid, serving as the basis for newer, but usually more generous, laws of admission. These differing legal situations resulted in the understandable wish for a unified control of trade, although justification for this wish should not be overvalued. Is it really a disaster if, when a retail business is opened in Flensburg, it is governed by a different ruling than in Munich?

Until the end of the first legislative period I successfully resisted pressure from the retail trade on the ground that a law discriminating against entry could not be combined with the spirit of market economy, and that it would not only have to correspond with the basic laws of the Federal Republic, but that this would have to be definitely affirmed.

Negotiations later on turned on the question of whether it was possible to formulate a law within this framework. Impatience with the length of these discussions led to a surprising manoeuvre behind my back in the Federal Parliament. Here, on June 11, 1953, shortly before the end of the first legislative period, the C.D.U./C.S.U. asked for a law for the temporary control of retail trade. This draft legislation failed to be passed, partly because the legislative period ended before it could be effected, but also because it aimed at splitting retail trade into several dozen branches, so attracting considerable public opposition.

With this situation in the Bonn Parliament I was forced to tell the Chancellor on June 20, 1953, that work on the law to control retail trade would be continued in the Federal Ministry for Economic Affairs, and that a positive attitude would be taken to the basic demand for a professional code 'to raise performance and secure competitive efforts in the retail trade'. On July 14, 1954, the Wiesbaden draft was made public, which was much discussed in retail trade circles. This was for them the final, and, from their point of view, the only possible and acceptable draft.

Detailed discussion within my own Ministry of this proposal, and also negotiations with other authorities, forced us to the conclusion that this draft, too, was not free from restrictive consequences, which could not be brought into accord with the basic principles of my economic policy. In turn, an altered draft was no longer acceptable to them. At this juncture, I took the opportunity in Hamburg on October 27, 1954, on the occasion of the meeting of delegates of the Association of the Retail Trade, to discuss once more this whole complex question. What I said then has been borne out, so that I have no reason to believe that these basic views are either changeable or wrong.

The Hamburg Declaration

I said in Hamburg:

> 'It would have led to a bungled economic policy if I had allowed myself to grant special favours to this or that group, this or that occupation or this or that economic branch, so that in turn everyone got something. That is impossible. In our days of rapid change, it is all too easily forgotten what Germany looked like six years ago, or in what a desperate and regrettable condition German trade was, or rather stagnated. You had become nothing more than executives of the State, State commissioners in a soul-less apparatus of power.

It is only as a result of economic policy that you have once again become responsible and free businessmen. . . .

'Retail trade has now regained its status in the minds of the German public; it is valued more and regarded in a completely different light than it was six years ago. This is already one factor playing an important part in our problem of occupation classifications. . . . I am firmly convinced that with, and in spite of rearmament, we shall succeed in increasing the turnover in retail trade even further in the future. (In fact the retail trade turnover between 1954 and 1956 rose by DM 10 milliard.) Above all it is essential to continue to sell a rising volume of goods. My continuing battle to maintain competition directly favours the retail trade, since it guarantees a healthy relationship between purchasing power and prices. And it helps ever-widening circles of the population to buy and reach for more goods. Eventually all this flows into the retail trade.

'For you, competition is the most essential element. All we do must in your very own interest spring from the intention of retaining competition. If this is so then the question of trade orders appears in a new light. . . . I admit that in recognition of the moral basis of retail trade I was inclined to examine the question of trade categories in the retail trade. . . . But right from the beginning I was not prepared to support a solution which was going to split the retail trade into—I don't know how many—occupational and commodity groups, and which would have required special permission for admission to each. . . . You go and tell the man in the street that, as is well known, anyone wishing to manufacture stockings can do so without hindrance, as everyone can work freely in industry. But must the man who sells stockings across the counter know more about what he is doing, possess special knowledge and demonstrate it?

'I doubt very much whether you can explain this to fifty million people; if you can, then I admire your powers of persuasion. . . . I do not wish to paint a black picture, but I do want to say that if retail trade shrinks, if the businessman in retail trade wants to rid himself of the responsibility of competition, if he denies the rationale of his activity, then matters will get hopelessly out of hand.'

I gained the impression at the Hamburg meeting that it would be possible to dissuade the representatives of the retail trade from their demand for a law to regulate entry and in its place to interest them in a law to further trade productivity, which would create the conception of the expert businessman and so lay the basis for an improvement in apprenticeships. A draft, worked out on this basis, was sent on March 15, 1955, to all interested associations. However, no serious discussions ever took place, since, in the meantime, retail trade had begun to look for support towards the Federal Parliament for its old favourite, a law to regulate entry. Unfortunately, they were not disappointed in this hope. On October 22, 1955, the C.D.U./C.S.U. parliamentary group submitted a draft measure about necessary qualifications in retail trade.

In the discussions which followed in the parliamentary committee on small and medium-sized shops, my Ministry, amongst others, reserved its position. In view of the decision of the Federal administrative court of November 3, 1955, which recognized the law of retail trade protection and made its enactment constitutional, it seemed inopportune to resist the draft too strongly. Nevertheless my Ministry strongly opposed all attempts to widen the area of application of this law.

No Trade Limitations

My reservations regarding this draft (which had certainly been weakened compared with earlier ones, and presupposed a certain expertise, and only exceptionally required examination in technical knowledge) rest on the belief that the hopes of many small and medium-sized traders that it would impose an effective embargo in respect of all new entry into retail trade would not be realized. And that quite apart from the impossibility, in principle, of combining a limitation of freedom to trade with a free economic order. It must be feared, therefore, that as soon as the law becomes effective, new restrictions will be called for to make the activities of all competitive undertakings more difficult.

I want to ask once more where it would have led to if I had not opposed these attempts? How could we have coped with the social and economic absorption of refugees in West Germany if—obsessed by group selfishness—we had given each group a special position?

At a time when we are trying to make the best of the limited space available to West Germany, there can be no room for erecting barriers in an economic area which has already become too narrow. This view cannot be reconciled with putting up barbed wire fences around individual categories of occupation.

Those holding different views should not forget that our economic policy has achieved a singular increase in turnover, which can be seen from the following table of retail trade turnover.

	Turnover in Mrd. DM	*Index of Turnover adjusted for price*
1950	30·8	100
1951	35·7	106
1952	38·8	116
1953	42·2	132
1954	46·1	144
1955	51·5	159

(These figures have been calculated on the basis of turnover tax statistics for 1950 and 1954, and the current representative statistics of the Federal Statistical Office)

In 1956 turnover rose appreciably, to DM 57 milliard at least.

Less Work—More Profit?

My opposition to laws about shop closing hours or the fixing or limiting of hours of work for the retail trade hardly needs further elaboration after all that I have said earlier. This, among other efforts, is aimed at a more comfortable life with a growing income and simultaneous security.

The magic formula is: less work and a better life for everyone. I do not hide my feelings about these aims. For such laws I have no sympathy, for in my economic policy I think, above all, of the consumer.

Trade must serve the consumer. I cannot imagine that the worker will welcome a Saturday afternoon in which he cannot shop, at least not until he himself is able to dispose of a completely free Saturday. It would be contrary to nature if on his only free afternoon the worker did not want to be able to go shopping in company with his family. No one holds the extraordinary view that on Saturday afternoon there should be no trains or postal deliveries or that no restaurants should be open. It is understood in a well-established economy that, in the public interest, some occupations have to reckon with special working conditions.

Certainly, everyone must have his free afternoon—this need not be discussed here. But fifty million consumers are interested in retaining the freedom to shop peacefully in their free time. It should be remembered that the German consumer does not go to sleep on Saturday afternoon; he goes out and spends his money. For that reason I have advocated the rotating Saturday.

I have discussed this subject, which interests me, with retail traders in the U.S.A. They had already heard of the German demand for a free Saturday afternoon. Their comment was something like this: 'Your retail traders must be doing well if they are prepared to forgo Saturday afternoon.'

It is certainly wrong to suppose that Saturday afternoon closing would not lead to a drop in turnover. People here behave as if the wants of fifty million consumers were a fixed and immovable quantity worked out rationally. People standing ready to buy in front of closed shops will not return to do their shopping just when it suits the retail trader. For that reason we should not take any steps which would certainly lead to a reduction in retail trade business.

Quite another thing is the demand of retail trade workers for a free half-day and reasonable working hours. Naturally, I do not deny that, if this demand were met, the retail trade would face a difficult problem. But other branches of the economy had to adjust their schedules to meet the difference between the hours worked by the undertaking and the hours worked by the individual worker. There are many ways of solving the problem.

If this particular question has been dealt with in some detail here, this has been done not to criticize any particular branch but, by citing a good example, to illustrate the problems arising from it.

German Miracle?

The reflections outlined above will have made it clear that the idea of supporting particular interests is foreign to my mode of thinking; I want this firmly established, for in my vision of the universe and in my thoughts on economic policy it is the human being who is at the centre of all events. All my economic policy measures are based on the criterion of how human beings will react to them, and what the consequences of any changes in economic circumstances would be for them.

Since all the successes which would have been achieved as a result of my economic policy can be traced back to the activities of those actively taking part, I do not believe that the idea of 'a German miracle' should be allowed to establish itself. What has taken place in Germany during the past nine years is anything but a miracle. It is the result of the honest efforts of a whole people who, in keeping with the principles of liberty, were given the opportunity of using personal initiative and human energy. If this German example has any value beyond the frontiers of the country it can only be that of proving to the world at large the blessings of both personal and economic freedom.

Chapter VII

CARTELS—ENEMIES OF THE CONSUMER

THE CONCEPTION OF the 'social market economy' has been found valid—and not only in Germany. Even the enemies of my economic policy no longer contest this claim. An economic policy may only call itself 'social' if it allows the consumer to benefit from economic progress, from the results of increased effort and increased productivity.

The best means to achieve this aim within a free social order is competition: it is the central pillar of this system. The social market economy obliges me to focus my attention on, and to declare war against, all efforts to form cartels and against those aiming at a limitation of competition of whatever kind.

Carlo Mötteli in his contribution 'Trade Unions and Economic Order' in *Wirtschaft Ohne Wunder* (Eugen Rentsch-Verlag, Erlenbach/Zurich, 1953, p. 303) rightly draws attention to the fact that a free economic order must not only resist all attacks by the trade unions, but that 'within the camp of the employer, honesty towards a true competitive order leaves much be be desired'. The tendency to curtail trade and industrial freedom through cartel agreements is hardly less strong than the urge of the worker towards collectivism.

In view of the importance and urgency of this problem I tried to get work going on proposals for a German cartelization law soon after I became Director of Administration of the Economy on March 2, 1948. This aim was first expressed in the 'law governing the main principles for controls and price policy after monetary reform' of June 24, 1948. In accordance with my proposals, Section III of the Law states: 'In so far as the State does not regulate the traffic in relation to trade and output, the principles of competition must be established. If economic monopolies are formed, they must be removed, and, until this can be done, State control must be exercised. A draft German law along these lines should shortly be submitted to the Economic Council.'

It is worth remembering that the first postwar German Parliament adopted this formula by a large majority. Some time before the Economic Council had made this decision, the U.S. and British Military governing authorities had promulgated broadly similar decrees—the U.S. Law 56 and British Ordinance 78—which, on February 12, 1948, prohibited the excessive concentration of German economic power and outlined plans for decartelization. The military governing authorities reserved the right to see this through.

According to Allied declarations, particularly those of General Clay, these military decrees were intended to be a transitory ruling, to be replaced later by a German cartelization law, which would nevertheless in those days still have needed the agreement of the military governing authorities. Thus the Bi-partite Control Office asked the Economic Council on March 19, 1948, to submit a draft law which, in accordance with the Havana Charter of March 24, 1948, would forbid cartels and similar restrictive practices, and all limitation of competition.

Out of this situation developed the first German attempt to deal legally with this extremely difficult question. At my request, a committee of experts submitted the first draft of a law to secure competition and also a draft law on monopolies, on July 5, 1949. The committee included, amongst others, the specialists on the law on cartels, Dr. Walter Bauer, Professor Franz Böhm, Dr. Paul Josten, President of the Senate, Dr. Wilhelm Köppel, Professor Dr. Wilhelm Kromphardt and Professor Dr. Bernhard Pfister.

Early Rebuff

The early demise of the Economic Council did not allow these plans to be pursued in Frankfurt. But during these months I repeatedly tried to explain in public my fundamental views on cartels. For example I explained quite unmistakably in the *Volkswirt* of December 16, 1949:

> 'I regard the development of competition as the best guarantee both of a continuing increase in efficiency and of a just division of the national income. In the interest of a truly "social" market economy I cannot possibly forgo the advantages of healthy economic progress. . . . Plans or controls imposed by industry appear to me to be no less undesirable and damaging than State controls. . . .
>
> 'With all its many facets, its tasks and aims, and, in spite of its infinite nuances and shades in practice, the implementation of cartel systems cannot hide from us that all market agreements, especially in the field of prices, aim eventually at a limitation of competition. . . .
>
> 'I regard all such attempts as a crime against the sanctity of life, whose inner meaning is change, movement and progress, and therefore cannot respond to the uncouth methods of planning regulations and stabilization.'

On December 27, 1949, I said on the Bavarian radio: 'Freedom reigns only where the power to suppress freedom is not misused, but where it has been incorporated into the moral and legal code, where it has become part of the general order and where society itself regards it as of great value.' At the C.D.U. meeting at Goslar on October 22, 1950, I described the future German monopoly law as the cornerstone of the social market economy; it was to 'prevent the private exploitation of positions of power, protected organizationally or juridically, in favour of free competition', and to give the Federal Government 'an effective instrument for dealing with open and secret price agreements'. This monopoly law was to 'utilize and make effective the best principles of our policy for a social market economy'. The law was to be a 'milestone in the history of German reconstruction'.

No American Orders

These statements could be continued indefinitely. I recall them only to show that every citizen who voted for the Federal Government in 1943 and 1953, in voting for the social market economy, also supported my views concerning cartels, unless he reckoned on the dishonesty of politics. Since even today the nonsensical and sly accusation is made in discussions that the work on the cartelization law had been undertaken as a result of American orders or in realization of an American idea, a few remarks are needed here.

In all these endeavours I have never come across orders from the American side, much less bowed to them. Nevertheless it is a very similar kind of thinking and feeling which has led the American economy to such obvious successes, and which, besides considerable detailed research, has strengthened my conviction about the damaging effects of limitations of competition.

For the sake of historical truth it need not be denied that the first Federal Government, when it first came into office, tended, in accordance with the rules of the time, to discuss its draft cartelization law with the Allied High Commission. The latter informed us on December 1, 1951, that expert discussions regarding this all-embracing law would have to take place, and in fact these were begun on December 11, 1951. These discussions, which continued over several weeks, are recorded in a volume the size of a dictionary.

The negotiations themselves continued in a matter-of-fact atmosphere. They concentrated on a number of main questions, such as the specific form of the cartel for rationalization, regulations concerning the acquisition and use of patents and patterns, and the Allies' wish to incorporate binding regulations protecting industrial freedom, and on the definition of so-called 'companies dominating the market'.

The draft which was finally passed by the Federal Government contradicted the principles of American law in its basic construction. The principle of outright prohibition is strictly enforced in North America; the alternative of making administrative exceptions, which characterizes the German draft law, is foreign to American law. This brief hint may show how unreal are all the unfair assertions about my dependence on American ideas in respect of monopolies.

The Federal cabinet of the first legislative period finally approved my Ministry's draft at the beginning of 1952. It was submitted to the Federal Council as a 'draft law against Limitation of Competition'. The Federal Council in plenary session discussed this draft on May 23, 1952.

It is worth recalling here that the Federal Council in its first deliberations supported paragraph one of the draft law which dealt with the much discussed principle of outright prohibition. This decision represented a remarkable victory for me, in particular since some months earlier a Commission of the Federal Council, which had been especially asked to deal with 'the preparatory work for the Federal Law against Limitation of Competition', had proposed that 'Limitations of competition through interventions conforming to the state of the market should be omitted in those cases in which cartelization would lead to misuse'.

The Federal Government reacted immediately to the suggestions of the Federal Council, and submitted the draft to the Federal Parliament on June 16, 1952. Ten days later, at the 220th meeting of Parliament, it was read for the first time. The twelve months available to the Federal Parliament during its first legislative period proved too short to deal with this difficult law. It had already become clear at the time that the many-sided resistance from the opponents of a general prohibition of cartels had influenced the deliberations of the Federal Parliament, an opposition which was both disturbing and time-consuming.

Principle of Prohibition Confirmed

I did not hesitate to submit anew a draft of the cartelization law to the Federal cabinet a few months after the formation of the second 'Adenauer Government'. The draft was identical with that of the first legislative period. In spite of violent and many-sided attempts to throw out the prohibitive principle which I supported, the Federal cabinet passed my draft by a considerable majority on February 17, 1954. With it the cabinet expressed the desire that during further parliamentary discussion the Federal Parliament should resume where the previous discussions of the first legislative period had ended.

The Federal Council made its position clear on May 21, 1954, when, in spite of violent and dramatic discussions preceding the meeting, the basic principle of the draft, expressed in the prohibitive principle of paragraph one, was approved by a majority. Several months then passed before the Federal Government decided to pass on the draft to the Federal Parliament. For this delay until January 22, 1955, I am responsible.

Trade and industry repeatedly attacked my draft on the grounds that it would expose the economy to unlimited competition, which was undesirable as long as the State, through taxation, took away too much from the reward of the labour of a working man. Since, from a material point of view, this argument was not without some justification, I agreed to a postponement during the period of discussion of tax reform. In addition it had to be taken into account that Parliament, as a result of its work on tax reform, was in fact overburdened.

The interlude afforded another chance of discussing the most important proposals of the draft law with interested economic circles, in particular the Federal Association of German Industry.

These talks led to a much discussed and frequently misunderstood summary on October 18, 1954. The Federal Parliament itself read the first draft submitted by the Government on March 24, at its 76th meeting. Thus Parliament had more than two years available before discussions came to an end—a period in which even a difficult law can surely be thoroughly reviewed from all angles.

There may be a tendency here or there to look askance at the slow progress made by this law. But I myself have clearly pointed to the many objections raised at many stages of the discussion. To be fair it must be admitted that we were dealing here with a legal formulation of a highly complicated matter, where the law makers had almost no experience to draw on.

Protection for the Consumer

That is why I believe it to be important to establish that during the different phases of parliamentary deliberations it was not only the technical manoeuvres of my opponents for a postponement that were decisive, but that by agreeing to a postponement I gratified my own wish to receive from Parliament a law which would be truly useful and which would reflect my basic views. I had hoped that with the approaching end of the legislative period Members of Parliament might possibly agree with my views, especially since this law protected the consumer. But these tactical reflections must not be continued here; I consider it far more important to give the outlines of my attitude to cartels which should remain valid beyond the questions of the day.

In the first place, I must state why I am such a definite opponent of cartels. In this connection a brief glimpse into the past is essential.

I start with the sound economic findings made by scientific economic research, that a competitive economy is at one and the same time the most economical and the most democratic form of any economic order. The State must only take a hand in the running of the market in so far as it is needed to uphold the mechanism of competition, or to supervise those markets where complete competition is impossible.

It is a historic fact, not disputed by any economic school of thought, that the liberal economic era at its most civilized stage was responsible for a considerable advance in human progress. After the guild society with its economic, but also ethical and guild aims had become a hindrance to economic progress, the principle of *laissez faire* released unexpected economic powers. While the guilds prohibited personal initiative and progressive ideas, the producer of the early 19th century was able himself to decide the What, How, Where, How Much and Whither of his production. Since all producers stood the same chance of free activity, competition developed and with it the 'market', which now became the focal point of all economic interest. Through the market price, based on supply and demand, production and consumption benefited all.

In the last decades of the 19th century, phenomena which, on the one hand, limited the effectiveness of the market economy and, on the other, led to increased social and political tensions, became increasingly noticeable.

To some extent the forces were part of the market economy, but, in addition, measures taken by the State led to a curtailing of the mechanism of competition through the formation of monopolies and other elements of power governing the market. The development of modern techniques itself encouraged a tendency towards monopolies.

Every monopolistic position conceals the danger that the consumer may be cheated, and allows economic progress to stand still. The negative results of tendencies towards monopolies were more clearly visible when the national economy was smaller, and more cut off from the free world markets by protectionist measures. This was all the more true when, protected by such barriers, private monopolies were even deliberately advanced by measures of economic policy.

All Must Participate in Success

I am convinced, and this is the nucleus of my attitude to cartels, that only as a result of free competition shall we liberate those forces which will guarantee that economic progress and improvements in working conditions will not be absorbed in greater profits, private incomes and other benefits, but that these benefits will be passed on to the consumer. It is the social rationale of the market economy that every economic success, wherever it is gained, and every advantage arising from greater efficiency, and every improvement in labour productivity, will benefit all the people, and lead to the greater satisfaction of the consumer.

The market economy therefore cannot be separated from a system of free competition; it cannot do without the function of free prices. Whoever wants to exclude the function of free prices—and it does not matter whether it is done by Government initiative or by industrial organizations through cartels—kills competition and allows the economy to stagnate.

In pursuing these thoughts to their logical conclusion I have regarded it as my most noble and important task, since the day of currency reform, to limit and reduce the many Government measures in respect of price formation. Since, therefore, everyone knows that I have based my economic policy on the principle of freedom, then a truly organic and harmonious order can only be guaranteed in a guided free market by a free competition of labour and a free formation of prices.

While I firmly oppose every kind of bureaucratic *dirigisme* and State controls, I am equally firm in refusing to allow other forms of collective economic influence. There is no difference in principle or in function between State and industrial economic planning. If we want to have a free economic and social order, we must not allow anyone or any group to have the right to interpret freedom according to individual taste, and then to limit it. In my view a free economy is synonymous with free economic enterprises. Entrepreneurs do not know what they are doing when they fight the system of a competitive economy.

As far as I am concerned, freedom is indivisible. In my view, political, economic and human freedoms are a complex unit. It is impossible to detach one part without making the whole collapse.

The Secret of Market Economy

Every politician solicitous for the welfare of the people in general must be conscious of the indivisibility of freedom, and after years without political freedom he must be prepared to grant the people this freedom. This sense of responsibility moved me, as soon as I had taken office, to rout these ghosts from the past that were trying to regulate the actions of those concerned with the economy in the interests of the State. I created in my sphere of work the basic condition for a true democratic order; I helped freedom to come to the surface.

The secret of market economy is just this, and herein lies its superiority over any kind of planning—that it enables processes of adaptation to take place almost daily and hourly, balancing supply and demand, national income and national product, both quantitatively and qualitatively. Whoever does not support competition and free market prices no longer has any argument available to oppose planning.

Some of my opponents may now ask whether the freedom of the entrepreneur, which I have so strongly stressed, is not circumscribed if the entrepreneur is no longer permitted to use his freedom in a way he considers proper—in other words, to use it in given circumstances to limit the free activity of the individual. I am pleased to admit that this is one of the central questions of modern market economy. To ask and answer this question means that we have to demonstrate the great difference between the social market economy, which we have been trying to realize in West Germany since 1948, and the liberal economy of the old days.

In my conception the social market economy does not recognize the freedom of the entrepreneur to exclude competition through cartel agreements; it imposes far more the obligation to gain the favour of the consumer through one's own efforts in competition against rivals. The State must not decide who should be victorious in the market, nor should an industrial organization such as a cartel; it must be the consumer alone.

Quality and price determine the form and direction of production, and it is only on the basis of these criteria that the selection is made.

In this sense, freedom is the right of every citizen, and it must not be short-circuited by anyone. The freedom demanded by supporters of cartels to limit or remove freedom is not the concept of freedom which, in the interest of the future of free enterprise, I should like to see put first. Whoever uses the word freedom must be honest about it. Freedom—I repeat—is and remains indivisible. It must not be either defended or rejected on grounds of expediency.

The opposite pole to economic freedom is represented by strongly marked economic power. Therefore it must be ensured by law that the advantages of a competitive economy are not wiped out by the disadvantages (which have been proved historically) of a serious concentration of power.

So the law maker is forced to give particular attention to the problem of economic power as a factor which may possibly disturb the balance of the market economy. Competition and the increase in output and progress which follow must be secured by Government orders and protected from all disturbing elements. In particular, there must be guarantees that nothing will hinder the production of free price regulating in a free market which acts as a guide to the trend of the economy.

The Basic Forms of Economic Power

Economic power in the main comprises three basic forms:

1. By legal treaty, or organization, or by trade agreement, independent companies bind themselves in such a way that a group of them agree to limit their own independence or to restrict or eliminate competition by regulating market factors.

2. On the basis of share capital, so that the power of decision of a legally independent enterprise will be influenced by interlocking interests or by a holding in another firm so that it cannot fully exert its ability in the market.

3. By the emergence of a single large concern which, because of its strong position in the market, exerts a dominating influence on supply and price establishment.

The market price, which in a perfect competitive economy cannot be dictated by a single market partner, could be wilfully changed by concentrated economic power, and with it the market trend, to the advantage of influential power groups, who could consciously and artificially control it. A price thus determined for a market organized on monopolistic lines is no longer a 'datum line' to which individuals have to adapt themselves to retain their ability to compete, but it can only be determined according to individual judgment and so manipulated. From it naturally grows the danger of cheating the consumer, but also the danger of national misdirected investment, and the possibility of a curtailment of technical and economic progress.

The law maker must regard it as his task to exclude factors which disturb market trends by

(*a*) preserving, to the greatest possible extent, competition between companies;

(*b*) preventing the abuse of monopoly power in markets where complete competition is impossible; and

(*c*) by creating a State organ to supervise and, if necessary, to influence markets.

An economic constitution drawn up on such a basis would be the economic counterpart of political democracy. As the political right of the citizen to decide is essential in a political democracy, so the competitive order assures the basic economic rights of freedom to work and freedom of choice on the part of the consumer.

The close relationships and interdependence between the political and economic constitutions make the legal settlement of basic economic rights urgent and essential. My efforts are thus aimed at establishing competition firmly as the driving force, and free prices as the regulator, of the market economy within a legal framework.

Whoever wishes to go beyond these principles, or disregards them, undermines the market economy and destroys the foundation on which our social and economic order rests. The reader may well feel that we are here dealing with basic questions of economic policy, and that in a discussion of cartel policy we are not dealing with just one of many points at issue. Here we are dealing above all with the central problem of our economic order. Only from this central position can the battles for a monopoly law which have continued for years be understood.

But let me illuminate, too, the social side of this question. I oppose cartels in principle, since a sound and well-intentioned social market economy—in which the word 'social' is consciously stressed—can only be guaranteeed if as a result of competition the superior achievement gains over the inferior, and if through this form of competition what is needed is supplied in the best possible quality and quantity and at the proper price. Simultaneously this principle ensures that a higher achievement gains a better reward, and that in this social aspect worthy producers reap greater security and new opportunities.

So far as the moral evaluation of cartels is concerned—and this is so often misunderstood—I want to say straight out that I am far from judging cartels morally, or even from imputing dishonest motives to individual industrialists and entrepreneurs.

For example, if a businessman believes that the price of his product should cover his production costs, no moral reasons can be opposed to this idea. Yet this view cannot be reconciled with the inner laws of a market economy, for it would guarantee an income even to the least efficient businessman.

No, with the best will in the world I cannot see any positive good in cartels. Above all, when evaluating them from a national economic point of view, I can see only their negative side. Often in recent years I have had the experience of people coming to me—from one branch of industry after another—asserting that unless they are allowed to make price agreements, they will inevitably collapse. I have never granted such requests, and the collapses which had been predicted have not taken place.

Exceptions are Necessary and Possible

If in past years I have defended the principle of the market economy with a toughness verging on obstinacy, there have been good reasons. Yet at the same time I am aware that the theoretical model of pure competition is not entirely valid everywhere.

A 'theoretical model' of this kind in no way means that it can be realized everywhere in practice and in its purest form. I am not so unrealistic as not to see thousands of examples around me from which it is clear that the theory of free competition has been mixed with other elements and thus diluted. Nor am I so dogmatic that I do not understand that there may be situations in which the prohibition of cartels could be or might have to be modified. In particular instances it is very possible to permit limitations or a loosening of restrictions against cartels. But in the meantime whoever makes fun of the 'theoretical model' of complete competition only shows up his own spiritual inadequacy.

In enacting the above concepts the Government's draft law is free of all dogmatism. Thus it does not start from the much-criticized concept of complete competition, but instead it recognizes possible justifications or even the necessity for intervention. Consequently the draft envisages conditional cartels as well as export cartels and possibly rationalization cartels. No one can declare with a good conscience that the just needs of the economy have not been taken into account, or that by adopting this procedure certain economic interests are being discriminated against.

Discussions of Principle Miss the Point

These observations would be incomplete if I did not mention the debate between the supporters of a law of prohibition and a law of misuse. According to my way of thinking this way of putting the question misses the point as much as an attempt at a moral evaluation of the problem. Thus I should like to stress once more that my opposition to cartels does not rest on the idea of deliberately evil aims or practices, which amount to discrimination, but that in my view collective price maintenance must be regarded as a grievance—even if these can be defended morally and mathematically. Thus any law on misuse would not be practicable.

I go so far as to say that the fixing of prices at too low a level can be as damaging economically as prices which are put too high. The only economically 'proper' and defensible market price cannot be defined. It emerges above all from the equilibrating function of price in a free market.

According to my view the total prohibition law is always logical. It makes the only possible deduction from the negative quality of every kind of law of misuse, yet allowing for those exceptions which may appear to be economically necessary.

The supporters of cartels make the big mistake (surely not by accident—which displays their weakness) that they measure the effects of cartel or anti-cartel measures only by the private economic results of the undertakings involved, leaving entirely on one side the general economic view. It is just those tight cartels that are successful in their aims which, viewed from a general economic point of view, must be regarded as the most damaging.

The cartelization law based on the principle of a prohibition of cartels must in no event be changed, or else it will become a farce which would render the whole policy of the Federal Government ridiculous in the eyes of the public. Also I believe that the cartelization law is a useful, if not altogether the best, means to silence the political attacks on the business economy.

The businessman is unassailable if free competition makes the function of the free businessman indispensable, and if as a result of free competition and the resulting progress, a price is reached which offers the best possibilities to the consumer. The attitude of the consumer towards our economic order will become increasingly more favourable if the citizen can be certain that through a free market he can be master of his fate, and that he is not exposed to anonymous economic forces and powers.

The supporters of cartels who demand a law of supervision or misuse are basically far more dogmatic than the supporters of the law of prohibition, since they rule out any refutation of objections. They persist even when it is pointed out to them that a law of misuse misses the point of the real national economic problem. I do not accuse cartels of misuse in a criminal or a moral sense. The 'misuse' is expressed in the fixing and immovability of prices—i.e. in doing away with the function of the free price. That is why I can do nothing with a law of misuse. In all these years I have never received a reply to this objection; and I agree that, from the point of view of the supporters of cartels, no answer is possible.

Essential Barometer

It is an illusion and a bare impossibility to form a nationally 'right' economic price through a cartel. Can anyone really refute my basic conception that in a free market, in which the free businessman produces freely and at his own risk, there can be no fixed prices tied by a cartel, because then the quantitative and qualitative balance of the various offers from producers, and the far greater demand of millions of consumers become logically impossible? The economy would have to become blind, the businessman could no longer take his bearings according to the state of the market, since he cannot tell where, when and what is being produced, and in what quantities, from price reactions. The balance of supply and demand cannot exist, if the economy stands still as a result of cartels.

What the layman regards as the more or less secret doings of a free national economy begin just where we ask the question: 'How does it happen that the millions of consumers choosing freely find just what they need in the market?'

No one can suppose that hundreds of thousands of free businessmen never make a mistake in their individual calculations. No, naturally, they are not infallible; too much is produced of one thing and too little of another, and not always the right thing as regards price and quality, i.e. not always what is in demand. And we all know how changeable the consumer is.

Public consumption changes all the time, but nevertheless supply must be able to absorb this peculiarity. That can only be achieved if every businessman who wants to survive has no other ambition than 'to be right' in the market, to retain the goodwill of the consumer, and to offer him all the time something better, in order to survive in competition with his rival. In this wrestling match for a position in the market the function of the free price cannot be excluded.

Indirectly, this means that the businessman cannot receive a guarantee that his production costs will be refunded to him in his price. If a cartel wants the support of such dangerous moral theses, then it would follow logically that the businessman could not justify his continued existence. His task would then be merely one of a technical and administrative officer. He could no longer lay a claim to a businessman's profits.

In a national economy the price will sometimes have to be high to balance supply and demand—it may have to be higher than one which might have been imposed by a cartel. On the other hand, according to the position of the market, it may be below costs.

Thus I must refute the views of those who base the case for cartels on the position of the undertakings in question. I have no objections to cost accounting; on the contrary I would wish that every enterprise had available people able to make the right calculations. Cost accounting has the one purpose of ascertaining the exact position of the individual enterprise, and whether and how far it can maintain itself in a competitive economy. But it is quite wrong to make demands or put forward a case for cartels on the basis of such calculations.

The German businessmen who rightly oppose excessive tendencies towards joint management have every reason to cease supporting cartels, for in fact the policy of free or fixed prices touches the problem of joint management closely.

The businessman can justify his existence only as long as he is prepared to fulfil the function of a free businessman, with all its opportunities but also with all its risks. He remains irreplaceable and untouchable only as long as he is willing to prove himself in free competition in a free market. As soon as the businessman tries to limit the risks by collective agreements, or attempts to remove them entirely—i.e. if he aims at shifting through cartels the individual decision from the level of his own undertaking to the level of branches and associations, then, I believe, the demands for joint management can no longer be opposed and certainly not with any justification or conviction.

By forming cartels the businessman deprives himself of his proper function; eventually he becomes an official and thus is replaceable. At the very same moment as the responsibility of the businessman is removed, and the fate of his enterprise and that of his workers are made dependent on collective decisions, then the attitude of the public to the businessman will change fundamentally. In the social climate of the mid-twentieth century it will then be no longer surprising if joint management is demanded to make such fateful decisions. If businessmen themselves decide to relinquish their freedom of movement, they undermine their political, social and moral standing; at that moment officialdom would reach for power.

I cannot omit to mention here the view which may be painful for the supporters of cartels, that the economy after 1948, while the sellers' market prevailed, was enthusiastically in favour of competition and free prices, but that a visible change of opinion took place when, with a balanced economy, the inner laws of a rising volume of goods made themselves felt.

Cartels to Overcome Crises

It is one of the main arguments of the supporters of cartels that economic groupings of the cartel kind are essential to prevent, or at least limit, the disastrous consequences of crises, whether of an economic or a structural nature.

Far be it from me to suggest that all economic crises are due to the spread of cartels—that would of course be stupidity. But I am firmly convinced that the attempt to try to save oneself from the crisis by cartel agreements is neither fitting for the national economy nor can it possibly lead to success.

At any given time the total supply of goods faces a fixed purchasing power, and that is why not everyone can gain immediately from more purchasing power. That would be like believing in magic. The first great danger of cartel-like agreements is that those branches of the economy meeting an essential need scoop off more purchasing power than they would in a free market. This advantage for those who benefit must logically work to the disadvantage of those for whose products only a relatively small purchasing volume exists.

What has been said here about the urgency of needs is also valid for those cases in which powerful interests demand preferential positions. Over and over again the supporters of cartels point to the necessity of preventing economic collapse; they believe they have found a cure for all such eventualities in fixed cartel prices.

But in this way the organic healing of the symptoms of crisis is prevented. For, if a certain product, at a certain price, can only be sold at a certain, but for industry, insufficient quantity; or if, perhaps as a result of changes in consumption, the demand for such products declines, then price fixing is useless. If a falling price can attract new buyers and encourage consumption to rise, while a higher price repels the purchaser, then a cartel wanting to control purchases and cover production costs can only bring about a forced cut in production at rising production costs. The calculation never works out—but the crisis deepens.

The inner laws of such actions inevitably lead to a progressive shrinkage of national economic activity. If too many were to act in the same manner we would come to a complete standstill in the market and finally to an insoluble hardening of the crisis. No cartel agreement will then suffice to reactivate the economy or to make room for new production.

In a free market, however, the distortions arising from crises are brought about less easily, for the free price reacts easily to the fluctuations and changes of the market, and through competition permits those forces to grow which make for assimilation and balance.

In a free market economy the tensions arising organically from the dynamic of expanding business can be cured. That is the only successful and satisfactory path for the economy and the individual undertaking. If in this process profits have sometimes to be forgone, or if losses are made, it has been proved again and again that a free business economy possesses the ability to adapt itself to an almost incredible degree, and that it is just this 'having to prove oneself' in the market which guarantees economic progress, and which permits the advantages accruing from greater effort to benefit the consumer, i.e. the people as a whole. In this sense our policy may rightly be called a 'social market economy'. The businessman can do no better in seeking a moral basis for his position than to be prepared to carry all risks openly, and not to seek refuge in cartels, nor to look for protection in collective agreements. It is a more than dangerous path when the businessman aims at a collective, rather than a personal, responsibility.

Nor can cartels be justified from a social policy point of view on the ground that they aim to protect business and to safeguard work, and that for this reason the workers are interested in supporting them. This is an untenable view for all those who understand even a little of the workings of the national economy.

What can be protected and secured artificially by cartels are, at best, unproductive jobs, with the resulting danger that the whole national economy will cease to progress—a state of affairs which in the long run must become fatal in a world of international competition—even if in view of our present export surplus this danger appears to be small.

Such a policy cannot be called social, since it inhibits progress and thus prevents the creation of new, productive and secure jobs. There have never been as many unemployed in German economic history as in the period when cartels flourished most strongly. Cartels always have to be paid for by a lower standard of living.

A Modern Fairy-tale

In the attempts to gain supporters for cartels all conceivable means have been used. The most remarkable which has recently been put forward is the statement that cartels would protect and further the well-being of the middle classes. That is, to put it mildly, one of those typical modern fairy-tales which does not even contain a grain of truth. Every market has as much purchasing power as there are goods available for consumption. And that means that all those offering supplies and services fight for a given purchasing power.

We know very well that not all branches of our economy are equally able or willing to form cartels. In basic industry and in heavy industry, and where agreement is easily attained, a tendency towards forming cartels, a desire for cartels and an ability to form cartels must be assumed to exist to an appreciable extent. But the nearer we come to the sphere of manufactured goods, the nearer we move to processed goods, the stronger changes in pattern appear, and the more difficult will any agreement be, and so cartel agreements become ineffective and useless.

Those who want cartels aim to gain a greater part of the purchasing power for themselves, i.e. for their product, than would be their share in a free market. As a natural consequence this greater purchasing power, which some groups demand for themselves, will be missing from other parts of the national economy. And it will be missing just where middle class existence is at stake, with a hundred thousand small and medium-sized companies. Here purchasing power is lacking, which the branches of industry able to form cartels have attracted to their own undertakings.

It is utterly clear that the sectors able to form cartels are not those in which the middle class participates. The middle classes work with processed goods, and in the manufacturing goods industry. We find them in consumer goods, in retail trade and in skilled crafts. It should always be remembered that cartel manipulations do not increase purchasing power by a single penny. The result is that in an economy containing cartels, existing purchasing power is insufficient to absorb the total supply of goods—unless it is at the expense of the non-cartelized branches of the economy; that is, in the main, the middle class sector.

If then, wiser by experience, the middle class sectors of manufacturing industry and the consumer goods branches also want to find their salvation in cartels, it will be shown that the divergent elements there can hardly be mastered, and technical difficulties will permit only hypothetical solutions. Even where agreements are possible it will be found that at the best the price can be saved, but turnover can in no circumstances be maintained. That, in turn, is not surprising; it is only natural. Suppose a national economy had the possibility or the power through cartels to raise its price level by 10%, then the real purchasing power of the consumer would have to drop by 10%. That means that the existing purchasing power would only suffice to absorb a national product which had shrunk by 10%. In a free market economy the phenomenon of an unsold supply of goods would lead to a new balance as a result of price pressures. Where cartels predominate such attempts lead to an inevitable crisis.

No New 'Dirigisme'

Another reproach against my conception of cartels is that the cartel bureau would become the starting point for a new State *dirigisme*.

I can hardly believe that this view can be taken seriously by anyone knowing the situation; nevertheless, since it appears again and again in the discussions, I want to mention it.

One almost tends to hear here a Babel-like confusion of tongues. On the one hand efforts are made to show that cartels are not so easy to form, and therefore the danger of a thorough cartelization of the economy does not exist. At the same time it is held that applications for cartels might be so numerous that the cartel bureau would not be in a position to cope with the task.

If the opponents of the Government plan really fear that a giant administrative apparatus might come into existence, they express thereby their conviction that large sections of the German economy want to return to cartels. Unfortunately I, too, share this belief, and that is why I regard a defence through my draft law against cartel formations as absolutely essential.

The cartel office, as explained before, will have to be as big as the German economy demands. So far as I am concerned it should be as small as possible. It is within the power of the economy itself to decide how large the cartel office should be.

So far as the much-feared State *dirigisme* is concerned, the contradiction within the argument is complete. The private cartel bureaucracies which are formed when cartels are permitted are never mentioned, although this privately organized economic *dirigisme* would certainly have to be vastly larger than any cartel bureau, which would have merely the one task of preventing the unjustified spread of cartels, to maintain competition and allow the market to function freely.

Here a not very convincing attempt is made to name a bureau as *dirigiste* which, quite to the contrary, tries to prevent the *dirigisme* of cartels and the growth of a new privately organized planned economy. With the best will in the world it is impossible to speak of State intervention, if the State attempts to safeguard the principles of a free democratic social order.

A Word to the Businessman

I have frequently been misunderstood by German businessmen during discussions about a cartelization law which have now gone on for years. That is why before concluding these observations I should like to say a word to the businessman:

The free businessman stands or falls, I believe, with the system of the market economy. In any other order he becomes more and more the mere executive organ of a foreign will and descends to the level of an official in a planned economy.

If the businessman no longer wants to meet the task of measuring up to free competition—if an order is established where the force, the imagination, the wit, the efficiency and the desire to create is no longer in demand, if the more able are no longer in a position or permitted to be more successful than the less able, then the free business economy will shortly cease to exist. A general flattening and avoidance of responsibilities would gain ground; the striving for security and stability would produce a mentality no longer in tune with the true spirit of enterprise.

I am aware that the offensive against the market economy by the collectivists of all kinds aims at undermining the function of enterprise. When the striving for collective agreements gains the upper hand in the camp of the businessman, then, much earlier than these businessmen would like to believe, the time will come for the question to be put politically: What defence is there for private ownership in production and what right has the businessman to make economic decisions?

If my conception of cartels is interpreted as enmity *vis à vis* the businessman, I must doubt the seriousness and honesty of such an interpretation. There is in Germany really no more glowing defender of the free enterprise economy. I have remained faithful to these views throughout the eight years in which I have been responsible for the economic policy of the Federal Republic, in the face of all suspicions, attacks and abuse, and I have forcefully defended the order of a free enterprise economy. History will show that in fighting for the cartelization law I defended the position and function of the free businessman more effectively than those purblind circles who see the salvation of the businessman in the cartel.

Chapter VIII

THE VALUE OF INDIVIDUAL OPINION

THE POSITION OF THE INDIVIDUAL within the State, or better still the attitude of the citizen to the State, should be a constant consideration of the politically responsible. On this point I want to make my position clear as a comment on the eagerness to organize (not to say craze for organization) which permeates the 20th century. Now the inherent passion of the German for associations, formerly much ridiculed, has taken on a new and dangerous guise. It has encouraged the conviction that, if only big and strong organizations can be built up, which would be in a position to demonstrate their aims in a politically powerful manner, then the State when faced by these interests would capitulate. Obviously many large pressure groups act in accordance with this principle. If this conviction grows, the State will necessarily become the plaything of pressure groups.

Hand in hand with this development goes another, which might almost be called tragic: the experience which I have gained over the many years in which I have been responsible for economic policy has taught me again and again that, in these collective expressions of opinion, 'mistakes in translation' of the worst kind take place. What the individual, of whatever rank or occupation, professes, has hardly anything in common with what the organization representing him makes of its mandate, i.e. what it puts forward as demands.

This statement can be illustrated with many examples. For instance, the results of the questions put on the occasion of the strike for joint management should be remembered. To the question 'Why are you striking?' only a small percentage of those questioned were able to give an even approximately accurate reply about the real purpose for which the strike had been called by the trade unions.

The facts of this case do not only apply to the relationship between employer and employee. Elsewhere, too, I have repeatedly come across examples of these crass 'mistakes in translation'.

Thus, when I spoke with individual businessmen about their attitude to demands by associations for cartels, or when I discussed the various trade laws with businessmen in retail trade, in short, when I discussed with middle class men their collective demands, I have repeatedly heard that the proclaimed 'collective demand' represents the individual's wish quite inadequately.

The Future of Democracy

On the basis of this experience I believe that an organization remains harmless only as long as it seriously aims at taking individual concepts and crystallizing them, but refrains from attempting to impose its own power policy.

This is one of the most difficult questions for our young democracy, still struggling to find its final expression. The solution of this problem is in no way the task of the State and certainly not in the first instance. It is the task of every individual to see to it that we shall return to a form of co-operation between human beings, in which first of all every individual feels responsible for his own fate, and is no longer prepared to vanish in a foglike anonymity—and so does not grant the unconditional right to an institution to carry out its mandate according to its own lights.

We must keep alive the will for independence and freedom, one of the most elementary forces of man, and strengthen it day by day. I cannot believe that anyone who confidently puts into the hands of an organization all he expects from the future can feel happy. And finally, I do not believe that the best arguments are always on the side of the strongest organizations.

It is a bad habit typical of our times to think and speak only in collective concepts. Is it not frightening if only one view is ever heard from the professional groups, if the absolute is always demanded? This is entirely unfruitful and leads to sterility. Thus, for example, I have had to listen to *the* conception of *the* economy, of *the* industry, of *the* trade. Who, I ask, is *the* economy, *the* industry, *the* trade? Can the views of members of groups really be so finely sifted and collectivized that some-one can justly speak for them in the singular? If it were argued that on this or that question a larger group held this view, another a different one, then such testimony would seem credible. The formation of collective judgment is usually a practical impossibility, if it is put forward on the basis that it is obligatory for all members.

These remarks are not meant to be a derogatory criticism of our forms of organization. It is merely a matter of recognizing the limitations of such assertions, to expose a serious problem of our social economy and thus of economic policy. I thus welcome every individual expression of opinion. When a large number of citizens turn to me in their letters, to present their personal requests, mentioning the points with which they agree, but naturally expressing their opposition to certain proposals, I welcome it greatly.

These freely expressed views have often served me well. At least they constitute a check on how the population is reacting to the events of the day. For example, when, shortly after currency reform on July 8 and 9, the spokesman of the S.P.D. said that as a result of currency reform and the measures arising from it practically nothing had changed—Deputy Suefferts saying: 'An improvement in supplies has not taken place'—I replied:

'If the previous speaker states that we cannot talk of a real improvement in the supply position, then, ladies and gentle-men, I do not know where the speaker of the S.P.D. has experienced currency reform. Not, it seems, in the street. If you come to my office I shall show you a whole heap of letters from workers and employees, from all sections of our people, who express their deep satisfaction with currency reform and with my economic policy.'

The psychological and political importance of such letters is in no way diminished because they can be divided into three large groups of clearly different values—first the letters from those who mean it honestly, expressing their own troubles and sincere wishes, and making suggestions which must be taken seriously; then the repeated letters of a few, who believe that they can offer a patent recipe which, if followed, would immediately solve all problems; and finally the letters from those written for reasons of opposition or sometimes even flaming hatred. Naturally, I regard the first category as the most sympathetic, and not only because it supports my case; luckily, it is also the biggest.

It is clear from a large number of letters how near to the heart of the German people is the stability of the currency, something that has been overlooked by the theoreticians who favour a slight permanent watering down of money.

To illustrate what I have been saying, here are some excerpts from the kind of letter which I receive daily:

On July 3, 1956, a citizen from Koburg wrote:

> 'Millions of Germans look to you in the hope that you will be successful in safeguarding our currency and economy in the face of all dangers. This is no easy task in a world which is split into dozens of sovereign economies, which sacrifices its natural cohesion to a misunderstood instinct for self-preservation. The same senseless attitude can frequently be noted within our own economy, but it is not in the final analysis one of the causes of worry for the security of our currency. Here too there exists only the same cure as in all other segments of society in our country striving for perfection: an increased knowledge of the way in which all human contributions to the world economy are interrelated.'

From Eggenfelden in Bavaria on May 1, 1956, I heard:

'Bravo, Herr Minister! I, together with many others whom I have asked, have heard your speech in Munich with great satisfaction. What has pleased us above all is that you, a man in a public position, have dared to express what every person feels—namely that today many have lost touch with what is possible. Unfortunately this goes right up to the top. . . . The mentality is always the same: to think only of the moment, to act only in one's own interest. . . .'

An engineer in Backnang wrote:

'. . . Economic miracle—inflation! I see and hear much of the one, while I fear the other. For the third time—to save in vain! And what will follow? The sufferers will always be us, the small savers. Those profiting will be the so-called owners of real property, those in debt and speculators. . . . The far from solid confidence in the State can no longer carry such a load. Inflation is an utterly immoral thing, a theft from the body of the people.'

Inflation—Wages and Agriculture

Questions are frequently asked about the cause of inflation. From Bad Kissingen this view was expressed on June 30, 1956:

'. . . In my view the currency question is causally linked with the regrettable practice of subsidizing agriculture, now common in all civilized countries. It is thus an agrarian question, indirectly linked to party propaganda for the votes of the peasants. Unfortunately, parliamentary seats are regarded as more important than the currency.'

Oddly enough, it is often the refugees who, frightened by the tragic experience of having lost all, raise their voice in warning.

Sometimes deep fury is expressed with what is taken to be the beginning of an inflationary trend:

'. . . If we could at last manage to lower prices noticeably, all decent people would be relieved, since then the vast differences between the newly rich on the one hand, and those who lost everything as a result of the Second World War on the other, would slowly disappear. It is high time that the lowering of prices took place.'

A hothead from Bad Ems wrote on June 28, 1956:

'. . . Do you believe in the fairy-tale of the Trade Unions, that they share no blame for the rise of prices? Who else? Is the loss in the value of money a natural phenomenon, or the work of fools?'

From Obermenzing a housewife wrote on June 14, 1956:

'. . . We, the citizens, are above all interested in the mark retaining its purchasing power at home. . . . Herr Minister, help all of us for whom inflation would spell disaster.'

An unusually high proportion of the letters came from Swabia, where many of the writers discussed the points in question with great thoroughness.

From Wendlingen on Main I received the following on April 3, 1956:

'The conviction that a creeping inflation continues is firmly embedded. Entreaties, unfortunately, do not help. The free play of economic forces knows no discipline; no one seriously considers moderation; every participant—businessman and trade unionist—tries to make the highest profit possible without a thought for the consequences. On the side of the consumer the same lack of discipline exists. In many cases purchases are made quite thoughtlessly. Even if on this or that side some reflection still exists, it cannot escape from the whirlpool. Thus it is a question of persuading producers and consumers to return to *terra firma*. And that is only possible by means of taxation. . . . Large-scale benefits for the saver are essential. Unlimited exemption from taxation of incomes and capital for all those deposits which during the next three or four years are paid into a savings account. . . . Besides the economic miracle, we could perhaps experience a savings miracle.'

Questions about wage and price policy are put even more frequently than those about the general problem of currency stability. Thus:

'. . . We want low prices, for what good is an increase in wages, if most of it goes on higher living costs. In addition the Deutschmark is progressively being debased, and finally German exports will be throttled by constant wage increases, which in turn will again bring about unemployment.'

From Wülmersen on May 29, 1956:

'. . . Can you do nothing, Herr Minister, about the way wages spiral? If not, then inflation cannot be kept at bay. Herr Minister, I want to raise my voice in warning. Be hard, not only with agriculture, but also with the German trade unions (DGB). If an inflation should recur the last shreds of the morale of savers would vanish.'

A simple woman from Pasing turned to the Minister for Economic affairs on May 16, 1956:

'. . . In forty hours it is impossible to work as much as in forty-eight hours, and that at the same wage. So an increase in prices takes place. Every businessman increases the prices of his goods and it is the consumer who suffers. Fifty years ago one worked from six in the morning until six at night and nobody died from over-work or got ill. People were healthier and happier. And don't put up wages all the time. . . .'

The wage demands of the trade unions are surprisingly often criticized. Thus a writer from Ulm declared on April 3, 1956:

> 'You have outlined clearly the question of a possible inflation, and I believe what you say. But as one now reads of new demands to be made shortly for wage increases from the trade unions, then the building trade will shortly follow. Allow them to make their demands, and give in to them—building will soon stop and the gentlemen can go for walks instead. I believe that the time has come for a period of calm in wages and salaries. Perhaps you will be able to use the measures you have announced before it is too late. Anyway, the constant wage increases give one cause to be afraid of a possible inflation. . . .'

The attempt to wage a psychological campaign for price stability provoked a vast number of letters, many correspondents mentioning their own 'private war' against rising prices. An arms manufacturer sent in his correspondence with a dealer, from which it is clear that he had always received a special rebate of 33⅓% for some tools. Then the dealer wrote: 'It has been reported to us that recently you have been using the resale rebate for special concessions to final purchasers. Please allow us to inform you that from now on we shall only allow you a resale rebate on 22%.' The businessman in question urged us to intervene, since 'these measures would naturally result in an increase in prices charged to the consumer.'

Not all Complaints are Well-founded

The sense of responsibility which should be shown by the sensible consumer is not always apparent. A citizen from Lenneper complained that for the repair of a chair seat and the handle of a small wicker basket she had to pay DM 50, and begged my Ministry to re-introduce measures to keep prices down. From the correspondence which followed it became clear that there had been considerable thoughtlessness in agreeing to the price charged. How could this housewife have agreed to give this job to a basket mender completely unknown to her without first inquiring about the price that she was to be charged for the work? This sort of correspondence is typical of many.

My appeal not to meet every demand for a price without questioning it has had a number of repercussions. Thus a traveller using the German sleeping and restaurant cars sent in details on May 14, 1956, about recent price increases, which my Ministry used in satisfactory discussions with the D.S.G. (Deutsche Schlafwagen Gesellschaft).

The owner of a small manufacturing concern with an average annual turnover of DM 60,000 told me that he had not increased the selling price of his product, in spite of a threefold increase in the price of raw materials. He continued: 'I believe that an association of businessmen honestly supporting your aims would be of value to you.'

A fashion store in Bavaria sent a notice and leaflets of which some 100,000 had been distributed, giving clients a guarantee that prices would not be raised between November 1955 and Easter 1956.

> 'Someone must make a start. That is what the German Minister for Economic Affairs Erhard has demanded from responsible traders at the Berlin meeting of the Federal Parliament. He meant that price increases must stop. Our firm has made a start. We declare that we shall not increase the prices of women's and children's clothing before Easter 1956.'

A citizen from Bielefeld on April 1, 1956, sent in an original letter received from a repair work room together with the repaired spectacle frame, which had cost DM 6·50:

> 'I turn to you as the "head" of the economy. Firstly, I want to thank you, Herr Minister, for your work in the reconstruc-

tion of our fatherland. But you, better than anyone, must realize where slowly, but surely, the selfishness of our traders and the self-indulgence of many of our people are leading us. . . .'

From many of the letters the point is made that the sensible approach is for people participating in economic processes to examine price demands critically and refuse to accept them blindly. To give an example, here is an exchange of letters. A correspondent from Heimbach-Weis ordered a certain valve, which was sent to him with an invoice for DM 74·20. Intensive research, which led, amongst other things, to an exchange of letters with the makers, finally produced the information from the manufacturers that the regular price was DM 35, or, at the most, DM 40. He then wrote: 'After I had finally been told of the price by the makers, and the supplier continued to demand DM 74·20, I returned it to him and did not pay.'

A writer from Langenau (Württemberg) drew my attention in mid-March 1956 to the fact that in sales talk the remark: 'Buy, prices are rising' was often heard. And many people are so lacking in conscience that they spread this poison.

Many letters are concerned with concealed price changes. One client who for years had bought certain pastilles reported, with considerable annoyance, that the normal package suddenly contained only 40 instead of 51 pastilles as hitherto. The correspondence between the manufacturer and my Ministry led to the former openly acknowledging that he believed that, with this concealed price increase of 20%, he met the wishes of his clients better than by an immediate and necessary price increase.

Lower Duties are Popular

Agrarian politics, or rather the criticisms regarding the 'Green Front', are a constant talking point. An unusually large number of letters discuss these questions. Here are some examples:

'Herr Professor Dr. Erhard, the people of all classes look to you. Thus I beg you to lead a relentless fight against your opponents, who, instead of lowering prices, want to raise them in opposition to your views.'

A housewife wrote:

'. . . We housewives read in the papers with great pleasure of your intention to bring about a lowering of prices of foodstuffs. . . . To lower prices cannot be so difficult, and in my view must begin with agriculture. It seems advisable to examine the trade margin of the abattoirs, the dairies and the retail traders. Meat cattle prices drop again and again, yet meat and sausage prices remain unchanged. And every butcher drives an Opel Kapitän or Mercedes. . . . Herr Minister, by bringing about lower prices you will win great praise, and we, the housewives, shall be especially grateful. We wish you every success.'

A citizen from Stuttgart-Degerloch was enraged by the wrecking of the original plan to include agriculture in the 30% tariff reductions:

'The result is, as it so often is, that the consumer will suffer; it is a well-proven way of allowing the consumer to carry the burden. The devil takes the hindmost.'

The same theme was discussed by an architect from a small village in the Odenwald:

'As regards the 30% tariff reduction I should like to tell you of my own experience: I have an estate in . . . a village with . . . houses. This area of the northern Odenwald is regarded as poor. During the past four or five years almost every second farmer in this village has put up new agricultural buildings and also new homes and—what is to be welcomed—has bought new farming implements. Every farmer's son has also bought his own motor-cycle. . . . I do not grudge the farmers, with whom I am on the best of terms, this greater prosperity, but I do not on the other hand understand the cries of woe about agriculture facing ruin and thus being unable to survive a lowering of tariffs.'

Sceptical voices are not only raised about agriculture. During the discussions about lowering tariffs for farm products, I received a furious telegram:

> 'Farm voters protest energetically against intended lower tariffs for agricultural imports. Measure hits agriculture with full force, and undoes effects of Green Plan. We expect withdrawal of your tariff plans, where they concern agricultural products.'

A carefully worded reply could not be delivered, in spite of all the efforts of the Post Office, and of a number of other organizations.

Such protests also bring about counter-protests; I received the following telegram:

> 'Consumers in the whole Federal area, especially housewives, to whom Chancellor recommends counting every penny, warmly welcome lowering of tariffs, and expect passing of your tariff proposals in full. It is high time to take effective measures, which will put a stop to the permanent increase in prices. . . . Do not weaken in the face of protests from agriculture, which, though it has its troubles, is basically no worse off than the millions of recipients of medium and small incomes, who hope for a certain easement of their position as a result of the tariff proposals.'

Another correspondent from Frankfurt wrote:

> 'We follow your deeds with admiration, but have nevertheless regretted that you weakened in the discussions. You will see that the people will continue to remain dissatisfied.'

On May 13, 1956, the Ministry received this from Rheinberg in the Rhineland:

'. . . The big economic successes of the past eight years were only possible since the people had confidence in you. . . . Surely there are enough ways to stop the increase in prices. Why don't you lower tariffs? Why is rearmament being organized at such a brisk pace? Why are no brakes applied to the building activities of the Government, the Länder and the local authorities. . . . ? Herr Minister, we, the savers, hope you and the Federal Government will be successful in keeping the currency stable.'

On July 18, 1956, a Munich citizen expressed his rage with the breakdown of talks for a comprehensive lowering of tariffs.

'I find it incomprehensible that the lowering of tariffs which you introduced should have foundered. It seems as if important positions were occupied by agriculturists or others who don't mind price increases, and for whom perhaps this means good business. . . .'

Some correspondents sent clear warnings. Thus, a citizen from Stuttgart on June 2, 1956, who had been following my efforts 'with increasing apprehension', wrote:

'. . . to preserve the German economic miracle from the fate of other miracles. Why do you not act with more energy? Is not the stability of prices the foundation of well-being? . . . I believe, Herr Minister, that a section of the economy no longer has the kind of social conscience which you expect from it. . . . Do not look to the coming Federal parliamentary elections, but instead secure yourself a place in the history of the German people. See that your principles, which millions of German people support, are energetically and logically applied. Our democracy needs a firm hand, if it is not to founder.'

The public here frequently overlooks that for any government there are frontiers beyond which it cannot act, and that the Minister for Economic Affairs cannot carry responsibility for everything important that happens in the economic sector.

From Stuttgart a letter of March 27, 1956, said:

'I read in the daily press that the hourly wages of building workers are to be raised again by 8 pfennigs from April 1, 1956. I am horrified. This damnable creeping inflation, where will it lead to? Do you know, Herr Minister, that this is open fraud.'

Very plain words were used in a letter of March 6, 1956:

'Dear Herr Minister, You promised us some lower prices. So far this has not come about. On the contrary, some prices have risen, and, unfortunately, it is your colleagues who have opposed your efforts. We are just where we were in the Third Reich. This cannot end happily.'

From Brazil, Hand-made Paper and Gold Coins

Frequently, reference is made to details. Thus some Brazilians and former Germans who emigrated to Brazil wrote at the end of 1955 from Santa Catarina, Brazil:

'In many ways we like you best of all of the Government people there in Germany, because you are decidedly a man of freedom. When you firmly opposed the attempts to form cartels we were one hundred per cent for you. . . . Monopoly capitalism opposes freedom; it is the opposite of freedom if one group of citizens takes advantage of the others. Now we have been asking for some years: Is not Erhard aware that a group of striking workers does just that, if, by threatening mass strikes, it uses blackmail for more wages. If cartels are suppressed then strikes must be suppressed too.'

Naturally, there are many letters which, following some unpopular measure, prophesy chaos. On May 12, 1956, a manufacturer wrote from Paderborn:

> 'If, to control the boom, credit restrictions are to be introduced, this can only be done in stages. If it were done in one go, a catastrophe would follow . . . our way so far leads inevitably towards Communism. . . .'

Frequently, well-known men comment on current problems. For example, on January 14, 1956, the president of the board of a well-known industrial concern wrote:

> 'I should be very grateful for your advice on how the . . . industry should behave in the face of price threats. It is fighting a hard battle for its existence, in view, too, of the totally incomprehensible price policy of your basic industries which, as is clearly shown by their recent balance sheets, work with large margins of profit.'

The desire to simplify the administration appears in many and unexpected ways. Thus a dentist from Giessen sent three communications from the Federal Association for Air Defence printed on fine paper, elegantly finished. He said: 'Unfortunately, this gives the impression that the much urged economic discipline does not apply to Ministries and public authorities.'

Besides letters of protest and criticism, there are others of appreciation, often containing valuable ideas.

During the discussion about the usefulness of the BDL measures a writer from Stuttgart declared on May 8, 1956:

> 'I very much hope that in co-operation with the BDL you will be successful in keeping the reins firmly in your hand, so that the Bill will tighten its restrictive policy rather than slacken it.'

On November 21, 1953, a writer from Cologne had this to say:

> 'I read in the paper your speech to the Association for Action for the Social Market Economy. Without a doubt your activities played the greatest part in the electoral success. Please continue to show the same courage, the same attitude, which you have shown in supporting competition, towards the administration. This vast administrative apparatus is insupportable for an economy which is itself up against stiff competition.'

A manufacturer from Remscheid-Lennep wrote on April 30, 1956:

> '. . . It is not flattery when I report to you that the economy is convinced that you are up to your job. I should not like to have your post. When I saw you a few days ago on television, I got the impression that you are perhaps too good-hearted. And it would be expedient if you dealt differently with your opponents.'

On February 22, a citizen from Bauschlott near Pforzheim commented on my advice to be moderate:

> 'In the past few days I have read your warning about the fresh dissatisfaction of all sections of the German population. That you have expressed such views is much to be welcomed. . . . It is bad politics for poverty to be discussed at meetings of industry and trade when in front of the meeting hall stand dozens of Mercedes cars. I have nothing against wealth, but I think it inappropriate to grumble all the time. But, unfortunately, it is just those sectors that have experienced a marked improvement and an increase in their capital who feel no sense of responsibility towards the Government, but instead would make agreements with the devil, if only something could be gained by it. . . .'

Among the many letters there are many curiosities. A retail trade business in a large West German city sent without comment several bags in which its goods are packed, on the back of which is inscribed: 'Erhard is right! Many prices would fall if everyone always chose the best offer. It is up to you.'

Several writers put forward this or a similar suggestion:

> 'The Federal Bank should mint a milliard gold coins, and while withdrawing a milliard of paper money put these into circulation in payments for wages and salaries. These gold coins would immediately be hoarded, and would reduce purchasing power possibly by a milliard.'

On July 14, 1956, a Berlin citizen ended a communication with this statement:

> 'I am in possession of the reply of your Ministry . . . to my letter to you, for which I thank you. Even if the answer falls far short of my expectations, I have at least the satisfaction that it is not true—as frequently stated—that letters sent to a Minister land in the waste paper basket of the ante-chamber. I shall now refute such remarks.'

Chapter IX

MARKET ECONOMY AND WAGES

MY CONSTANT BATTLE to secure true and free competition aims at supporting in the first place those forces in our country which are beneficial, and which above all should help the German economy towards a permanent progressive increase in productivity. Where there is no competition, there is a standstill which eventually leads to general stagnation. Everyone then defends just what he owns, that is, he is no longer interested in increasing his own efforts—so important a factor for the prosperity of the national economy.

This increase in economic efficiency is by no means an end in itself. The facts of the case of the social market economy can only be regarded as completely fulfilled when, in keeping with growing productivity, prices are lowered, thus making increases in real wages possible.

I shall never cease to work towards this end—and I shall continue to do so even when many no longer believe that a policy to cut prices is possible or likely to be successful. This aim must not be lost sight of just at that phase of economic development through which we are now passing. Did we not face a similar problem during the Korean crisis? At the C.D.U. meeting in Goslar on October 22, 1950, when the waves of price movements ran high, I could point to the fact that the Volkswagen works had lowered its prices by 10%, in spite of higher raw material costs and a simultaneous increase of 10% in wages and salaries. I explained that such a policy 'completely corresponds to the aims of a social market economy'.

These pointers may suffice to make clear the close link between the effort to maintain competition and the desire for a higher standard of living. In the long run it is economically impossible to want the one and simultaneously to forgo the other. This indissoluble relationship can also be presented in another way: only competition can ameliorate the consequences of rising prices which we have experienced during three periods in the past eight years—namely in the second half of 1948, as a result of the Korean conflict, and now as a result of boom and full employment.

To maintain a competitive economy is in every sense a social obligation. We can learn from our own past, but also in looking at countries beyond the Iron Curtain we can see that in the planned economy, and even more in the State-controlled economy, the proportion of wages in the national income is and has always been smaller than in the market economy. The proportion of wages is always smallest in the State-directed collective economy, as at present under Bolshevism. It would be remarkable if it were different, for not only does the bulky bureaucratic machinery in the nature of things consume a large part of the national income, but the composition of the national income also shows that it is not meant to satisfy human needs. No one wishing to be taken seriously can declare or even wish to prove that the social and economic performance of a State-run economy can be greater than that of a market economy.

If I have here remarked that in the market economy competition is the ideal means of increasing productivity, and that this in turn makes lower prices and higher wages possible, then an historical explanation is needed.

A Rule for Businessmen

I have found it necessary to discuss publicly the trend of wages when this threatened to go beyond what was economically possible, and there was a danger that the limits set by the trends in productivity were going to be exceeded for political reasons. This state of affairs came about twice during the period when I was responsible for Germany's economic policy—in the recent past and during the Korean crisis. During the other periods I have never raised general objections to a rise in wages, even though these were considerable. Those who are familiar with my economic beliefs know that an important part of them is reserved for a generous development in wages.

That is why I have repeatedly declared that the often exercised opposition of employers to wage increases in principle (which thanks to a rising yield of our national economy were not only possible, but necessary and sensible to maintain the stability of our currency) is not appropriate to the system of the market economy. Such opposition utterly disregards the aims of market economy as I understand it. To me it appears ill-founded if the employer himself never takes the opportunity to increase wages, except when the unions press him. Especially during the phases of a quiet economic upward trend employers, if they were prepared to raise wages on their own initiative because of improvements in productivity, would act with economic propriety and psychological astuteness. Naturally, the margin available to cut prices should not be entirely given away. A crass alternative would be to prefer cutting prices to increasing wages.

The objection that the trade unions must show victories to their members, and that therefore the position I recommend is inadvisable, cannot be regarded as justified in the national economic sense.

If the actual progress in productivity is regarded as setting limits to the activities of the trade unions, and to the scope for a voluntary increase in wages on the part of the employers, then the question now arises as to what protection can be found to prevent an infringement of these limits.

Wage increases not covered by increased productivity must always lead to price increases. But first it should be said without passion that employer and employee agree easily during a time of boom; both are concerned with production and tend to hope that the results even of a doubtful agreement will not directly affect them. But every agreement which ignores its broad effect on the national economy adds to the burden of other groups in the economy whose incomes change less quickly, and for whom every increase in price, above all of important goods, is detrimental in its effect.

Thinking of the Future

I have already drawn attention to these social—or rather anti-social—consequences of disregarding the limits of healthy changes in wages, when I discussed the question of the so-called 'active wages policy'. This kind of expansionist wages policy, which tends to shake the price structure, must be damaging, unless for different reasons an inflationary trend is welcome. I do not and never shall accept such a conception, for a policy of this sort would slowly but surely inflame the inflationary trend until all desire to save was killed.

In evaluating a policy which gives a small place to the stability of purchasing power, the general economic effects must be considered, quite apart from the anti-social results. In Germany if we are not in the long run to damage our exports we cannot and must not thoughtlessly raise wages and salaries. Even in a period in which we sometimes regard our export surplus as an evil, we must not forget that our goods are not being bought abroad just because they are German, but only when and for as long as we are prepared to persist in our efforts. As part of the world economy we must understand the connection in the sphere of wages. It must not be forgotten how much our proud successes in the field of foreign trade depend on the stability of our currency and on confidence in the constant value of our money. Only a policy directed in this way can impart the feeling of security for economic transactions, in the larger field of the national economy as well as in the smaller, i.e. in the sphere of the household.

This attitude must remain. These statements and views remain valid even in a period when the favourable trends in our foreign trade are safe from any danger that could threaten from that side. If a policy with an inflationary trend is accepted, or if such a policy no longer finds any resistance, then there will be no stopping of the consequences. The depreciation of money and increases in prices which would follow would mean that our surpluses would melt away like snow in the sun.

I believe equally that all employees should participate fully in the increasing productivity of our national economy, as I expect that the trade unions should show that responsible attitude in their wage demands which will guarantee the security of our currency and the further salutary upward trend of our economy. This warning for moderation can nevertheless only be justified so long as the employers do everything possible to reduce prices or, at the very least, maintain the stability of the prices of the goods they produce and sell, and in particular of consumer goods.

Autonomy and Responsibility

The question of joint management is connected with these problems. My views on this point are well known. Now, as previously, the Federal Government, the coalition parties, probably the whole of the Federal Parliament, want to give and preserve freedom of decision for joint management so far as wages and working conditions are concerned. This freedom is necessarily linked to the responsibility to use it sensibly, that is not to pursue a policy which would lead to higher prices, and so cut purchasing power, reduce the ability of the German economy to compete, and in the final instance endanger the currency. Freedom, without responsibility and a feeling of obligation, can only result in degeneration and chaos.

At the International Fair at Frankfurt on March 6, 1955, I was able to say with full conviction: 'I am pleased to be able to declare that both sides in joint management are clearly acknowledging their responsibility. Until I have proof to the contrary, I am confident that from this direction no elements will disturb the German economy.' But the trend since the spring of 1955 raises some doubts whether these confident statements, based on a belief in innate human good sense, are still valid today. A glance at the differences between the trend of wages and productivity confirms these doubts, especially since the growth of wages in 1956 far exceeds progress in productivity. During the first nine months of 1956, productivity rose by 3·8% over the same period of 1955, while the gross weekly wages of the industrial worker over the same period increased by 8·6%.

In this connection I should like to quote the views of a leading advocate of the market economy, Walter Eucken. He says:

> 'If it is right that it is only possible to distribute what has first been produced, then the first concern of all social reformers must be with that economic order which is most effective. Only after that can other questions be asked. When in any kind of economic order all go equally hungry, then this is neither a solution of the problem of just distribution, nor of security nor any other social question. Nor is it impressive when efforts are made to render the effects of a bad order more palatable by ethical embroideries and appeals to the common interests of all.'

The Cake Must Get Larger

That is why I want to stress once more that my aim to raise the standard of living is concerned less with the problems of division than with problems of production and productivity. The solution is not to be found in dividing but in multiplying the national income. Those who pay attention to the problem of division frequently make the mistake of trying to distribute more than the national economy produces.

This does not mean that the present division is ideal or 'just' in every respect. In the long run changes are possible. But such changes, particularly if they are to be made quickly, bring in their train violent discussions, battles for more wages and perhaps even strikes. The economic energies of the nation needed for these purposes would be appreciable. That is why it seems to be more sensible to use this same energy to increase productivity, in order to obtain more for all in this, the only fruitful way.

What I have said here is brought out by trends in national income. Between 1949, when the Federal Government began its work, and 1955, we have succeeded in raising the gross national income (expressed in 1936 prices) from DM 47·1 milliard to DM 85·8 milliard. In the first six months of 1956 the national income, at roughly DM 44 milliard, was almost as large as that for the whole of 1936 with DM 47·9 milliard. The net income of employed workers correspondingly rose from DM 34·101 milliard in 1950 to DM 61·367 milliard in 1955 and DM 31·909 milliard in the first six months of 1956. Income during the first half year is usually well below that of the second half year, e.g. first six months of 1955, DM 29·393 milliard, second six months, DM 32·974 milliard.

The rates of increase in private consumption are particularly illuminating, having risen by DM 5·205 milliard in the first six months of 1955. If private consumption (all price changes being left aside) is calculated in 1936 prices, then these are the rates of increase for recent years:

Rates of Increase Since 1949

Private Consumption Expressed in 1936 Prices

1st Half-year							
1950	compared	with	1949	+DM	1701	million	12·6%
1951	,,	,,	1950	+DM	1848	,,	12·2%
1952	,,	,,	1951	+DM	1037	,,	6·1%
1953	,,	,,	1952	+DM	1684	,,	9·3%
1954	,,	,,	1953	+DM	1761	,,	8·9%
1955	,,	,,	1954	+DM	2182	,,	10·1%
1956	,,	,,	1955	+DM	2372	,,	10·0%
2nd Half-year							
1950	,,	,,	1949	+DM	2485	,,	15·9%
1951	,,	,,	1950	+DM	772	,,	4·3%
1952	,,	,,	1951	+DM	1844	,,	9·8%
1953	,,	,,	1952	+DM	2040	,,	9·9%
1954	,,	,,	1953	+DM	1625	,,	7·1%
1955	,,	,,	1954	+DM	2955	,,	12·1%
Calendar year							
1955	,,	,,	1949	+DM	21934	,,	75·5%

The great responsibility of every economic and social politician can also be seen from a new trend in economic developments. On the threshold of the age of automation, at the beginning of a phase which many (if with some Jules Verne-like fantasy) would like to call the beginning of a second industrial revolution, we have here in Germany, as in other highly industrialized economies, a great need for capital, which must be satisfied in an orderly manner. In theory there are only three ways of dealing with it. The demand can be met through the free capital market, in which every citizen should participate as far as possible. Here capital comes to be generally available as the result of the small individual savings of the many. That is why this method must be regarded, not only as the classical one, but also as the healthiest. Unfortunately it must be said that, besides political mistakes, clearly due to the population's worry about price trends, and in spite of increasing prosperity, savings have recently fallen (see graph on savings since currency reform on page 65).

If this natural way of finding capital through the capital market becomes blocked owing to the action of the people, then there are two further possibilities. One is finance through higher prices. But I do not believe that any of my readers will think that this is a useful or—in the long run—a politically defensible method. If we were to try to exploit this procedure then I am firmly convinced that our social and economic order would soon break down. Such an attempt would contain so much social dynamite that it could only lead to a catastrophe.

As a final solution there remains the appeal to the State; that is, the State should make available the necessary means for investment. As so often is the case with such transparent political demands, no one asks where the State is to find the necessary means. Without endangering the currency and without disturbing the price level no State can lend out more in capital than it has first received in taxation from its citizens. Thus this method means not only confiscation without compensation in favour of mammoth State capital ownership, but forces every individual citizen into the position of slave-like dependence on an all-powerful State. A free national economy based on private initiative is then doomed to moulder.

If the Socialists support an 'active wages policy' and acknowledge the need to increase investment, yet at the same time stick to the view that the problems of automation cannot be solved by private economy, then little imagination is needed to detect that the Socialists believe that they have found the hook on which to hang a social revolution. Soon State planning and a new *dirigisme* will be introduced as the answer to the apparent need to deal with the new technical developments. I can only say that I warn those who feel tempted.

Finally, there remains the possibility of letting the demand for capital slacken—i.e. to let investment, which is needed for the national economy, fall away. It is clear that we would then leave the circle of the modern industrial economies and would slowly but certainly drop back to a more primitive existence.

If we are to tread the path which seems to me to be the only fruitful one, then we must lay the basis for creating sufficient capital. We can achieve this aim only if and so long as the German people have confidence in the stability of the political, social and economic order. But for the man in the street this is symbolized by the price which everyone pays for the essential things of life. That is the focal point where our efforts for an appropriate wages policy, and for securing the stability and basis of the economic, social and political future of our people, must meet and combine.

From these reflections it will become increasingly necessary for the individual to become conscious of the limits to his own demands or to those of his group. Some wage increases, for example, seem beneficial to the worker, and even appear particularly tempting, but if they shatter the price structure they will carry the seed of evil in them and, as is the nature of things, will injure those who hoped to benefit.

Though man has been successful in splitting the atom, it will never be possible to explode that old economic law which tells us to live reasonably and within our means, and which forbids us to consume more than we can produce or want to produce.

Chapter X

DOES PROSPERITY LEAD TO MATERIALISM?

IN RECENT YEARS the idea that the policy of the social market economy clearly leads men more and more towards a corrupting materialism has been gaining ground.

This view should be critically examined.

Beyond the differing economic standpoints, the work of all those who participate in the economy, as well as the urge for the constant improvement of our productive capacity, makes economic and social sense by opening up improved and freer ways of living for the whole people. Egyptian pyramids were not built for their own sake; no, every new machine, each new power station, every new factory and any other means whereby productivity can be increased, serve in the final instance to enrich all who live and work within the sphere of the social market economy. I shall never tire of ensuring that the fruits of economic progress will benefit ever widening circles of the population and finally everyone.

Without production no income is possible in the national economy, but it is also not possible to produce without consuming, except in a totalitarian system. This point of view dissuades me from granting any privileges demanded because of political or economic strength. Those who try to exploit positions of power must be conscious of the fact that in this way they damage the interests of others.

From this point of view I consider it one of the most important tasks of modern economic policy to apply recent knowledge to overcome former violent swings of the economy, once thought inevitable. If this can be achieved, much will be gained towards increasing the prosperity of all, and at least every diligent and hard-working member of the community will have a better chance of proving himself and of succeeding.

The Will to Consume

A permanent, evenly balanced economy, which at one and the same time keeps alive the forces that lead to expansion and progress, presupposes a dynamic population which is basically willing to consume. Only this will to consume, which I have often mentioned, permits production to develop uninterruptedly, and keeps alive efforts for greater efficiency and improvement. Only if consumption (including productive consumption) exercises a constant pressure on the economy will that force remain active which adapts itself in the sphere of production to increasing demand and undertakes corresponding risks.

It is and remains the ultimate aim of any economy to liberate man from material want and stress. That is why I believe that the better we succeed in increasing prosperity the rarer will be man's tendency to adopt a purely materialistic attitude towards life, because an increase in prosperity creates the ambient in which man is lifted from a purely primitive materialistic way of thinking. I am convinced of this postulate, since man remains bound to material considerations only for as long as he is overwhelmed with the cares of everyday life. Conversely, all human beings who, thanks to prosperity and social security, are conscious of their own worth, their personality and their human dignity, can look towards the possibility and the happy prospect of freeing themselves from materialistic thinking.

Thus, the new refusal to permit economic expansion to slacken, while there are still some people whose social standing is unsatisfactory, is based largely on social-ethical considerations. But it is quite another question whether it serves any purpose to regard the will for expansion as a constant factor in all phases of development, and to proclaim it equally loudly.

So long as expansion springs not only from the desire for a

better way of life, but for greater output, harmony is assured. But if the wish for expansion brings with it the danger that, without reference to the output of the national economy, men demand more from the national economy than it is able to provide, then the socially beneficial effort lacks a real and moral basis.

The outlook which aims to increase the yield from one's own work—expressed in wages—yet simultaneously envisages a reduction in the amount of work done (perhaps by reducing working hours) without reference to improvements in productivity, has little in common with that will for expansion which I have advocated here.

No German Austerity Policy

In its proper sense expansion means an increase in the total yield of the national economy, when all are able to share in this increase. Today we are experiencing that unwelcome trend in which groups are bargaining for their share of the national income.

There is no sense in harbouring illusions. No national economy can grant more than it is able to give as a result of the total effort made by men and the products of their labour. It is just at a time of full employment and boom that the limits of consumption for every individual have to be strongly emphasized. It is to be hoped that no one will deduce from this that I want to speak here of a special kind of German austerity policy, a policy of self-denial. Nobody can accuse me of saying that I have ever used such words as 'pulling the belt tighter' or 'to do without and to renounce', etc. Such proscriptions do not conform with my basic economic views.

My record over the past years denies any suggestion that I am pursuing a restrictive policy as regards consumption just for its own sake, or that it could possibly be my aim to ruin a favourable economic situation. No, I affirm that the success of our economic policy has always been founded on the fact that we have not been discouraged by difficulties, but have found the solution by dynamically moving forward, that is, by looking towards expansion.

Is it then really justifiable to declare that the achievements of the social market economy, since it is leading the German people along a path of soulless materialism, are being shown up as apparent rather than real, and that this economy will atrophy with prosperity?

It should first of all be asked whether this apparent impoverishment corresponds to actual fact and whether—if this question is answered in the affirmative—there exists a true causality between growing prosperity and increasing materialism. A confirmation of this assertion would mean the death sentence for the principles and aims of the free Western world.

I do not believe that the trends in Germany since 1948 towards a broad and rapidly rising improvement in general living standards can justify such tragic conclusions for our people and destiny. We must soberly reflect on what has taken place during the past years.

A poverty-stricken and hungry people, deprived of the most rudimentary ways of making a living, and suffering under the soulless economic *dirigisme* robbing it of any individual freedom, succeeded in a relatively short period in regaining its vigour and freedom. What could be more human than to consume and to enjoy in the full flush of one's renascent energies?

It must be added that, with the democratization of the masses, a social change is taking place which has particularly increased the material well-being of the employee. As a result of this development, it is almost a matter of course, and even unavoidable, that ever-increasing numbers of people are able to afford a higher standard of living, that is they are able to buy more goods in a variety which has hitherto been out of their reach.

I have consciously worked towards this end, and I am happy with its success. Is it not pharisaical if the better-off or rich sectors of our people complain about the pleasure-seeking and desires of those who basically have no other wish than to act like them?

I regard the material rise of the German workers and other

sectors of our people as an absolute political, social and economic gain.

I want to ask bluntly whether the radio receiver, or the vacuum cleaner, or the refrigerator, represent different things in the house of the worker than they do in the house of the rich man? Is it in one instance the expression of civilization and culture, and in the other evidence of a materialistic attitude? I fail to see—leaving aside the difference in the amount of noise—where in this valuation the motor scooter differs from the motor car.

Such foggy thinking will not contribute to saving our people from a material impoverishment of life. The size of income is neither a yardstick nor a frontier in a moral evaluation of consumption. For this reason I do not understand why, and how far, the human soul is likely to be endangered by prosperity and wealth. Logically the counter-question should be asked: At what income level does the human soul escape the dangers of wealth? But merely putting the question shows that it should be rejected.

Those sectors which now enjoy higher consumption more and more must not be criticized, since, first of all, the goods they are now able to purchase represent the fulfilment of a long-felt want, or because they are not yet able to place spiritual, cultural and material values in their proper order in satisfying their wants. With greater security of social well-being the stage will surely be reached when the differences between the good and the bad, and what is valuable and what is not, will be more clearly recognized.

False Impatience

On the surface it may seem indisputable that some consumption demands appear primitive. We do not have the right, nor does it serve any useful purpose, to be snobbish about this. It is part of the inalienable freedom of man that he may consume freely; we must not be intolerant in this respect. Let us not forget the long period of want experienced by the German people, which makes it all the more comprehensible that they now want to consume the fruits of their honest labour.

No argument will destroy my belief that poverty is the surest way to the deterioration of man through the small material cares of everyday life. Perhaps genius can triumph over such conditions; in general, material worries enslave men increasingly and they remain imprisoned in the material sense.

I do not wish to overestimate the purely economic factors. I believe that a well-functioning economy must be secured, both for the individual and for the people as a whole, as a basis for all higher efforts and the fulfilment of spiritual demands. Only as a result of a secure material basis will men become free and ready for higher things.

If we are today striving for new forms of civilization and culture, then in this broad spiritual discussion, particularly with the East, we shall only begin to succeed if men find that inner freedom and satisfaction which alone can guarantee true freedom. An economic policy which aims at increasing prosperity must, of necessity, be a good foundation for this goal.

This statement naturally does not attempt to change the thousand-year-old problem which is mentioned in the New Testament about the rich man, the camel and the eye of the needle. The thought which is expressed here is to lead wider sections of the people towards greater prosperity, but not to smooth the path for that kind of wealth and abundance which is said to lead to gluttony and vice.

Finally, it must be remembered that the material and the spiritual sides of life cannot be as sharply separated in practice as appears possible in the abstract. If, for example, men live in beautiful apartments, if they also sense in their own home something of the progress which surrounds them at work, if mothers and wives need no longer spend their evenings exhausted in the kitchen, but by virtue of material progress can dedicate themselves to their families, then much will have been achieved towards the unfolding of spiritual powers.

Surely it is proper to want to see better results from one's income than merely a larger number of beefsteaks and cutlets.

All this is indisputably right and important, but it should not be forgotten that it is not the first duty of Ministers for Economic Affairs and political economists to educate people accordingly.

The Spirit Cannot be Commanded

I do not hesitate to voice my great desire to see the German people turning towards more spiritual things as their standard of living rises. But I refuse to give orders to that effect. There is evidence that the luxury of today will become a matter of everyday use tomorrow. These seemingly material changes also alter the conception of what should be a higher living standard and what helps to increase social status and social position.

In my capacity as Minister for Economic Affairs, I should surely not be asked to become responsible for the spiritual well-being of all the people. In my job I have a particular task. I understand it to be to get enough out of the national economy in the way of energy and productivity for everyone to be able to live free from worry and want, and for everyone to be able to acquire property and thus become independent. In this manner, everyone will be able to develop his dignity as a human being to a greater extent, and so will no longer depend on the favour of others, or even on the favour of the State. It seems to me that with the achievement of such an aim the Minister for Economic Affairs will have made his full contribution to the overcoming of an apparent or actual materialism.

In these explanations I am conscious that there are certain limits in evaluating the material. With increasing productivity and with higher efficiency of human labour we shall one day reach that stage of development when we shall have to ask ourselves which is more valuable: To work more, or to lead a more comfortable, fuller, freer life and thus consciously forgo some pleasures. But I do not believe that we have got that far yet. Some time will still have to pass before this question will be ready for honest discussion.

Certainly it is to be hoped that the people will then have

reached the stage when they can use this 'longer leisure' more sensibly. The experience of certain countries is not encouraging and teaches us that leisure, demanded and granted out of a wish for higher material things, has not increased the spiritual well-being of the individual nor made him any happier.

Special German Situation

The German way should therefore find a slightly different expression. Our task is to sense slowly but increasingly the wishes of the individual and of the group, so as not to move mechanically, but in an effective manner, towards increasing general satisfaction. This is certainly no easy task.

It also cannot be denied that the problems here discussed overlap my immediate sphere of work. Even I, as the man responsible for economic policy, must take a stand about the 'social atmosphere', and, in so doing, I clearly sense the strength of the general intemperance—consciously nourished—which threatens to oppress good sense and truth.

Altogether the German people tend to lose relatively rapidly all sense of reality—a defect of character which in the recent past has led us to a tragic fate. It may be psychologically comprehensible that, with the end of want and with the boom, here and there signs of *hubris* are noticeable. It is all the more important to keep this within bounds, so that our people, who in austerity demonstrated the most admirable virtues, can also behave appropriately in happier times.

The appetite comes with eating, and so it has happened that with a flourishing economy more and more new wants have been awakened. The very same people who in 1956 are dissatisfied with their economic fate would never have dared in 1947 or 1948 to hope that they would arrive eight years later where they find themselves today. But that, nevertheless, does not prevent them from being dissatisfied. Envy is the complex which possesses them. It seems that the German is so made that he cannot bear another, a neighbour or a friend, being better off. However good his own position may be, he is then envious and dissatisfied. This particular kind of insatiability represents a special danger for our country, which must be recognized and fought against by every intelligent human being.

Final Aims

I am often asked what is the final aim of my economic policy. The question implies a fear that an endless projection of present trends might lead to a complete dissolution. The way of putting this question is certainly justified, and I do not wish to avoid answering it.

My reply is clear and unmistakable: I do not believe that, in drawing up our present economic aims, eternal laws have to be expressed. We shall certainly arrive at a point when, quite rightly, the question will be put whether it is still right and useful to produce still more goods, to increase material prosperity, or whether it would not be more sensible, in forgoing such 'progress', to gain more leisure, more time for thought, and more rest. But this is not a question for the Minister for Economic Affairs alone, but concerns the theologian, the sociologist and the politician.

The problem is complex and can be understood only in philosophical terms. Yet we must not avoid another more difficult question: Are people today sufficiently relaxed and happy to use their leisure in this higher sense? What remains to be done and on what level should it be done to achieve that inner maturity which will lead man to regard a renunciation of material things as beneficial?

It will also have to be borne in mind that more free time will bring with it a changed attitude to life, and naturally to the economy. All this can neither be constructed nor organized; it has to grow organically.

As long as we adhere, politically, to the motto: 'Let us work less so that we can consume more', we are taking the wrong path. But if trends which have now begun continue, in the sense that our people, assured of the essential security of their material life, will increasingly regard spiritual enrichment as useful and valuable, then eventually we shall have to correct our present economic policy. No one must then be so dogmatic as to continue to regard further expansion as a benefit for all.

Today we must not occupy ourselves unduly with speculations of this kind. If, for example, we compare Germany and the United States, then it is obvious how much scope there is in the way of expansion, in increasing prosperity, and in freeing people from material want. So until further notice I am of the opinion that, now as before, it is our job once for all to free millions of men, who are still burdened by the cares of everyday life, from their afflictions. Far too many human beings still live only in the shadow of prosperity, and therefore we must not cease our efforts.

Chapter XI

THE PSYCHOLOGY OF MARK AND PFENNIG

'IF WE ARE SUCCESSFUL in changing the economic attitude of the population by psychological means, then these psychological changes will themselves become an economic reality, and so serve the same purposes as other measures of economic policy taken so far.' In this sentence, spoken on behalf of the Federal Government in the first economic debate in the Federal Parliament on October 19, 1955, in Berlin, I expressed a fundamental principle. And it is this which has led me to use psychology as an instrument of equal worth to those well-known methods of traditional economic policy.

From a purely theoretical standpoint, this method of exerting influence on the participants in the market during the boom, at the same time as an attempt to influence prices, may not quite fit into the usual type of market economy. But I can see no reason why I should forgo this aid for purely doctrinaire reasons.

I have often been accused of being too true to a system. Therefore I should not be criticized if, as a political economist, I deviate on occasion from the 'ideal' of the economy. In my view, I do not offend against the market economy in its proper sense. It is a simple question of economic psychology: economic events are not guided by mechanical laws. The economy does not lead a life of its own like an automaton, but is fashioned and applied by man. If that is so—and surely it cannot be doubted—then the whole structure of the economy will have to change considerably according to our actions and attitudes.

So the consequences of the methods of psychology must not be underestimated.

Against this general background the objections of orthodox liberals, who would work exclusively with classical methods, cannot be entertained. The ultra-liberal critics must not worry over my lack of loyalty. I might even go so far as to state that the methods which I have mentioned here have been neither appreciated nor applied enough in theory and in economic policy.

Modern psychology demands precisely that the national economic process be not merely considered in the technical sense. It is equally important that the human beings who animate this machinery be included in national economic calculations. How we ourselves act is of decisive importance for the trend of the economy. Whether we are optimistic or pessimistic, whether we speculate on a boom or on a slump, whether we want to save or to consume, all this is expressed in economic statistics. In turn, these statistics, in the form of lower, stable or rising prices, colour our actions.

It would be wrong to suppose that the idea of psychological influences had only been discovered in recent times with the boom and full employment. If in recent years I have been criticized by some sceptics because I have left my desk to deliver speeches all over the place in a far from bureaucratic manner, I have done so for just these reasons. Nevertheless these reflections have only in recent times found proper expression or systematic use. I am convinced that the psychological campaign which I have conducted will in future become indispensable as an instrument of economic policy.

It may well be too early to compile a text book of systematic psychological guidance for the economy. In the next ten years, when more experience has been gained, economic science may well produce such a volume. However, I must make the point here and now that the world would react unfavourably to any attempt to appeal to its moral sense.

Naturally in turn this is not meant to imply that I consider the economy and the economic activities of people as perhaps amoral. But there is no sense in appealing to the people if they feel that they are meant to make sacrifices for the sake of a Minister or the Government. Above all, the people must be made to understand that to follow the voice of good common sense and of economic reason will, in the long run, result in their benefit.

Permanent Boom

An appeal must be made to the self-interest of all those who, during the boom, have nothing to gain by selling their labour or goods at a higher price if, in return, all the advantages so gained have to be paid for by higher prices. In this way everyone loses, for this sort of reciprocal climbing of prices on top of wages, and then wages on top of prices, destroys any kind of economic order and the power to compete.

This view once made me declare that I did not intend to put up a roll of honour for those obeying my well-meant recommendations. If in past months workers and trade unions have repeatedly been warned by me to be moderate and disciplined, it was in their own interest. Similarly I also called upon businessmen to oppose wage increases that went beyond the limit of possible progress in productivity, which is not incompatible with keeping prices stable.

I attach importance to relying on people's understanding and honesty, for we want to enjoy the boom, and not return to the automatic economic cycle with all its disadvantages. Since preventing this danger must be our major task, I have repeatedly demonstrated that, if people deceive themselves by wanting to seize every personal opportunity, they are sure to lose more than they could possibly gain. If, on the other hand, men show themselves to be up to the task of the hour, then I am convinced that the happy position of the boom can be maintained without inflationary trends.

From this it will be clear that I applied, during the boom and the so-called full employment experienced in Germany since about the middle of 1955, the psychological principles that

I have advocated. The biggest danger threatening the boom and economic progress does not—as is sometimes said—lie in too great an exuberance of materialism. My belief is that the threat of illusions nourished by demagogues should be taken far more seriously.

Increasing demands which, if they were to be met, would soon lead to a fatal inflationary development are based on a totally unrealistic conception of the nature and function of the national economy. For that reason it has to be said repeatedly that the inner connection between consumption, savings and investment is rarely completely understood.

Apart from political delusions which find expression in the so-called 'active wages policy', the connection between wages and prices cannot seriously be denied. The game that has now gone on of first higher wages and then higher prices proves either that this knowledge has not taken proper root, or that it is submerged by political considerations.

Our success in making people aware of the relationship between work and productivity, and between wages and the standard of living, and in acting accordingly, will determine whether we can face the future either with confidence or with apprehension. At this stage of economic development there is no cause for considering our economy as unhealthy. The disturbing influences, in my view, come entirely from inappropriate attitudes to what is economically possible.

For the sake of thoroughness it should also be mentioned that, besides the dangerous overestimation of the real possibilities, the boom is here and there regarded as a suitable platform to acquire economic power by unscrupulous means. In such cases any attempt to influence trends by psychological methods is bound to founder. Here massive counter-attacks will have to be launched.

The Nightwatchman State Belongs to the Past

I have already dealt with those critics who believe that it is impossible to combine modern psychology as one instrument of the contemporary political economist with the conception of the market economy in its classical form. Such a mode of thinking stems from the virtually outmoded Manchester School liberalism. I am unwilling to accept without reservation and in every phase of development the orthodox rules of a market economy according to which only demand and supply determine price, so that the political economist has to refrain altogether from interfering in price matters.

My views on this are fundamentally different; a modern and responsible State cannot afford to return to the role of the night-watchman. It was precisely this wrongly understood freedom which buried freedom and a free order. Such an attitude is all the less justifiable today, since, without a truly free world market and freely convertible currencies, the function of international prices is not in full play, and thus does not act as a healthy regulator in world-wide competition.

If the relationship between the classic method and the new political economic instrument of psychology has to be explained, it can be done very simply. I want to explain it by reference to existing conditions within the Federal Republic.

The Bank Deutscher Länder, as well as the Federal Government, are responsible for securing the stability of the currency. So I wish to achieve exactly the same end as the BDL does through its monetary, credit and currency policies. In reference to the so-called overheating of the boom, I commented at the opening of the German Industrial Exhibition on September 24, 1955, as follows: 'If you want to put it that way, the Bank Deutscher Länder and I are running a race.' The usual economic, financial and currency measures aim at influencing the trend of events in a definite direction. If, through psychological methods, I succeed in changing the attitude of people, I shall succeed in re-grouping data and facts in a manner which I regard as economically sensible. Whether people act differently owing perhaps to their being forced to do so by the policy of the Central Bank or whether they do so from a realization of their own interests is in the final instance unimportant. So we are not dealing with a polarity, an enmity between two different methods, but with two complementary means. Those who—as I do—value common sense as the strongest force, will be confident that in the future methods of psychological persuasion will find their place in economic policy as an instrument of freedom.

In this careful evaluation it must be remembered that in the contemporary social economic progress not only individuals but, above all, groups, determine events. To me it thus appears to be all the more necessary to communicate ideas and knowledge, to awaken good will and to appeal to common sense in order to help economic good sense to win through.

I regard it as a special advantage that psychology can be used in an early stage of any danger that might threaten. For example, I was able to state at the beginning of the boom, and the Bank Deutscher Länder agreed, that, so far, not the actual price level, but only the price climate had deteriorated. At that time to have intervened with firm traditional measures would have been precipitate, unless one had wished to slow down in the early stages that favourable economic trend which was rightly called a boom. Clearly we were then dealing with a psychological phenomenon. The danger does not threaten from the boom as such, but from a false evaluation of its chances and possibilities for material gain. It was not the economic trend but man who created difficulties. Nothing has materially changed in this situation since then.

Price Consciousness v. Inflation

In this psychological campaign for economic reasoning I have not limited myself to gaining supporters at large meetings only. I have also tried in many talks with individual branches of the economy to mobilize forces to prevent a too heavy increase in prices. Since the autumn of 1955 I have taken part in several such talks. The public knows only of a few of my efforts—perhaps that of keeping coal prices within reasonable limits or of my attempts to postpone by several months a rise in the price of pig iron.

The aim of such discussions was always the same: I wanted to create an atmosphere in which every purchaser would consider whether the price of the goods he wanted was reasonable, and in which everyone making or offering goods would once more ascertain whether his price really corresponded to the need to keep the price structure stable, and thus the security of our whole economy.

It can be justly doubted whether I have succeeded in achieving this aim completely. But it must be taken as proved that without these many attempts we in Germany, as in all other European countries, would have had a higher level of prices than in fact we have.

In this connection a glimpse at the actual trends of the cost of living will suffice.

Price Index for the Cost of Living
(Average Consumer Group (1950=100))

June	1950	99	June	1954	108
Dec.	1950	101	Dec.	1954	110
June	1951	108	June	1955	109
Dec.	1951	112	Dec.	1955	112
June	1952	109	June	1956	113
Dec.	1952	110	Dec.	1956	114

In brief, my aim is, through constant talks about prices, and through repeated public statements, to prevent the eruption of an economic sickness and to localize any crisis. In such an unstable situation price trends have to be mentioned daily, so that people might become immune to an epidemic of wild price increases. It is not a case of faith-healing for the German economy. Far from it. But I must repeat once more: the attitude of the people is and remains decisive.

Chapter XII

WELFARE STATE—THE MODERN DELUSION

EVERY TIME I SPEAK on the theme of 'social security' I am in danger of being accused of going beyond my brief. If I speak less as Minister for Economic Affairs and more as a political economist, it will seem natural to those knowing the subject that within the sphere of the social market economy the Minister for Economic Affairs has every reason to interest himself in further developments of our social policy. The social market economy cannot flourish if the spiritual attitude on which it is based—that is, the readiness to assume the responsibility for one's fate and to participate in honest and free competition—is undermined by seemingly social measures in neighbouring fields.

If one is prepared to think this problem through, one will understand the unwisdom of drawing the limits of discussion too narrowly. A watertight division could only be defended if the actions of all those influencing economic conditions stemmed from a common attitude, if they supported without reservation that order which the market economy wants to bring about. Put briefly, all would have to pull in the same direction.

I have repeatedly stressed that I consider personal freedom to be indivisible. With this conviction I have worked since 1948 to reduce all economic restrictions. A free economic order can only continue if and so long as the social life of the nation contains a maximum of freedom, of private initiative and of foresight.

If, on the other hand, social policy aims at granting a man

complete security from the hour of birth, and protecting him absolutely from the hazards of life, then it cannot be expected that people will develop that full measure of energy, effort, enterprise and other human virtues which are vital to the life and future of the nation, and which, moreover, are the prerequisites of a social market economy based on individual initiative. The close link between economic and social policy must be stressed; in fact, the more successful economic policy can be made the fewer measures of social policy will be necessary.

It should not be denied that in modern industrial countries even a good economic policy will have to be complemented by social policy measures. On the other hand it is true to say that every effective social aid will have to be based on an adequate and growing national income, which means an efficient economy. Thus it must be in the interest of every organic social policy to secure an expanding and sound economy, and to take care that the principles guiding this economy are maintained and extended.

As a result of the transfer of incomes through social budgets, which today play an important role in the process of economic distribution, there is now a close interdependence between economic and social policy. A national economic policy of neutrality and autonomy is thus a thing of the past. It has to make way for a social policy which is closely tuned to economic policy. Social policy must not damage national economic productivity even indirectly, and must not run counter to the basic principles of the market economic order.

If we desire to guarantee a permanent free economic and social order, then it becomes essential to achieve freedom with an equally freedom-loving social policy. That is why, for example, it is contradictory to exclude from the market economic order private initiative, foresight and responsibility, even when the individual is not in a material position to exercise such virtues. Economic freedom and compulsory insurance are not compatible.

Other special relations between economic and social policy

will be mentioned later in more detail. Here it should be noted that any social policy which does not regard the stabilization of the currency as of first importance must create the greatest dangers for the social market economy.

The Hand in the Neighbour's Pocket

This danger must be energetically countered. More differences of opinion exist on this point than on any other problem. Some say that the happiness and well-being of the people are based on some form of general solidarity, and that one should progress along this path at the end of which, of course, stands the power of the State. The calm and comfortable life so pursued might not perhaps be luxurious, but it would be all the more secure. This form of living and thinking is visibly expressed in the so-called Welfare State. On the other hand the natural efforts of the individual to be thrifty on his own account and to think of his future, his family and his old age cannot be abolished—even if great efforts have been made indirectly to kill the human conscience.

In recent times I have frequently been alarmed by the powerful call for collective security in the social sphere. Where shall we get to and how are we to maintain progress if we increasingly adopt a way of life in which no one wants any longer to assume responsibility for himself and everyone seeks security in collectivism? I have drastically described this flight from responsibility when I said that if this mania increases we shall slide into a social order under which everyone has one hand in the pocket of another. The principle would then be: I provide for someone else and someone else provides for me.

The blindness and the intellectual inertia which are pushing us towards a Welfare State can only bring disaster. This, more than any other tendency, will serve slowly but surely to kill the real human virtues—joy in assuming responsibility, love for one's fellow being, an urge to prove oneself, and a readiness to provide for oneself—and in the end there will probably ensue not a classless but a soulless mechanical society.

This process is particularly incomprehensible because, with the spread of prosperity and the growth of economic security, our economic basis becomes increasingly solid; the need to safeguard the achievements from all future dangers overshadows all other considerations. Here there exists a truly tragic mistake, for one meets with an apparent refusal to recognize that economic progress and prosperity based on effort cannot be combined with a system of collective security.

This call for security, which naturally must permit more State intervention, shows up the contradictions contained in this dishonest policy. If the words of these demands are reduced to a simple formula then what is being demanded is no more and no less than a lowering of taxation simultaneously with a greater demand on the public purse. Have the defenders of such a thesis reflected where the State is to find the power and the means to meet such demands which, taken one at a time, might be justified?

The Need for Security

In the final instance this way of thinking leads to utterly antisocial results. If the State refuses to sin against the currency, which would destroy everything so far achieved in reconstruction, then its purchasing power—whether in the form of social service payments, credits, loans or subsidies—is limited to what has first been collected from its citizens in taxation. I regard a policy which allows the State to gather capital in this manner, in order to enable it then to make private loans, as utterly immoral.

Those who do not shrink from thinking this problem through will rapidly recognize that the quest for security is an illusion. Just as a people cannot consume more than it has first produced, so the individual cannot gain more real security than we, the whole people, have gained as a result of our efforts. This basic truth cannot be concealed by attempts to veil it with collective schemes. It is for just these well-intentioned ventures that a high price has to be paid. Efforts to free the individual from too much State influence and too much dependence on the State are thus brought to nought; the tie with collectivism becomes stronger. The apparent security, granted to the individual by the State or by any other group, has to be bought dearly. Whoever wants protection of this kind must first pay in cash.

It is also wrong to believe that we should only move towards a Welfare State when collective security is granted by the State either completely or in part from general taxation. Nor can these dangers be avoided by imposing a comprehensive compulsory insurance, in which payments are financed from contributions.

General compulsory insurance—whether it is fed from one source or from many—is only different in degree, not in principle, from the ordinary citizen's pensions. The trend towards a Welfare State begins when State compulsion extends beyond the circle of the needy, to include people who as a result of their position in economic life consider such compulsion and dependence as unwarranted.

Here the important question must be asked: Does penetration by the State, by the public authority and by other large organizations into human life, and the resulting budgetary increases, accompanied by greater demands for taxation of the individual, does all this really lead to the greater security of the individual, to an enrichment of his life and to a decrease of individual anxiety? If I put this question in this absolute form, I should like to answer it equally clearly in the negative. The security of the individual, or at least his feeling of security, has not increased with the State or the group assuming a larger share of the responsibility; it has decreased.

And Finally the 'Subject'

The just demand to give more security to the individual can in the end only be met by increasing general prosperity, thus instilling the feeling of human dignity and, with it, the certainty that the individual is independent. The ideal I cherish is based on the strength with which the individual can say: 'I want to prove myself by my own efforts; I want to meet the risks of life myself; I want to be responsible for my own fate. You, the State, must see to it that I shall be in a position to do so.' The cry must not be: 'You, the State, come to my aid, protect me and help me', but the other way round: 'Don't bother with my affairs, but give me sufficient freedom and leave me enough from the results of my labours so I can shape my own existence, and that of my family.'

The result of this dangerous road towards the Welfare State must be the increasing socialization of incomes, the growing centralization of planning, and the extensive tutelage of the individual with increasing dependence on the State or the group—together with the deterioration of a free and well-functioning capital market as an important pre-requisite for an expansion of the market economy. In the end we shall find the 'subject' and a guarantee of social security by an all-powerful State, but we shall also have a paralysis of the economy.

It seems to me to be particularly dangerous to make way for these tendencies towards a Welfare State at a time when the objective, or the material facts, are clearly all against such a trend. If we had to presume that in the modern national economy, in spite of the progress in technique, economic trends and the living conditions of the people are becoming worse, then this longing for complete collective security would be understandable. But it seems to be almost certain that the living conditions of the people who realize the true market economy will continually improve. Since we should count on rising incomes and a rising standard of living, from a social point of view it seems proper to ask the individual to increase his responsibilities accordingly. This demand is all the more justified since the Welfare State, from all existing experience, means everything but 'welfare' and must finally spell 'poverty' for all.

This fundamental discussion about questions which cannot be avoided in an analysis of social policy does not mean that I wish to ignore the special requests which have recently been made. As the reader turns over these pages, social reform will probably have found its legal expression.[9] Nevertheless, I am doubtful whether the discussion about the aims of social reform will have ended. A glimpse at those countries which in recent years have made similar attempts shows to what extent such reforms have become no more than the starting point for the achievement of a sensible social order.

My criticism about the disastrous pressure for a Welfare State must not be misunderstood as a wish to change social security as we know it. I believe that a further extension of social security is perfectly possible. But what I consider as totally wrong is that people who, having acquired freedom as a result of their profession and their position in the national economy, should wish to move into a collective scheme, or worse still, to be pushed into it.

Limits of Social Insurance

In judging social insurance in its contemporary setting it should be remembered how much economic forms and principles have changed in the past decades and to what extent the social and political structure has changed. The man of the 'proletariat' who cannot provide for his own old age, or who does not want to provide and thus has to be protected by the State, will soon vanish if the present economic policy continues. Living conditions for the worker have improved infinitely and have become freer since the era of Bismarck. Compulsory State protection should end where the individual is in a position to provide for himself and his family on his own responsibility. For wage-earners, this applies at least to those who have a higher income and thus occupy a responsible position in the economy or in the administration.

Furthermore, it would be serious for our social life if such citizens were forced into insurance, for as a result of their position and functions it might be expected that they would want to prove themselves by their own efforts. It is perhaps understandable that war and currency reform, and the great changes which followed, have brought with them a demand for collective security. But it would now be wrong and ominous to base security from the general risks of life on such an eventuality which, it is to be hoped, will never recur.

From what I have said it can be seen that I should like to limit the area of collective security rather than extend it. To avoid all possible misunderstanding it should be stressed that I regard it as a natural duty for the community to see to the security of those who are now old and who, through no fault of their own, have lost their savings as a result of policies leading to two inflations. Here no social differences exist; the old workers and employees have to be helped in the same manner as the members of the free professions, the independent workers, the natives and the refugees. But this special problem, arising out of Germany's particular history, must not lead to that confusion which regards compulsory insurance and collective security as something which can be taken as a matter of course. The tragic consequences of inflation, experienced twice within one generation, does not tend to increase confidence in one's own strength. These tragic experiences must be taken into account; but they should, on the other hand, lead to a more careful examination of all economic and financial measures to make sure that we do not again take the same path, which can only lead to a serious devaluation of our currency.

Attempts to include the independent workers in collective insurance should be particularly scrutinized. A readiness to cope freely and responsibly with the hazards of life is essential to independence in a free economic and social order. Independence in the market economy means undertaking some useful job of one's own accord and on one's own responsibility, and thereby becoming a pillar of enterprise and initiative. On the one hand, the independent individual has open to him all the chances arising from economic progress but, on the other, he must be ready to face the economic risks involved.

In no circumstances can such a position in the economic life be guaranteed by the State under the system of the market economy. It must, above all, be earned anew day by day by economic achievement, by the readiness and the courage to face risks, and, above all, by a will to be individually responsible to shape one's own life, if it is to have meaning. As a result those who are independent within our economic and social order must also show responsible foresight for themselves in facing the risks of life.

It is paradoxical and, moreover, an irresponsible privilege to give every citizen an opportunity to work independently and by means of a free economic policy to further the pursuit of independent living, and then to take away from these independent people by State compulsion the responsibility to shape their lives.

This compulsory insurance, which is essentially of the model type, loses sight of the fact that in the independent trades and free professions one deals with heterogeneous and differentiated groups, and that here, therefore, as a result of individual thrift, it becomes impossible to meet the needs of each case. A critical discussion cannot avoid the question of where it would lead if the free professions started—each group for itself—to build up a system of group provision.

No Out-of-date Solutions

Have we not, in the past eight years, learned by tragic experience where it leads when the national economy is fragmented, in particular when every section and every class and every group believes that it can live its own life? If, for example, members of the free professions, be they doctors, lawyers or accountants, want to cut themselves off in respect of their pensions, then this security within a smaller framework will become increasingly problematical. In this manner selfishness is cultivated, a damaging mania for the ego, so that this clannishness becomes simply out of date—especially as it is taking place at a time when we are beginning to free ourselves from protectionist and nationalist thinking and, in this way, to achieve wider horizons of individual and social life. It should not be thought that, on the one hand, tightly-knit groups can find security in a collective scheme, and, on the other, can break their ties to move into a wider field.

From other aspects, too, such wrong-headedness leads to grave problems. For example, the attempt to apply the principles on which old age pensions are based for workers and employees to individual professional groups must necessarily fail. It would be practical only if there were no chance of considerable structural changes during the next few decades. Even if for the mass of dependent workers a continuation of present trends can be expected, nobody can foresee how specific developments will affect certain of the middle-class sections: for example, craftsmen or retail traders. There, at least, the possibility of considerable structural changes has to be taken into account. The smaller the circle that wants to adopt the new principles of large-scale social insurance is, the greater the problems and the insecurity of the basis on which such an order is made will be.

These considerations must necessarily be relevant to the much discussed pension reform, whether one speaks of an index pension, or a productivity pension based on wages, or of any other kind of pension. The decisive point is that the pension is meant automatically to change with the economic situation. This 'movable' pension is based on the steady increase in productivity which is part of the market economy. It bases itself on the general experience that the increase in productivity is expressed less in lower prices than in higher nominal wages. Such a productivity pension related to wages is harmless only as long as no currency or economic disturbances result from wage movements. If these are expected, then this scheme to adapt pensions to wages increases the danger of upsetting currency stability. A cumulative effect may possibly be expected, the results of which will be discussed later.

A Good Social Policy Demands Currency Stability

From a political point of view some thought should be devoted to the question of whether too close a link with wages will not essentially lead to lower resistance to excessive demands from trade unions in wage negotiations. This connection is based—more or less clearly—on the equally dangerous and wrong precept that 'the stability of the currency has nothing to do with social policy'.

It seems to me in every respect impossible to base every new social reform, such as pension reform, on such a criminal catastrophe as the last inflation. It is a great mistake for a people, or a State, to believe that it can introduce and pursue an inflationary policy, yet insure itself against the results. This is to try to lift oneself by one's own bootlaces. On the contrary, it is essential to concentrate all efforts to prevent an inflation, and to reject and so forestall it.

Inflation is not the result of a curse or a tragic fate but of a frivolous or perhaps even criminal policy. Every change in old age pensions, which brings about an inevitable rise in prices, thus reducing purchasing power, cannot lead to happy results. Larger groups of our people will want to escape from their responsibility to themselves, and will try to gain an apparently absolute but yet quite illusory security.

To translate a wage policy (the so-called 'active wage policy') which must result in permanently increased prices into the field of pensions must quickly reduce general support for currency stability, and thus start a disastrous trend. A general interest in maintaining the real purchasing power of our money is one of the most important counterbalances that oppose an inflationary policy in a well-ordered State. Furthermore, it must be asked how the formation of investible funds, so essential for technical progress, is to be achieved if social laws openly count on the likelihood of continually increasing prices. If all the people begin to lose confidence in the stability of the currency, and as a result of the aim for complete security demand such large contributions, then they would, in fact, have little or no incentive for individual saving.

During the discussions on the pensions index I clearly stated that it would be unwise to lay aside the idea of a movable pension. It is in favour of such a dynamically devised pension scheme that our idea of a minimum standard of living, that is, of a dignified way of living, is constantly changing. Pensions based on a full working life calculated on the classic contributory formula should, when pensionable age is reached, be regarded as insufficient—the more so, the stronger these changes are. The real danger, the almost destructive effect of a dynamic pension, is to be found less in their mobility than in their being linked to wage trends, which may well exceed what can be combined with monetary stability.

On a modified basis there exists the possibility of a flexible adaptation of pensions to changing living conditions and standards. This would be the case, for example, if as a guide for such a pension scheme the current increase in productivity were taken. Then there would be a guarantee that even the pensioner participated in real progress.

The formula would have to be something like this: to the extent that the national income, at constant prices, divided by the number of the workers or the population, shows an increase in productivity, the basic pensions will be raised by the same percentage. The pensioner would then share in increased productivity, but his interests would constantly be directed—even during his active life—towards constantly improving the performance of the economy. This worker or employee (or pensioner) will not regard saving as superfluous, but will be aware of the fact that investments financed by savings serve to improve his well-being, and provide for his old age and for that of his family. As with an active man, so also the pensioner becomes a centre of resistance to every attempt to pursue an inflationary policy.

In conclusion, it must be said that social security is certainly a good thing and desirable to a high degree, but security must first of all come from one's own efforts and one's own endeavours. Social security is not the same as social insurance for all—it is not achieved by passing individual responsibility to some group. At the start there must be responsibility for oneself, and, only where this is insufficient, the obligations of the State and the community begin.

For the benefit of our people it would be better if we showed less desire for collectivism and more social sense. The one kills the other. That is why finally the question has to be put whether, united by the wish and the obligation not to see any German exposed to want, we are acting rightly by strangling the best virtues in the ideal of collective security, or whether, by striving for greater prosperity, and by opening up more and better chances to gain personal prosperity, we should not declare war on the destructive spirit of collectivism. My own views are clear: I hope that my warning will not remain unheard.

Chapter XIII

REARMAMENT AND THE MARKET ECONOMY

REARMAMENT MUST BE SO ORGANIZED that it will not upset our free social economic system. I have held this view ever since the rearmament of Germany was first discussed. It is not dogmatism but anxiety to secure our social existence which has led me repeatedly to stress this. It is important that every contribution to defence should not merely maintain but also strengthen the freedom-loving order of the West. It would be paradoxical if in making our contribution to defence this freedom-loving order were threatened or given up.

The fundamental condition of reconciling economic consequences of defence with the market economy is anything but theoretical. It imposes on us utterly concrete and important conclusions affecting our lives.

To begin with, world opinion should be reminded that it is the experience of history that rearmament in Germany has, as a general rule, disregarded the principles of financial stability and economic order, thus bringing about a decay of the currency. This bitter memory is based on two unfortunate experiences. Everyone has been affected by this lack of responsibility. If the last (price-freeze) inflation could be said to be due to the cost of the war, its roots certainly lay in the methods of financing rearmament. To ask the people to go through such dreadful experiences for a third time is impossible. We must resist all attempts to disguise the costs of rearmament by debasing the value of our money. In a people as experienced in inflation as the Germans, the smallest deviation from the right path tends to lead to disastrous effects. It is therefore essential to remain honest, and to finance rearmament exclusively by transferring purchasing power through taxes, and not by misusing the Central Bank. All manipulations in this field, however cleverly veiled, must be met by a hard, unconditional 'No'.

Currency Stability Not Endangered

In spite of acknowledging the economic severity of any defence contribution this refusal must be made all the more decisive—so that foreseeable expenditure will not go beyond what our expanding economy is in a position to offer. Our economy, for example, has for years managed to carry a contribution to occupation costs amounting to about DM 7 milliard without bringing into question the stability of the currency, or similar points. The proposed defence contribution is DM 9 milliard per annum. In spite of all the criticism that has been made for years, no one can say that this figure has been exceeded. The increase of DM 2 milliard a year compared with the occupation costs can be traced in the yearly increase in the national income, which in recent years has amounted to between DM 10 milliard to DM 20 milliard (1953: DM 134·3 milliard; 1954: DM 145·46 milliard; 1955: DM 164·0 milliard; 1956: approximately DM 180 milliard.)

This increased burden of DM 2 milliard must not be taken lightly, but it cannot with a good conscience be described as in any way endangering economic stability. In past years we have financed the occupation costs without inhibiting or preventing German reconstruction; the defence costs which are to take their place are unlikely to do so either.

The amount of DM 10 milliard can nevertheless be regarded as inconsiderable only if the market economic policy, with its inner stability, is continued. It is thanks to the pursuit of these principles that the national income since 1949 has been raised by about DM 100 milliard. If the Federal Republic continues on this path, it should be in an increasingly better position to meet the needs of defence without detriment to its obligation to increase the standard of living of the German people and, above all, to increase social services. The expansive force of our economy creates the best conditions for success. The German people are thus able to look forward towards future development in this sector with calm.

If the relationship between the market economic order and rearmament has just been discussed from the point of view of financial policy, so should the production of armaments; in this sector, too, the rules of the market economy should be applied. Wherever possible the function of the free market must be allowed room, or its principles must be sensibly applied. That is why I have always stood for the principle of open tendering. As in the civil sector, this alone ensures that everyone interested can make his offer, and that the one in a position to offer the goods at the best price will receive the order. (It does not mean that the cheapest price will always win.)

This method—with some variations in detail—should be possible within the usual trade machinery. But with special armaments a market price of this kind cannot be determined. With public tendering, however, the most important principle of the market economy will be laid down. Thus I want to oppose strongly all attempts to make the market economy responsible for any deficiencies in deliveries.

These deficiencies are due not to public tendering, but rather to handling it in too bureaucratic a manner, and not least to the machinery of placing and accepting orders, which is only in its infancy. Thus, for example, according to the regulations, the price contained in the offer is not decisive for its acceptance. Other circumstances, in particular the suitability of the company and its actual ability to deliver, must be taken into account. In placing orders the definition of quality should be so clearly met that the goods on delivery could be examined to see if they correspond to the standards laid down.

The smallest amounts of standard trade goods will, of course, not be tendered for, but bought in 'the shop'. A principle can be ridden to death, and a sensible principle can in this way be sabotaged. Every method of public tendering presupposes a certain number of offers. It thus loses its justification where—

perhaps in the case of heavy arms such as tanks—there is no market. Yet even there the choice of firms should be guided by the spirit of the market economy. With any given means the best result must always be secured; in applying this general economic law it is necessary to reflect whether and how far German readiness for rearmament in this sector is practical and responsible.

Clearing House for European Armaments

The development of a home armament industry raises serious doubts both in respect of savings and in respect of the enormous investments required for such production. What is invested here cannot be invested elsewhere in the national economy. This is certainly a very simple statement, but in a country with a struggling capital market it is also very important.

These heavy armaments, whose production in West Germany for the Federal Republic alone would demand a greater output, thus immediately offer possibilities for European collaboration. I have represented Germany in the talks for the formation of a 'Permanent Armaments Committee' and hope that the idea of forming a kind of clearing house for European collaboration in the armaments sector can soon be realized. No country should be possessed by the ambition to achieve self-sufficiency in armaments.

Unfortunately the first attempts to collaborate have not led to a concrete solution. Perhaps the points of view are too different. Possibly, one country may believe that we in West Germany could produce too many armaments, while another may think that we are producing too little. These differences in attitude have perhaps contributed to the lack of a firm plan for common rearmament.

Now that there exists a general idea of the material needs of the German forces, one must repeat a strong appeal for a systematic division of work in Western Europe. There is still time to prevent false developments and wasted energies. Once the national armaments industry—and it need only be the beginning of it—demands to be heard, it will become more difficult to ban the spirit of autarchy. Such ideas then acquire a certain weight and so are correspondingly less easy to correct.

The wish to give preference to a European agreement before the creation of a national armaments autarchy stems—apart from political and military viewpoints—from economic considerations. Above all, rational production with considerably larger quantities can be built up here, and all the advantages of mass and batch production are effectively exploited. To renounce home production, and the necessity arising from it, for heavy equipment, would also be an excellent means to reduce our trade and payments surpluses. Here again the armaments sector should be regarded only as a part of the whole economy.

Actions Not Talk

In only a small number of cases has there so far been agreement for common European manufacture, and even with agreement about standard models, not much progress has been made. This unsatisfactory state of affairs must not be accepted as unchangeable; to accept such a fatalistic attitude would mean transferring belief in European unity into the realm of the fairy-tale. I believe that this field offers an excellent opportunity to realize fruitful liaison rapidly without necessarily calling special conferences to work out complicated detailed agreements which take years. The organization and technical framework for it already exist.

This acceptance of European co-operation does not mean, though, that there will be no research and development commissions in Germany. Such work is valuable for every modern national economy beyond its specific use for the armaments economy. So far as the private economic sector is concerned, a form of orders must be devised which will not lead to eventual demands for protection or even a monopoly position for such production. Such a procedure would be neither in keeping with the principles outlined above, nor with the desire to leave a free hand for later collaboration within the European framework.

If the task of economic rearmament is guided by the principles of market economy the right decision will be made possible. To mention only one of many examples, the inclusion of West Germany in the NATO community will call for a certain amount of stocks, in particular of strategically important goods. To allow the State to do this stocking up, and to advance perhaps towards the building up of vast government stocks, would not be in accordance with the principles of the free market economy. Nor would the accumulation of stocks by compulsion be in keeping with a free economic order. Thus the aim must be to offer special concessions to the economy, perhaps in the form of tax reductions, to achieve that decentralized building up of stocks which, from the point of view of defence, is so desirable.

The same principle, not to permit the State to take over what the private economic sector can itself achieve, naturally forbids the State to build up its own armaments industry. This idea, which has repeatedly been mentioned, must be turned down with equal vigour.

No Useful Economic Impulse

The desire to include the armaments sector in the general economy is having technical administrative consequences. For this reason I suggested the formation of the so-called six-member committee, within which the Ministry for Economic Affairs and the Ministry of Defence freely discuss those questions which come under the jurisdiction of their Ministries. This committee, according to the unanimous view of my colleague Strauss (Minister of Defence) and myself, has done excellent work in solving all the economic problems of defence.

In considering these tasks the German people must never forget that the Federal Republic has not for one moment allowed itself to be swayed in its decisions by ideas of combining rearmament with the stimulating of the economy. We know that we have not made such mistakes. What appear to us to make rearmament essential are not economic reasons, but exclusively important political considerations.

The disowning of any independent economic interest gives the Minister for Economic Affairs the moral right and the opportunity to raise his voice in the future if the danger should ever arise that our free and social market economy might be destroyed by rearmament, or by its methods. The events, still so fresh in our minds, that rearmament means economic and social disturbances must not be accepted as causal; it means no more than that we trod the wrong path. But there does exist the orderly harmless way, and it is this which we shall use in the future.

Our defence efforts strengthen the consciousness of the free world of belonging together, and that in turn gives us the certainty of preserving peace.

Chapter XIV

POLICY THROUGH DIRECT CONTACTS

'IN WHICH PART OF THE WORLD is the Minister for Economic Affairs now?' has been asked several times during the past few years, when I thought it useful to leave my desk at the Ministry in Bonn, to avoid the mistake of thinking Bonn to be the centre of the world. The fact that I repeatedly felt the need to talk with persons both at home and abroad, to explain German economic policy, and to find supporters for this system, has frequently led to misunderstandings and to many critical remarks. But I regard these activities outside Bonn as an important and indispensable part of my work, and I should like to believe that the positive results prove me right. This attitude becomes all the more understandable, since elsewhere in this book I have clearly stated how essential it is to keep in mind and, where necessary, to influence the formation of opinion of those participating in the economy.

Out of this grows the desire to keep people within the economy as well informed as possible, be they industrialists, workers, employees or consumers. It is for the purpose of cultivating such direct contacts that I have delivered dozens, even hundreds of speeches since I became 'Director for Economic Administration' in March 1948.

There were several occasions when I paid particular attention to maintaining close contacts because of the economic situation of the moment. There were even months when all depended on finding among the whole population real understanding of the economic situation and of economic policies. I am thinking here especially of that turbulent period after currency and economic reform when success depended on getting people to face the economic facts in a sober manner. Another such phase was the time after the outbreak of the Korean conflict, when everything depended on keeping everyone in the market—producers, traders and consumers—informed of the actual economic position to prevent them from going astray. Finally the third period of this kind was the boom within recent memory. Here it was still more important to demonstrate to what an extent our own economic fate depended on the understanding or the lack of it of all economic men.

The danger arising in every boom of overestimating what is economically possible had to be countered by repeated appeals to be reasonable. Even now it seems urgent to bring to the attention of every individual the immediate connection between the stability of the currency and his own attitude. This is essential partly to prevent wages from rising too far and in turn pushing up prices, and partly to prevent a thoughtless exploitation of the boom. Without this carefully cultivated and almost continuous contact it would have been almost impossible to explain the philosophy of the social market economy to the broad masses of the population. The reader might be interested to know how extensive these effects have been in the past few years.

This work, based on an appreciation of the great role played by the formation of public opinion in any modern State, was not limited to Germany only. In many trips abroad I have tried to address those people who were interested in our economic policy and in the successes we had gained in West Germany, and also to cultivate personal contacts.

Trade Policy in a New Style

This aim of making direct contacts reflects the changing importance of economic policy in forming relations between Government and Government and people and people. These changes of emphasis are also expressed in the novel position and importance of trade policy. I believe that to regard trade policy as a servant of foreign policy, or even as an instrument of Government power policy, is a thing of the past.

Unfortunately it has to be admitted that some, not fully comprehending the conception of a free economic policy, even today often think of trade policy as the sum of those measures which, in different ways, are expressed in bilateral agreements, dealing case by case, commodity by commodity, and country by country. This policy, which to me seems almost undignified in its arbitrariness and lack of consistency, is certainly not suited to the conduct of peaceful economic relations between the peoples and countries of the free world. It can only be disturbing. Though it is important and valuable that there should also exist bilateral relationships between peoples, and though it must be very much the task of foreign policy to achieve and establish such relationships, it would nevertheless be a fundamental misunderstanding to consider bilateral economic agreements as useful in building up or establishing relationships.

Economically, this method inevitably means to discriminate against third countries—which is certainly not desired by its defenders. It produces uncertainty and mistrust and also in every case reduces the potentially useful consequence from interchange between Governments. The fact that, following the destruction after the last world war of a free economic order, the world has been using this form of trade policy so far does not sanction it; at best it must be regarded as expedient in difficult phases of transition, and perhaps in the case of a special structure of linked economies as existed, for example, for a considerable time in South America.

As a result of the economic crisis of 1929 this form of trade policy spread its net of bilateral agreements across the world, and increasingly divided the world into different camps. It lacked, however, all basis for a unified economic policy and pushed national economies into isolation and atomization. The economic policy and practice introduced since the second World War, which I have defended almost passionately, is on the other hand distinguished by the striving for an all-embracing free world market, for multilateral agreements and non-discrimination, after overcoming protectionist and nationalist narrowness and doing away with counterfeit competition of every kind.

If the tasks and aims of economic policy are understood in this way, then there remains as little room for an independent trade policy as for a trade policy subordinate to foreign policy. Trade policy regarded as an arm of foreign policy will be misused. When bilateral trade could be exploited with the principle of 'the carrot and the stick' it inevitably led to the formation of sides and conflicts. This branch of economic policy did not then serve to link peoples, to overcome frontiers, or to bridge differences. The advantages of a market economic policy lie just in the way in which these things can be achieved.

Overcoming the Past

Wherever I have seen any chance of doing so, all my aims have been directed to ensure that countries should forgo a separate trade policy which differs from country to country. The less the exchange of goods and services between countries is an instrument of State policy, the smaller will be the danger of poisoning the international atmosphere. Only this attitude can free foreign trade policy from the curse of the past. Sober businesslike reflections then take first place; honest competition is able to develop between national economies. The realization of this demand leads Governments to agree to forgo the right of one-sided intervention in a free world economic order.

Here the Federal Republic in particular should be increasingly obliged to prefer such reflections to purely political considerations. Quite apart from questions of principle, this demand is supported politically by the heavy dependence of the German national economy on imports and exports. It should be remembered that the importance of foreign trade as part of the gross national income has steadily grown in recent years. Year by year an increasing part of the goods and services produced in the Federal Republic crosses our borders in exchange for equivalent services from other national economies. In this way foreign trade and, in particular, the ideal of the social market economy, without which the growth in foreign trade would be unthinkable, becomes increasingly important.

In the long run this state of affairs cannot be ignored even by those who still believe that trade policy should not be determined by the needs of economic policy, but should be used for other aims and purposes. It would thus be ridiculous to rob a visibly successful economic policy of its unity by splitting off trade policy. As it is, we are suffering from a splintering of economic policy into differing areas of competence.

Year	*Gross national income*	*Imports*	*Exports*	*Foreign trade turnover*
1949	100	9·9	5·2	15·2
1950	100	12·7	9·3	22·0
1952	100	12·9	13·4	26·3
1954	100	13·3	15·2	28·5
1955	100	14·9	15·7	30·6
1st half-year 1956	100	15·3	16·9	32·2

The development of the turnover in foreign trade (shown above) as part of West German gross national income urgently underlines what has been said here.

The reader would deceive himself if he concluded that the principles outlined here were being recognized everywhere without dispute. In Germany, too, in the recent past, passionate discussions took place about the realization of these principles, needing every ounce of my energy to prevent a handing over of trade policy in its entirety to the realm of the foreign policy makers. Much explanatory work remains to be done. This decisive question does not face Germany alone; it is important that all forces which support the idea of a world-wide and free economic policy make every effort to turn these ideas into facts in every single country.

The meetings of responsible political economists may here contribute much that is valuable. Thus I believe that negotiations for the creation of a 'Common Market'—an important problem of economic policy—fall under the jurisdiction of the Minister for Economic Affairs.

Chapter XV

DESTINATION EUROPE

AT THE OPENING of the International Autumn Fair in Frankfurt on September 2, 1956, I declared, not for the first time:

> 'The integration of Europe is more necessary than ever, it has become almost overdue. But the best kind of integration which I can imagine does not depend on the establishment of new offices and administrative procedures or a growing bureaucracy; it depends in the first instance on the reconstruction of a free international order, as best and most completely expressed in a free convertibility of the currency. Convertibility of the currency, of course, includes complete freedom of movement for goods, services and capital.'

These few words contain my basic views on the question of the purpose of European integration. In my view the world offers untold opportunities, if only we are able to make use of them. The benefit to be derived from a world-wide free economic policy can hardly be imagined. But the exciting prospects of tomorrow still have to face the hard realities of today.

In spite of far-reaching agreement to achieve European unity, and in particular a Common Market, it appears to be essential to clarify certain particular points. To air these problems is a basic pre-requisite to any serious discussion of the future shape of Europe.

In the light of the Messina Powers agreement made several years ago, some space should be devoted to the question of whether creation of a unified Europe by amalgamating partial groups should be pursued, or whether experience and knowledge point the other way. This question played a considerable role in recent years when it threatened to become the fashion for every section and every large branch of the economy to form its own association. I believe it to be wrong if economic integration—whatever sectors it may include—is limited to individual products, i.e. if thinking is confined to the integration of parts only.

It must not be overlooked that the spiritual fathers of the Messina Union were conscious of these shortcomings. They did not wish to confine European co-operation to the Messina Powers or to the sectors of coal, iron and steel. They regarded Messina as a first step only, which would compel the powers to sit together at one table to discuss common national economic problems, and to settle them peacefully. It soon became clear to sympathizers that one could also speak of other questions, for example, investment and economic policy and currency questions. The success of the experiments of the Messina Powers will greatly depend on the speed, extent and direction of further progress towards true forms of integration.

Since no decisive progress has been made in recent years, we find ourselves today (in spite of the Brussels discussions about a Common Market) at an interim stage.

The Aim: Comprehensive Integration

Serious though these problems are, and however much we thus tend to seek new solutions, it must not be forgotten that the true success and the fruitful solution of the problems raised by the Messina Powers lie elsewhere.

We seek integration in absolute terms. Above all we must create the basis for true integration. But in my view this is to be found above all in a different sector—in a currency political order. We must begin with the theoretical knowledge that the national economic order is not based on the sum of partial orders, any more than the national economy can be understood as an assembly of sections. It is a matter of function, of something complete and inseparable. It is a question of relations of a human and material kind, which are indissoluble, and which cannot be separated and then put together at will.

In this connection another point deserves mention. Today there appears to exist a certain lack of enthusiasm for competition, which necessarily follows the creation of a larger market. It is a mistake to think that conditions for free competition would be too unequal to permit the principle of the market economy to be introduced in an integration of this kind. One should—so some economists say—first of all level out these differences, that is, even them out before opening the doors to free competition.

Such attempts could lead to modest success within narrow limits. But it is a complete illusion to imagine that in a competitive world equal conditions relating to separate cost factors could be brought about at the start. Even to attempt such an aim must lead to a form of *dirigisme* and dilettantism which is bound to be unfruitful right from the beginning.

We can altogether accept that favours are more or less equally and 'justly' divided. God did well when he gave one country some natural advantages in this or that field, while other countries enjoy different advantages. In whatever way the cost components are made up, they will be integrated in the price. Price alone is the economic yardstick by which to judge performance, and which in the nature of things includes quality. For this reason it is necessary to think of integration not merely in a mechanical or quantitative sense, for then we should return all too rapidly to the errors and shortcomings of the past. For anyone with any insight integration means free and comprehensive competition; it means economic collaboration on a functionally higher level.

Sicily is not in the Ruhr

These critical remarks of course also apply to equally wrong ideas under a different slogan—that of 'harmonization'—which under this banner strive towards a levelling out of all economic conditions. I do not exaggerate when I report that wages, pensions, holidays and overtime payments are considered in this context. If one is prepared to acknowledge the thesis of harmonization then there are no logical limits, and demands for taking into account the costs of electricity and transport or taxes can be made with the same justification.

If an attempt were to be made to harmonize all costs relating to the position of companies from country to country and over a larger group of countries—that is, to balance them so that competition would cease to be 'disturbing'—then this does not mean integration but disintegration of the worst kind.

In this statement I do not wish to deny that every national malady would certainly disturb inter-State relationships at the same time. Yet this must not lead one to acknowledge the right of any one country to ask its partners in the common market or perhaps to force them to apply its own doubtful principles.

With the catchword of 'harmonization' the demand went so far as to suggest that at the end of the transition period the level of wages in the individual member States should be equalized and that their total working costs should be 'equivalent'. It would be possible to ignore this demand, since economically it is simply unrealizable, for between Sicily and the Ruhr equal productivity does not exist and there cannot, therefore, be 'equal' working costs. To practise this principle would lead to economic death. Wage costs at their respective levels are determined by productivity and not by an assumption of equal performance.

Nobody can wish to believe that it would be possible to set the same standard of productivity right through all participating countries for all industries, and to achieve the same progress in productivity. Even if the same starting conditions could be set for a given day through artificial manipulations, the next day would already show changes, since the ideas and attitudes of peoples towards saving and spending, their achievements, their industry and so on, can never be brought to a common denominator even in a common market.

Such demands rest on an utterly fallacious interpretation of economic laws and facts, but at one and the same time it characterizes a spiritual attitude which must under no circumstances triumph, unless human initiative and creative forces, yes, even life itself, are to be suffocated in an integrated Europe.

These ideas rest on the illusion that these natural factors can be changed, and the structural conditions artificially balanced between country and country until every country will work in every sector with the same costs. I do not regard this as in any way desirable—quite apart from the impossibility of ever achieving this questionable aim. There would then be no obstacle to a return towards national isolation, since if everyone can offer goods at the same price why—I ask—should I buy them elsewhere? Here the exchange of goods between countries would lose its final and real purpose. The point is just that all countries work with differing conditions, so that here the advantage is on one side, there elsewhere, so that the one can achieve more here, the other there. It is from this fact that the need for reciprocity and its fruitfulness arises.

The supporters of the theory of harmonization must not dodge the question of who is to make the sacrifices and how the bill is to be paid. In the nature of things such a delusion will lead in practice to justifying the setting up of a fund from which all those who are at a disadvantage, or believe themselves to be so, will either be compensated or helped to improve themselves artificially. But these are principles which do not accord with the market economy. There is no incentive to achievement here, but the contrary is true: the weaker member—for whatever reasons—is subsidized. This does not seem to me to be the right principle to further real progress—that rapid progress which we need so badly in Europe. Along this way the aim to improve the life of our people and that of other European peoples cannot be achieved.

As regards these theses, I have repeatedly pointed to the fact that this 'social romanticism' expressed here is extraordinarily dangerous. But I do support the idea of making common means available to increase productivity as well as to maintain some vital branches of the economy. It is not a matter of whether a common market is to be brought about as soon as possible or not; it is a question of the principle of order and spiritual direction.

No Bureaucratically Manipulated Europe

A Europe that does not live within the hearts of men, which is not regarded as a true community of fates worth making sacrifices for, which does not regard freedom as a first principle but wants to keep it on a lead, and finally a Europe whose spiritual and political outlines are not yet visible today cannot appeal to either the world or the European peoples. A bureaucratically manipulated Europe, breeding reciprocal mistrust rather than a sense of community, apparently materialistic in its whole attitude, will bring in its train more dangers than benefits for Europe. West Germany, by its policy of stability, has become immune from the attempts of infiltration from the East, and for that reason alone a common market must apply the same laws. To surrender this policy would mean to sacrifice the basis of this fortunate immunity from Communism.

Besides the political danger, connected with so-called social harmonization, this conception is theoretically insupportable. Social harmonization does not stand at the beginning but at the end of integration. It cannot be realized by a painful construction, but only through assimilating forms and conceptions of life within the rhythm of the progress of integration. Although I support a common market, I believe that even in a Europe thus integrated the conditions of life and production will never be identical. On the contrary the function of a common market rests on the possibility and on the need for a fruitful interchange between the individual countries, according to their special and different abilities and the variety of their natural and structural conditions.

If neither the path of partial union, nor that of a soulless equality, can be said to be possible, it must be asked whether a new Europe can be created through a new institutionalism? In view of present conditions in the national economies it is understandable that there is a general tendency to create new institutions to achieve supra-national co-operation.

Order with a Light Touch

From the economic point of view Europe must not be regarded as an organization or an institution; it must be conceived as a function. But then the question must be asked what we can do to enable this Europe to develop its functions. It is almost tragic if we have to believe that we are so hardened that we can understand order only within the conception of 'organization'. We have lost the sense for a true order, which reigns most strongly and in its purest form just where it is not noticed and noted as such.

By this I do not mean to say that I oppose European ties in principle. But I want to create the basis for such links. First of all I wish to make secure the inner order in national economies, since otherwise integration will inevitably have to lead to supra-national *dirigisme*.

Europe cannot be built with little means; it can only be understood as a complex economic and political function. The idea that certain sectors should be progressively withdrawn from national sovereignty and handed over to supra-national administration, and that at a given moment the weight of supra-national influence would then automatically lead to a total conquest of national responsibilities, appears to me to be less than realistic, and does not bear theoretical economic examination. The totality of the national function cannot be split into different competences.

The growth of supra-national authorities may perhaps have some political importance, but it can hardly contribute anything decisive to the solution of the economic problems mentioned here. My fears for that reason remain that we tend all too much to visualize European integration as the creation of institutions; in other words, that we overvalue the institutional as opposed to the functional—a fear which in the recent past has been increasingly recognized as being valid.

A word should be said here about the hope of some planners, that those of their ideas and ideologies which they were unable to realize nationally can now be realized on a European plane. In the light of our national experience it need not be explained further why the principles of the planned and directed economy are unsuited now to develop the productive forces of Europe. This economic conception is not even suited to the most primitive division of labour, let alone a fruitful and easy collaboration between national economies.

For goods and services, money and capital, in the treatment of customs policy and in view of the freedom of man to attain ever larger freedoms, no other way is open to us than to forgo all Government manipulations which contradict these principles. Where institutions are necessary to establish these principles of freedom, I am in favour of them. It appears to me that a truly good European wishes to see this community of action and attitude as an obligation on all participants.

If I have pointed to the fact that the politician may want to see the question of supra-national organization in a different light than the political economist, then, speaking for the latter, I must express my concern that the proper priorities may be lost sight of, and that the political forms of Europe may be settled before equivalent economic integration has been achieved. The great danger still exists today that we all want a free Europe, but that, if politics move forward without corresponding economic developments, a centralism might arise—a centralism which might stifle all that is colourful and different in this old European culture.

The Success of E.P.U.

Such considerations must necessarily lead to a critical analysis of existing European institutions. I have already spoken of the role of the Messina Powers in opening the door to rapid and comprehensive European integration. It is surely not the fault of the Messina Powers if this expectation has remained unfulfilled. How much they can do now to create Europe must be left to individual judgment. In their own sphere the Messina Powers can certainly perform useful services.

So as not to be accused of overlooking the wood for the trees, attention must be drawn here to the great successes which we have achieved with the European Payments Union. It is thanks to this common multilateral system that the member countries were able to rise above bilateral trade agreements, and that with it the development of European economic forces took a decisive step forward. A short glimpse at the statistics confirms this statement. For example, the exports of the West German Federal Republic to the E.P.U. area rose from DM 6·32 milliard in 1950 (the year E.P.U. was founded) to DM 18·53 milliard in 1955. In detail the increase of our exports to the E.P.U. countries was as follows:

Foreign Trade with the E.P.U. Area

	1950	*1951*	*1952*	*1953*	*1954*	*1955*	*1956 (Jan.-Nov.)*
Imports	7·87	8·87	10·15	10·62	12·3	15·49	4·36
Exports	6·32	10·63	12·19	13·24	15·78	18·53	5·64
	−1·55	+1·76	+2·04	+2·62	+3·48	+3·04	+1·28

Trade between member countries of O.E.E.C. rose from \$17·5 milliard in 1949 to \$30·0 milliard in 1954 and to \$34·176 milliard in 1955, and for the first six months of 1956 to \$18·066 milliard.

In spite of acknowledging these successes it is impossible not to point to what is still insufficiently organized, still incomplete, and what still cannot be achieved in the future within the scope of the E.P.U. Here again criticism of this institution does not indicate a turning away or a condemnation but, quite the contrary, an appeal for decisive action.

What is wrong with the European Payments Union? The answer is that the individual national economies participating within the Payments Union cannot be forced to keep to an orderly economic and financial behaviour so as to maintain inner stability in their national economies. Even in the European Payments Union, national sensibilities, falsely understood concepts of the autonomy of economic policy and national sovereignty still play an important role. No European country is prepared to accept generally binding principles. At best the European Payments Union can recommend but it cannot force a nation to act on its recommendations.

'Stability Begins at Home'

In America they say 'stability and convertibility begin at home'. That is exactly what is lacking in Europe. To the extent that participating countries do not show the courage and the desire to impose order, the Common Market will suffer the same fate as now befalls the E.P.U. Participation by a country in communities of this kind demands a certain behaviour in the field of economics and finance. A member State can only become ready for integration if it is willing not only to establish its inner order but also to preserve it without fail.

When one reflects how torn Europe was and still is today its present state appears less surprising. How much dogma the individual national economies have had to try out, what different ideas of economic and financial possibilities are still alive, and how many theories have motivated men's minds! One should, for example, recall Keynsian principles, 'deficit spending', the 'policy of cheap money', and all that goes with it, to understand that it will be extraordinarily difficult to arrive at acceptable common action and a unified rigorous policy in this sphere. Such unity is, however, the condition for freely convertible currencies.

If at the time of the gold standard any sovereign country believed itself able to dispense with an orderly economic and financial policy and a responsible credit policy, or—expressed differently—if any country had indulged in any sort of ideology which contradicted this assumption of inner order and balance, then the consequences of its behaviour would soon have become noticeable. It would have had to carry the consequences itself. If, under the rules of the gold standard, no more capital could be borrowed, and the reserves of gold had become exhausted, then no power in the world could preserve the rate of exchange from going downhill. In the times of the gold standard neither institutions nor persons gave any orders. An anonymous order existed, controlled by the system. It was not burdened with ideas of national sovereignty, nor with the delusion of national economic autonomy, nor whatever else exists in the way of prejudices and national sensibilities. Unfortunately we have not yet progressed this far again.

We use the European Payments Union, so to speak, as a crutch. Only when all member countries in the European Payments Union have begun to realize that it is their responsibility to keep order in their own house will the minimum conditions exist for meeting the real aims of the European Payments Union.

From the start the E.P.U. had this as its main thesis: by liberalizing their trade in goods and services members should find their way steadily towards free convertibility, which means that at the end of the attempts at liberalization all partners should be rewarded by freely interchangeable currencies falling into their laps like ripe fruit. It is certainly no denigration of the achievements of this system if I ask how many still believe and have confidence today that the E.P.U. can either gain or enforce this aim.

Equally it must not be overlooked in this evaluation of the European Payments Union that the system in its practical application maintains discrimination against the dollar area, even if it does not increase it, and thus inhibits integration within the larger framework of the free Western world. America, which helped Europe and wanted to help Europe, can only expect and fear that the flow of trade will increasingly bypass the American market. During the many Paris meetings I repeatedly emphasized that we are dealing here with a fault in construction, since a greater freedom of movement between the European countries and the dollar area will indirectly be felt as an impediment to the effectiveness of the E.P.U. While constantly enlarging our dollar liberalization to what is now 90% we have repeatedly come across this false assessment.

About Bilateralism

That bilateralism today can never lead to satisfactory results hardly needs further elaboration. It is simply inconceivable that the requirements and desires of two countries can be so completely and organically dovetailed that a balance satisfactory to both partners would follow. In such arrangements someone must always remain dissatisfied, for the total volume of any bilateral exchange of goods is automatically set by the ability of the weakest partner to deliver or purchase. The total exchange of goods then remains at such a low level that the economic aim of maximum or even optimum collaboration can never be achieved.

The work of the E.P.U. and of O.E.E.C. must naturally be judged by taking into account the terms of reference of these two institutions. Though we have progressed towards greater liberalization within the framework of these institutions, we know full well that so long as currency restrictions remain the objectives can never be reached.

How then, my readers will ask, do I imagine that Europe will emerge? At the beginning of any attempt to develop concrete ideas must be the statement: All efforts for political and economic integration will founder if all participants do not have the courage and the energy for a progressive liberalization of the exchange in goods and service and capital, a rapid lowering of tariffs as well as other protectionist barriers and manipulations, and act in this sense. What belongs to a free and common market, as formerly with the gold standard, is not wealth and strength but only a modest recognition that a Government, no more than a people, can live 'above its income'.

From the economic point of view I would clearly give preference to this free approach which is not limited to individual countries or groups of countries, before attempts at integration within smaller areas. Also I believe that this path towards the greater whole would from a rational point of view be the best for Germany, particularly as its prosperity is built on its relations with as many markets as possible.

Europe—Island of Disintegration?

If politically we tread the same path as the six Messina Powers, we must remember particularly that liberalization and freedom of movement must plainly progress faster within this smaller area of integration than within the total area of the Western world. In no circumstances must the removal of the barriers which still separate the different national economies progress faster within the greater international framework of the West than with the future common market area of Western Europe. It would be regarded as particularly grotesque if this European Union were in this way to become an island of disintegration.

Such a European integration, with as its first aim a Customs Union, appears to be morally, economically and politically justified only if this community in turn does not itself trigger off new differences and tensions. This means that the trading policy of the customs union as far as the outside world is concerned must be handled liberally, and that there must be no discrimination against 'third' countries.

One must point to the highly important British proposals in the early autumn of 1956 to widen the common market area of the six Messina Power countries to that of the free trade zone. I understand only too well London's view that a tariff wall protecting the smaller European common market from the rest of the world could not be in the general European interest. Behind this formula lie the same dangers which I had previously wanted to express.

Even if one hesitates to say so aloud, these ideas would have as their result the abolition of currency controls and the return to free convertibility. A national policy which even today barricades itself behind these primitive arrangements precludes any true and liberal economic and social progress. These inhibitions are so vast that only the lack of knowledge of actual facts prevents a spiritual rising of all free men and all free peoples.

Nor must we forget that it is by removing these barriers—and probably only in this way—shall we regain the basis of a true social order in the true sense of the word.

The more we succeed in making men feel as individuals, so that as a result of their personal freedom they become conscious of their power and dignity, the better and the more beneficial the general social order will become. This will be imbued with a much higher social quality than a society which always requires new organizations and institutions to cope with the chaos arising from an economy torn from its context. I gladly accept the unpopularity of being one of the loudest advocates of freedom—out of an anxiety for the shape of the free world and for the collaboration of the free peoples. Even within the supra-national framework I desire an honest order. To it belongs firstly the preservation of human freedom. We must recognize the principles of order which secure free and true human relations—in economics as much as in politics.

In achieving this aim we must be careful that we do not only have procedures and techniques, as perhaps before 1914, but that we arrive at a common spiritual aim, which will permit us to overcome national egoism and protectionism by new forms of real intercourse. True integration would lift us spiritually and morally to a higher plane of collaboration.

Here the differences rest more in quality and less in the quantity of collaboration. Integration and convertibility are not counter-poles, where the striving for the one might hinder or render the other superfluous; they complement each other. For example, if we speak of competition in a common market, we understand a form of collaboration that will overcome the deficiencies of the narrower limits within the European framework. It must be repeatedly asked why the European economies are so much less productive than the American economy.

The enormous discrepancy does not follow from the fact that people in the United States are so much more industrious and efficient than the Europeans. It is the result both of the size of the economy and of greater freedom. Both lead to a higher measure of productivity and to a greater utilization of human and technical productive powers.

This comparison should teach us to aim at these objectives

and to accept their realization as a European goal. We must reconstitute ourselves. Above all we must find a new spirit and establish that solidarity which will unite the European economies and peoples for the sake of this aim.

From these reflections it is clear that functional integration, whose characteristics have been repeatedly explained, must first take place. As in all my economic and political thinking I start here from the basic precept of the indivisibility of freedom.

Freedom is Indivisible

For me it is natural that the man standing for a free economic society at home belongs also in the van of fighters for a free economic division of work in the world and for close inter-State co-operation. Out of this realization of the indivisibility of economic freedom in all international spheres and institutions, the Federal Republic has strongly pressed for the freeing of international trade from short-sighted regimentation and small vexations.

Let me also touch briefly on a question of principle which appears repeatedly in discussions, particularly in private circles, but also in public: in a free world must the prosperity of one country provoke worry or fear in its neighbours?

Naturally this must be emphatically denied.

It is an economic truism that one partner can only do well if the others flourish. No business is possible with beggars.

It is as much my conviction as my experience that all that is valid and regarded as proper within a nation can and must be valid beyond its frontiers. As we in our countries face the necessity to free people from poverty and want, to increase the number of people sharing in a higher standard of living, to offer people the chance to expand freely and to become independent of the power of the State, yet accept the obligations of the order of the State, so the same principles must be used in economic collaboration of the free world.

Whoever sympathizes with the seriousness of these efforts

will agree with me and demand that freedom must not be choked by one-sided Government measures. So long as such a possibility of regression remains, a declaration for European integration will remain a declaration of platonic love.

That is no longer of use today.

This principle must in the nature of things also apply to the Common Market and the Customs Union put forward in the Brussels recommendations. It would surely not be sensible to allow individual members to slide back on the path towards integration, so that the balance of payments protective clauses could perhaps be invoked to meet a new outburst of sovereignty. It is also not a good solution if the country concerned—as was proposed during the Brussels negotiations—can afterwards be forced to lift these protective clauses, if a decision to do so is taken by a qualified majority. Little imagination is needed to realize that since such a decision would be regarded as an unfriendly act it could hardly ever be taken. Moreover such regulations would not demonstrate the lively consciousness of a community linked by a common destiny. But it is just this which needs to be kindled, for so long as it is lacking we shall never reach the goal, never find sufficient energy to form a true community comparable with North America.

In this field we need deeds. Sufficient words have been exchanged.

Much as wise men may want to discuss it I am firmly convinced that the problem could shortly be brought to a successful outcome if only we handled it with a little more courage. In my life I have repeatedly found that freedom, and above all courage for freedom, have always been worth while. All that has been begun in this way has always turned out well, but wherever we lacked the courage for freedom things have ended in disaster.

Unfortunately I find that on this theme I have to add some water to the wine. As things seem at the moment (January 1957) it cannot be expected that the future structure of the Common Market will do away with the possibility of utilizing the so-called protective clauses. But in return the lesser evil that a standstill or even regression of one country might inhibit other partners in unfolding their dynamic progress must be prevented. Should this happen, relations with the country which is hesitating must always be consolidated to secure the progress achieved.

To me it does not sound convincing if European integration is spoken of with emotion, while alongside free trade in goods and services, people are not to have the chance of working freely everywhere. It is an impossible position when there are still millions of unemployed in one European country while other countries do not know where to find sufficient hands and brains to cope with all the tasks facing them.

This is not a statement which I have just made today or yesterday. I have always taken the view that only when every citizen can find in every other country the same free opportunities of work is it possible to speak of one Europe. As long as this is not the case, then our creed in the last analysis is dishonest.

So long as we do not have the courage to deal with these crucial points, vague talk about integration or a perfectionist mechanism of purely economic rules of action appears to me unsuited to achieve the political, economic and social aims.

Insofar as all attempts to integrate Europe can be brought under one denominator it must be this: to realize freedom in all sectors of life.

Liberalization as the Best Medicine

Let me show by an example what freedom can achieve even when it is in no way complete. The effects of liberalization on our foreign trade are so convincing that they lose nothing in validity when I point to the fact that Germany at the turn of the year 1950/51 experienced one of its most serious—perhaps the most serious—crises of the post-war period. At the time it gave many people the occasion to regard my policy as finished. When in 1948 I accepted office in the Bi-zone, the average monthly export figure moved at around DM 200 million, and was in the main a forced export of coal, wood and other raw materials which were also urgently needed in Germany. Finished goods figured in our foreign trade only negligibly. Today the monthly export figures move between DM 2·4 and 3 milliard—to E.P.U. countries alone they come to DM 1·7 to 2 milliard. These convincing results were achieved not least thanks to the liberalization policy of Western Germany, which has for some time exceeded 90% with the E.P.U. countries and also with the dollar area; as regards the E.P.U. members it is being widened to 100% for industrial goods. Even in international relations, as I have already said, the granting of freedom does pay; it is not a one-sided gift, but produces reactions and results with fruitful and healing effects.

To strengthen the case a short glimpse is needed at the structure of our exports. The proportion of finished goods, which is decisive for the West German economy, has now risen to over 80%. This is a particularly clear demonstration of how much the freeing of trade—in my view far from complete—leads nevertheless to a pattern of exports suited to meet the structural needs of each national economy according to its nature.

What has taken place in recent years is most clearly illuminated by the following figures. I choose the year of the foundation of E.P.U. as the base (September 19, 1950), and deliberately omit the first post-war years when foreign trade was all too much burdened by forced deliveries.

Exports in DM million (monthly averages)

Monthly averages	*Total exports*	*Raw materials*	*Semi-finished goods*	*Finished goods*
1950	697	97	131	452
1951	1,215	110	176	888
1952	1,409	107	212	1,058
1953	1,544	124	227	1,153
1954	1,836	141	240	1,412
1955	2,143	131	272	1,683
1956 (Jan.-Nov.)	2,529	142	311	2,001

Does it not prove to be utterly ridiculous when we speak of this worst form of disorder—I mean the control of foreign currencies—under the heading of 'order'? We must surely free ourselves once and for all from the view that the most order reigns where the largest number of people have to be employed to enforce this order to keep disorder at bay.

If no one is to be seen preserving this order then far too many people wrongly believe that no order exists. The same is true of my belief that, in all talks about Europe, we must not only think of what will have to be arranged; we must equally bear in mind what can or must be discarded to enable an organic natural growth of Europe to take place. Since convertibility would bring about a true and at the same time the best solution to many problems, it should be expected that the effect of this order would radiate into almost every sector of social life. Economic policy would then gain a far clearer expression. I go so far as to declare that whoever manages to do away with foreign currency control will have done more for Europe than all politicians, statesmen, members of parliaments, businessmen and civil servants put together.

My constant appeals and admonition to create a new Europe by giving first place to securing its 'function' must not be misunderstood in the sense that I completely oppose every institution on a European level. What I do decisively oppose though is the idea that by creating institutions we would succeed in effectively overcoming the real difficulties. It is just here that the real differences of opinion exist.

Who is a Good European?

Every institutional attempt to find a solution brings with it the danger of getting stuck in illusions. There is for me no 'either/or' in this complex of questions, but an 'as well as'—with the accent clearly on priority for functional integration.

I myself have repeatedly found how fruitful it can be when people sit down together to find common solutions. But it is crucial that work based on institutions should not push aside, replace or cancel out the functional work. The institution must serve—and exclusively serve—to support the function of the common market; it must help to open up freedom. If the institution itself wants to 'order' it is out of place.

Modern man is in fact quite trained to being able to imagine a true order only if it is expressed in an organization or in an army of officials and, if possible, if sand can be heard in the machine. So it happens that the path to freedom proposed by me is being constantly attacked. I am said to be a 'bad European'. This situation led me to explain my position in detail in the *Deutsche Korrespondenz* of July 21, 1955, about 'Who is a good European?' I said:

> 'I am not prepared to let my European attitude and my beliefs in Europe go unrecognized because I put questions about it differently and because I have asked those participating whether there was only one path and one method to save Europe, or whether another way might not perhaps lead more rapidly and more effectively towards the goal. I wish to say clearly that I do not wish a lesser but a greater Europe than is expressed in the proposals for further partial integration.
>
> 'Every true function is indivisible. Therefore because I care for Europe I fear that such aggregations and combinations will never achieve either the economic or the political aim. Further I do not oppose European links, but quite the reverse. I am trying to create a basis for them when I remind people that in the first place the inner order of the national economies must be secured nationally, since otherwise integration will inevitably lead to a supra-national *dirigisme*.
>
> 'From this attitude it is clear that I do not tend to regard Europe as the final and absolute goal of economic order. The political economist may differ here from the foreign policy maker. For me integration means a first step, visible to our eyes, in which it is important first of all to reduce the barriers standing in the way of an international exchange of goods.
>
> 'In all circumstances I am striving towards free and liberal

relations with all countries of the Western world, in particular of course with our European partners. Europe is in this sense a form of integration of an economic or political kind. But the aim goes further—namely that we must not divide the Western world once again into different economic sectors.'

Chapter XVI

THE PHOENIX ARISES FROM ITS ASHES

IT IS WORTH WHILE paying more attention to the basis of the obviously successful foreign trade policy when looking at the monthly export figures of the Federal Republic, which rose from DM 300 million at the beginning of 1949 to almost DM 3 milliard at the end of 1956.

The principles can be reduced to two basic themes repeatedly mentioned in this book: on the one hand, the assumption of the absolute superiority of freedom over all attempts by the State to plan, guide or keep on a leash economic events, and on the other, the acknowledgment of the indivisibility of freedom.

Such an outlook does not allow any hesitation and knows no bargaining for position. Even less can this spirit be reconciled with ideas of a bilateral balance in trade relations between Governments. A foreign trade policy of this kind aims to achieve the same ends as economic policy at home is trying to realize. It is a matter of reducing protection in its various forms, such as foreign currency control, the quantitative limitation of exports by erecting high tariff walls and other administrative manipulations, and by overcoming the narrow-minded selfish thinking which has made life in Europe a torment. This 'back garden ideology' type of thinking has to be rapidly and thoroughly removed.

Thus when in 1948 we began to reintroduce economic freedom to Germany, it was for me almost a moral obligation to reach at the earliest possible moment the point where a policy of liberalization of foreign trade became possible. In spite of German backwardness in industry and other unhappy conditions, by the end of 1949 the degree of liberalization of private imports within the O.E.E.C. countries had been raised to 58·2% of the datum period between October 1948 and September 1949, and in October 1950 a further increase to 63·7% took place. We did not at that time make this change out of arrogance or even for reasons of an illusory imperialism; no, it was bitter need which forced us to expose our belief in the superiority of freedom to the hard test. The ruined German economy could not offer a living to the German people if it did not succeed within the shortest possible period in catching up with the level of output of the most progressive countries of the world.

The Switch to Success

We had to face the alternatives without pity or prejudice. If the German economy and the German still had sufficient power and energy to permit the experiment of a return to the world market through competition, then the path for German reconstruction was open. In particular there was then a chance to give the millions of refugees a decent occupation and to open the way to a standard of living for the German people commensurate with Western civilization. Insofar as this energy was lacking, successful reconstruction would have been unthinkable. Without relations with the world market and its best achievements there would have been no happy German future. Germany is inevitably dependent on the world market, whether as a purchaser of raw materials or as a seller of finished goods.

In this connection the Marshall Plan merits the special gratitude of the German people. This generous support deserves to be appreciated above all for its moral effects. It gave the German people the feeling of being no longer written off by the rest of the world but, on the contrary, of being able to share in the progress of the free world. But its economic and financial importance was no less great. Even so the Federal Government has never forgotten that it is its own responsibility to create from its own strength the ability to pay for our foodstuffs and raw materials by finished products. This policy made it imperative to open the doors, and to make the experiment, considered almost brutal, of forcing the German economy towards a higher level of achievement.

So from the moment when it became the responsibility of the Ministry for Economic Affairs, German trade policy was guided along the principle of liberalization in the widest sense of the word. This became particularly clear during the German E.P.U. crisis, when, in February 1951, as a result of our threatening indebtedness within the E.P.U. we were forced temporarily to suspend liberalization. Then recommendations were made to me from many quarters to betray the principle of freedom, and finally to forgo the idea of taking the lead. The Opposition said that, in the attempt to free European trade, we should take on the role of a modest fellow traveller. (cf. Chapter on 'The Market Economy Conquers Planning', p. 81.)

In the face of such short-sighted advice it was in our interest to use our own energies to encourage those countries which were not suffering from the same pressure to break through existing difficulties.

The German share of exports in the world market did not even reach 3% at that time and at this level was insufficient to support a successful programme of reconstruction. All German measures during this E.P.U. crisis in 1950/51 were taken with the intention, not only of safeguarding the principle of liberalization for ourselves, but of safeguarding it in general, and so enabling us to return to liberalization as soon as possible.

Liberalization All Round

This aim was achieved on January 8, 1952, with the return to liberalization to the extent of 56·8% of private imports (relevant year 1949). This policy finally triumphed on November 30, 1956, when the list of goods which could be imported from the Member States of the O.E.E.C. countries without limitation was so greatly enlarged that the Federal Republic, with a few exceptions, had in fact liberalized private imports from the

O.E.E.C. area by almost 100%. This statement had been true for some time of private imports from the non-participating countries (i.e. those that use E.P.U. facilities but do not belong to the O.E.E.C. countries, e.g. Australia, New Zealand, India, South Africa, Vietnam).

Here a beginning had been made with bilateral liberalization early in 1952 and, since March 1954, a gradual change took place to general liberalization within the O.E.E.C. area. Of private imports from the non-participating countries 97·9% (relevant year 1953) are now liberalized.

Germany thus has made a considerable contribution towards overcoming protectionism. This statement is all the more justified, as the Federal Republic is also pursuing the same kind of policy of decreasing quantitative limitations *vis-à-vis* other trade areas. Thanks to measures taken since February 14, 1954, and in particular the further broadening of liberalization during the middle of 1956, we succeeded in increasing the range of free private imports from the dollar area to 92·8%.

On May 16, 1956, a unified list of liberalization was put into force for a further group of countries, such as Brazil, Chile, Finland, Japan and Uruguay. This generous policy meant that at the beginning of 1957 about 90% of all private imports—calculated on the basis of 1953—and about 80% of total imports, were freed from quantitative limitations. The difference is explained by the fact that besides the few private imports still controlled by quantitative limitations, some Government traded goods (i.e. in West Germany the products from the controlled market in agriculture) remain outside the liberalized sector. The principle of freedom which has always characterized our foreign trade policy is best expressed in this abolition of quantitative limitations.

Universal Rules

Our conviction that bilateralism represents one of the worst relics of a tragic past made us readily agree to support all plans and methods to find unified rules for large areas. This above all is true of German participation in O.E.E.C., in the association of E.P.U. and in G.A.T.T. and in the International Monetary Fund. On this supra-regional plane there is no room for individual and limited rules of a bilateral sort which necessarily contradict the principle of freedom and discrimination. My ideal of a happy trade policy in a free world can only be regarded as fulfilled when trade policy between the different countries is no longer split, but rather when the whole of the free world has agreed to universal rules and principles. These thoughts have been explained in more detail in Chapter XIV.

The reduction of bilateral agreements has meant that the Central Banks no longer act as the providers of credit as in the recent past. That is not their function. With the overcoming of bilateralism on the other hand, international criss-crossing of credits will increase, which will make the balancing of payments a purely business affair on a private economic basis.

Liberalization, as also multilateralism, opens the way to an economically sensible flow of trade. Once foreign trade is freed from all restrictions then in international trade, too, goods will be exchanged according to the greatest national economic needs.

These generous principles must be adhered to when using other weapons of foreign trade. That is why for some considerable time I have tried to remove all special export subsidies. They are to be avoided in whatever form, for they almost always result in distrust. Insofar as on the German side they are a hangover from the past, the excuse may serve that for all too long we have had to abjure freedom in foreign trade. For that reason I particularly welcomed the date of December 31, 1955, when the Law to Encourage Exports expired. In the so-called Butler-Erhard statement of May 8, 1954, I undertook to oppose any prolongation of this law.

The Best Way to Encourage Exports

Those members of the German economy who every now and then demand export subsidies may like to listen to my old thesis, which has proved itself in the recent past, that the best help for exports is to keep the German price-level steady—at least more steady than that of other countries. The truth of this policy is at present expressed in our favourable foreign trade position; at the very least it promises greater successes than the use of questionable methods to encourage exports. To overcome export subsidies which disturb every natural flow of goods I proposed years ago that all measures in all countries to encourage exports should be permitted only within the framework of legal and clearly recognizable settlements. Moreover I suggested years ago—at the opening of the Frankfurt Fair on February 22, 1953—that a European institution should receive a list of all the measures taken by the various countries to encourage exports. Such publication should create the basis for international discussions to reduce these artificial protective measures.

The demand to remove all obstacles to trade must naturally also be expressed in tariff policy. On this point I have always stood for the principle—as in discussions about liberalization—that what is right in principle does not need to wait for an equivalent contribution from a trade partner to be realized. So, since 1955, when the domestic position of the Federal Republic made it appear sensible to reinforce competition, I have aimed to bring competition into Germany from beyond the frontiers by lowering tariffs. An autonomous reduction in tariffs was carried out in several stages, even though, according to my taste, more could and should have been done than the Government and Parliament allowed.

Some of the milestones on the way should be mentioned. The first tariff reduction on April 1, 1955, concerned 700 separate tariffs; they were followed by the 'economic policy' tariff reductions, which on July 1, 1956, were widened to include all products of the economy. A top tariff was laid down of 21% of value, and for the rest a graded reduction of tariffs was undertaken. Simultaneously an individual reduction of tariffs was foreseen for different foodstuffs, so that the tariff reductions agreed at the G.A.T.T. Conference of 1956 came into force almost without exception before their due date.

The List of Liberalization

A complete account of the comprehensive attempts to free the movement of goods, payments and capital from restrictions would require a list of many other measures. For example, one should point to the introduction of a general exemption limit for smaller payments abroad; to the progressive reduction of the obligation to offer foreign currencies to the Government, the reduction in regulations on unpaid transactions for imports and exports; the removal of annoying individual permits for the transit trade. Also worth mentioning are the increasingly liberal regulations concerning foreign currency allowances for travel abroad, and the liberalization of the insurance business. Above all the reader should bear in mind the loosening of regulations concerning investment by foreigners in Germany, and investment abroad by Germans. Finally, the different stages of simplifying administrative procedures regarding imports and exports should be mentioned, and the permission for 'every man' to import, even though here the ideal of a total 'debureaucratization' has certainly not yet been achieved.

Without a doubt these measures are important steps on the way towards a free market within the area of the free world. Nevertheless there should be no illusions that freedom will find its final complete expression within the framework of collaboration in O.E.E.C. and E.P.U. and within the competence of these institutions. That I have to make this statement six years after the coming into force of E.P.U. is not meant to denigrate the great success which E.P.U. can claim for itself, in particular as regards the defeat of bilateralism. Thanks to this institution, with the help of G.A.T.T. and the International Monetary Fund, we have today achieved an appreciable increase in the international exchange of goods in spite of the lack of an international price level which works. Thus, for example, the exports of the O.E.E.C. countries have more than doubled, from DM 71 milliard in 1948 to about DM 150 milliard in 1956.

The Final Percentages are Decisive

The remaining obstacles in the path of realizing a free foreign trade must neither be overlooked nor diminished. As we approach this critical frontier, where changes will have serious and noticeable effects nationally, the opposition of the protectionists will become stronger. To put this in a simpler but clearer form: to liberalize from nothing to 79% is relatively easy. Up to this limit it is almost in the national interest to grant freedom. In liberalizing from 80% to 90% the situation becomes more problematical, but when we arrive at 90 to 96%, then every one per cent of freedom becomes almost a dramatic affair. In this sector the true sentiment has to prove itself, for it is here that liberalization leads to healing results. Too many European countries stumble before this last hurdle, and only a few have the courage to overcome it.

In the same way as there are few chances to achieve the removal of quantitative limitations within the framework of E.P.U., so, unfortunately, one can hardly count on the possibility that convertibility as an instrument for overcoming currency control can be achieved with the help of this institution. Within the system of E.P.U. one speaks of structural debtor countries and creditor countries. This makes one think that the basis of accounting is too narrow to find final, fruitful solutions. Someone may (as I do) love the 'European Payments Union' with all his heart; but he would not want to deny that a widening of this regionally limited payments union, which to be complete leads to a world-embracing order of freely convertible currencies, must in every circumstance be preferred.

The Sign of Evil

The spirit of liberalization and the sterility of currency control are like fire and water. Currency control of any kind symbolizes everything that is bad for man. Only through mismanagement can the individual national economies conceive the crippling idea of having to stop competition. With it foreign trade becomes more and more an exercise in government power politics, and fulfils less and less its task of serving the economic well-being of all citizens in a free world.

This statement immediately raises the problems of the present German foreign trade situation. Unlike the time when I first took office, this is no longer distinguished by the anxiety of how to pay for apparently vast imports through exports. On the contrary, today it is a case of dealing with the difficulties which have now existed for over five years—apart from some interruptions—of an almost steadily increasing export surplus. In 1956 imports rose by about 16%, while exports at a level of nearly DM 1·5 milliard more rose by about 21%. The assumption generally made in 1955, that in the future imports and exports would level out more and more, has thus been proved wrong. The gold and foreign currency reserves of the Bank Deutscher Länder have in the meantime grown to almost DM 18 milliard; the development can be seen in detail from this table:

Gold and Foreign Currency holding of the Bank Deutscher Länder (in DM milliards)

End of year	*Gold and Foreign Currency holdings*	*End of year*	*Gold and Foreign Currency holdings*
1949	+0·38	1953	+ 8·17
1950	−0·66	1954	+10·95
1951	+1·52	1955	+12·81
1952	+4·64	1956	+17·58

These surpluses certainly express the real productive efficiency of the German economy, which should be acknowledged. Yet it would be false to attribute these trends exclusively to this productive efficiency. To a considerable extent this surplus is an expression of the fact that West Germany compared with other national economies has resisted the temptation of inflation relatively more courageously, or, put differently, that we have sinned less in this sense than some of our trading partners.

Our trend of prices internationally compared is still relatively favourable. The cost of living index at present shows a level of 114 (1950 = 100), while our most important European partners in trade show price increases of 135, 140 and even more. Naturally this position offers great chances for exports. Yet it would be wrong to base export policy in the long run on the speculation that other countries will continue with this dangerous price policy.

With boom and full employment in almost all the main countries participating in world trade, we sense more than ever how greatly we lack a stabilizing factor beyond the limits of the domestic national economy. I come repeatedly to the same point: it is an odd, not to say a grotesque position that, in spite of different trends of prices in the individual national economies, the rates of exchange have remained immovable, as if between these two factors there existed no inner relation. Out of such a contradictory policy a considerable shift in the opportunities for export must inevitably result. In any case this is an important reason why the Federal Republic achieves ever-increasing export surpluses, which on the debit side make the taming of the boom at home more difficult.

Inevitably this development has led to the postponement of convertibility which I demanded again and again. In my view only the free convertibility of currencies can form a sane basis for a truly functioning free world market. According to all practical experience only in this way will a unified economic and financial policy which aims at stability be enforced in the national economies. With it the present distortions, as also the extreme positions of payments balances, would vanish.

The all-embracing function of convertible currencies can never be replaced in as complete a fashion by other measures. All attempts which have been directed in this way usually went no further than the beginning, and they have always remained unfinished. In my attempts to reduce the extreme creditor position of Germany I shall definitely not make use of those false measures of using currency policy as an instrument of trade policy. This seems to me to be no less harmful than the sterile attempt to neutralize the unrealistic rates of exchange by means of trade policy. In using such methods one asks: Who deceives whom? Here in practice there is only one way—to relinquish finally that practice which has led to a falsifying of the rates of exchange. Even though I am conscious of the political, tactical and technical difficulties and considerations, I regard it as absolutely essential to discuss this problem, which cries out for a solution on the broadest international terms.

We face today the great danger that the attempts to free world trade will become stuck, if we do not seriously begin to establish a working international currency order, and unless we agree on common rules for economic and trade policy.

Facing the Solution

As much as I am convinced that only in this manner can the imbalance be adjusted which has led to an extreme creditor position within the E.P.U. for Germany, I also see that the present situation demands independent German action. It would not become us in international discussions to brush aside all mistakes, or unrealistically to demand from our partners that they should bring their price levels down to the lower German level. What is expected of us is rather a way of changing our trade policies in such a manner that the debtor countries in particular, in spite of this price situation, will find better and new chances to export to Germany, or that in some other way the flow of their gold and foreign currency towards Germany will be slowed down. The following table of the monthly net movements on foreign exchange accounts gives a good idea of the size of these movements.

Net Movements in Foreign Exchange Accounts—1956
in DM Million

Monthly Averages

1950	−25	1954	+227
1951	+168	1955	+160
1952	+203	1956	+389
1953	+299		

In view of the present situation it seems to be almost essential to proceed logically to free the whole of foreign trade from Government shackles. Wherever possible liberalization must be enlarged (and not only within the E.P.U.), remaining quotas must be raised, and a further reduction in tariffs, which have repeatedly been cut in the recent past, is also desirable in the interest of Germany. Further, it should be demanded that everything possible should be done to make administration simpler.

A policy based on increasing imports must not lose itself in the thicket of narrow-minded domestic German sectional interests, since not one of the reductions in tariffs has so far worked out to our disadvantage. In the long run I also regard it as impossible to continue unchanged the import policy which we have so far pursued in agriculture.

The aim of arriving at an increase in our imports and simultaneously at a slackening of the tense position of our balance with the E.P.U. will have to be supported by a series of other measures. For example, the plans to increase stocks appreciably and the supply position of the German economy, which have already been discussed, should be borne in mind.

Generosity is Right

If every conceivable easing of imports is attempted in this manner, which in the long run will mean the abolishing of Government limitations of imports and the specially raised prices for some imported goods (foodstuffs), the question arises whether a reduction in the West German creditor position cannot also be achieved through financial measures: for example, through early repayments of debts. Proposals to establish foreign exchange credits to E.P.U. as a whole, or to individual foreign trade partners, or some other forms of financial help, need serious and sympathetic examination.

In these considerations we should remember that West Germany would here have the chance to express its gratitude for the aid granted to it in the early post-war period in a psychologically effective manner; and further, perhaps Germany could also settle its accounts from a purely political view in an honourable way. It is only logical if the chances of a truly private export of capital are examined, even though the possibilities in the immediate future should not be overestimated. In the Federal Republic itself a shortage in the capital market will persist in the foreseeable future.

Great Importance of Foreign Trade

To turn briefly to the trends of German exports in the past few years, the total volume of foreign trade in 1956 ran at DM 59 milliard. In interpreting this figure it should be remembered that in the year of the foundation of E.P.U.—in 1950—the value of imports and exports at DM 19·7 milliard was exactly a third of the present value, even though the Marshall Plan imports, which were not paid for by German efforts, were included. The proportion of the turnover of foreign trade of the gross national income has now grown by more than 30% (imports 16·3%; exports 16·9% = 32% of the gross national income); the proportion of imports in 1949 was 9·9%, of exports 5·2%—a total which is less than half of the present figures with a national income which has more than doubled. It is also remarkable that during past years foreign trade has constantly increased in importance within the framework of the whole economy; its share today is appreciably larger than in the period of the last pre-war years. In 1936 it was only 24% of the gross national income.

Imports as well as exports have constantly risen in recent years, the steady transition from total currency control and absolute bureaucratization of foreign trade to increasingly freer forms has shown clear advantages. The statistics of foreign trade prove the truth of this statement (cf. graph on page 63).

This favourable development allowed Germany to move back into third position in world trade. Though the lead of the U.S.A. is still considerable, that of Great Britain has decreased in a not unappreciable way during the past few years. Even a few years ago the German proportion of exports in world trade was much less than that of Canada and France.

Exports in Percentages of World Exports

	U.S.A.	*Great Britain*	*Federal Republic*	*France*	*Canada*
1950	18·3	11·0	3·6	5·5	5·3
1955	18·6	9·8	7·4	5·8	5·3
1956	20·7	9·8	8·1	5·1	5·4

The details of the West German share in the world market are clearly reflected in the following table:

Proportion of German Foreign Trade in the World Market
Federal Republic

I. in % of World Imports			*II. in % of World Exports*	
(1) 12·9		1913	(1) 13·1	
(1) 9·1	(2) 6·5	1929	(1) 9·9	(2) 7·5
(1) 8·1	(2) 5·7	1937	(1) 9·4	(2) 7·1
	4·6	1950		3·6
	4·4	1951		4·6
	4·8	1952		5·5
	4·9	1953		6·0
	5·8	1954		6·9
	6·7	1955		7·5
	6·9	1956		8·1

(1) From 1913 until 1937 for the German Reich.
(2) Estimated by the Ministry for Economic Affairs for the Federal Republic.

The picture given here would remain incomplete if we did not take a glimpse at the structure of our foreign trade. This is all the more necessary since foreign trade can only fulfil its task when it creates the basis for a complete balance of the national economy, and, in the special German situation, opens up the possibility of giving employment to millions of refugees.

It is significant that the proportion of finished goods has constantly increased and today constitutes 80% of total exports.

This development is also expressed in a constantly shrinking proportion of exports of raw materials, which is now barely 6%, while in 1948 a quarter of our export income came from the sale of raw materials.

Breakdown of Trade into Percentage Rates

	*1948**		*1953*		*1954*		*1955*		*1956*	
	Imps.	*Exps.*	*Imps.*	*Exps.*	*Imps.*	*Exps.*	*Imps.*	*Exps.*	*Imps.*	*Exps.*
Foodstuffs	49·2	2·0	36·6	2·6	37·0	2·3	31·2	2·7	32·7	2·7
Raw Materials	26·2	25·2	32·6	8·0	28·5	7·7	29·7	6·1	29·4	5·6
Half-finished Goods	13·7	29·5	15·2	14·7	18·0	13·1	20·1	12·7	18·7	12·4
Finished Goods	11·0	45·3	15·6	74·7	16·6	76·9	19·0	78·5	18·6	79·1

* Combined economic area

The favourable trend of our foreign trade is well expressed in the index of volume (1950 = 100 as a basis), and when internationally compared is particularly impressive. To avoid wrong conclusions all price movements have been eliminated from the picture given below.

Index of Export Volume (1950 = 100)

	Fed. Rep.	*France*	*Great Brit.*	*Norway*	*Switz.*	*Canada*	*U.S.A.*
1952	154	104	93	102	119	123	130
1954	223	125	99	120	136	117	133
1956*	335	113	125	157	183	139	153

*September or October figures

Chapter XVII

OUTLOOK: CONFIDENCE AND ANXIETIES

SINCE THIS BOOK makes no claim to be theoretically systematic, but is meant rather to give to the German people some sort of account of progress so far, it seems a good moment to look into the future. This is not a matter of economic prophecy, but rather an evaluation of the present forms of our economic and political life, and finally an attempt to outline clearly the various possible alternative courses for our social and national existence.

Here, therefore, I speak as the Minister for Economic Affairs, whose daily experience is that his work does not involve 'pure economics' alone but the whole sector of 'political economy'. Thus he has constantly to aim at conciliation and at finding a happy compromise between sound economic sense and scientific knowledge on the one hand and political and even party political demands on the other.

Even the title of this book, *Prosperity Through Competition*, presents a problem, for I am not convinced that even with the achievement of this aim the German people will live happily and will be satisfied, and that prosperity by itself can suffice in guaranteeing social harmony and order.

It is too much to expect of the Minister for Economic Affairs that he should be made responsible for the spiritual well-being of a whole people. After eight years of successful German reconstruction it is certainly true, in spite of some poverty here and there, that we no longer suffer greatly from material pressures, and that in this field lies the real and final solution to secure a happy future for our people. Yet we are enveloped in uncertainty, and not only our minds, but our hearts and souls are puzzled. Perhaps—I should like to say certainly—many of us in concentrating all our human energies in regaining and securing the material basis of our life may have gone wrong, and in so doing the sense of a true and proper scale of values has been lost. Whether we shall be able to answer this urgent question in a satisfactory manner will decide our fate.

Not by Bread Alone

If in spite of all efforts to awaken the dynamic forces in our national economy, I have repeatedly pointed to the fact that though the purpose of the economy can only be to serve consumption, this must not also become at one and the same time the only reason for our economic activity, I have to thank my old teacher, Wilhelm Vershofen, for this understanding. The sense of the economy flows from the all-embracing life of a people, with its ultimate roots in values which cannot be rationally grasped. This means, in other words, that at least the members of Western civilization are not at this time experiencing the benefit of a united and common attitude to life. If we succumb to an attempt to reduce the values of our surroundings to a formula, and aim at marketing it, we shall find that happiness cannot be bought.

However, is our present situation without hope and without a way out? Here, too, I find sufficient courage to deny it, since I believe and sense that doubt begins to gnaw in the minds of many, and an inner unrest presses towards greater reflection. I believe that this demand is overlaid, even sometimes suffocated, by collective statements which know nothing of such feelings and which often do not wish to recognize them, so as not to upset the much-famed common fronts. Clearly the human conscience cannot be harmonized with collective demands of organizations for power. That is why in public we hear only language which complains and demands, but lacks every inner truth. But this reflection leads us back to the practice of politics.

To be sure, the Minister for Economic Affairs would be wrong if he did not examine and take seriously the troubles of economic men. He will gladly admit, for example, that the demands for greater flexibility, for more economic security, for the easing of the excessive tax burden, for a just division of the national income, or for security of employment, each have some justification. Yet he has continuously to warn against demanding too much. Those who put forward these demands must be made conscious of the fact that so soon after the collapse not all the fruits can be ripe today, but that there is a tomorrow to wait for.

But it is just this wisdom and modesty, which could strengthen us, that are not among the German virtues; quite on the contrary, for with every improvement in our material existence we are ever more strongly affected by *hubris*, thus losing all sense of what is possible and becoming. Although no one can deny to his conscience that in eight years of reconstruction we have almost achieved the impossible, and that the Federal Government is honestly trying to let all sections of the population participate in progress and prosperity, sounds of dissatisfaction can be heard everywhere. To avoid all possible misunderstanding I should especially like to stress that these expressions of *hubris* do not come from those who earn their living only with difficulty to meet the bare necessities of life. Naturally there is no occasion here for rejoicing. To improve further the economic position of just these sections of the population, which still number millions, the continuation of our economic policy is essential. That is why it is particularly important to take a stand against threats to block this path, which amongst other things also provoke the *hubris* of which I have just spoken.

Freedom Means Sacrifices

This is my first and greatest anxiety for our German destiny. Things can be mastered if only the spirit can be tamed. And do not let us forget here that we do not live alone in the world, but that our well-being depends both on the fitting of our country into the free world without tensions, and on friendship and confidence between the peoples. It seems to me that those looking at us from outside no longer understand us, and that perhaps we even give the impression of a people which in its complacency appears to be losing the feeling for a common responsibility and for a true solidarity of the free world.

So far we are not guilty, and this judgment may even be wrong. But false and shrill voices are heard everywhere, assuming in their delusion that the rest of the world must grant a reunited Germany protection and security without our making our own sacrifices. Also other countries carry material burdens for the sake of preserving freedom, which but for the external threat they would certainly prefer to devote to purposes of social welfare. But in Germany we hear sounds as if the Government were working against the welfare of the people, because in order to secure this welfare it wishes to collaborate with the free world in defence of our freedom. Whoever has remained unmoved by the events in Poland and Hungary, and who in spite of this show of brutal lust for power still believes in right and law from that side, is beyond help. He must, however, also be denied the demand to frame German destiny.

That, then, is my second anxiety, that we all too easily delude ourselves, and that thus we not only gamble with our prosperity but also with our historical existence and our very life. A people who for the sake of freedom no longer wishes to make any material sacrifices will in the long run be condemned to extinction in history.

The European Community is Essential

In what I have just said it has been implied that we are as little in a position to find fruitful solutions by ourselves as any other nation. I do not want here to view the problem from political aspects, even though these before all others deserve to be taken seriously. The free peoples of Europe will only be able to preserve their influence in the world if, supported by the friendship of and in close community with the United States, they become conscious of an indissoluble political community. But how shall we achieve this aim, and to what extent are the forms of existing economic co-operation to be regarded as suitable and sufficient to develop their own political force?

Because I am looking to the future, I will not reminisce about the Messina Powers, the O.E.E.C., the E.P.U., G.A.T.T. and the International Monetary Fund, but instead deal immediately with the plan put forward by the six Messina Powers to create a Common Market and a Customs Union. I should like to state here, too, that there can hardly be a firmer defender of European integration and even of a European confederation than myself; from this position I claim the right to be critical where I seem to recognize dangers confronting this aim.

It is just because I know how much the principles of an economic order may determine the form and the spirit of a social or political community that I should like to see some guarantee that the Common Market will not result in European *dirigisme*, and there tie and paralyse progressive and expanding forces. On the contrary I should like to see in this larger European entity the flame kindled which will grant to all men and peoples participating in the Community the security of a happy political, social and economic future. Whoever chooses to believe that institutional ties alone would suffice, disregarding the spirit of economic collaboration, out of the natural forces of progressive development through mistakes and errors would probably delude himself completely.

We can see how decisive the economic principles of order are for the life and spirit of a nation, and also how far the different fates of the people in the wider sense become a disturbing element in collaboration between Governments. But I do not wish to imply that the rules concerning the Common Market —as I have described them here—are wrong in principle. Yet I cannot hide my belief that the various compromises so far reached do not in every particular correspond to my ideas of a free inter-governmental order. Even though in the area of the free world a common market must, of course, be based on the principles of competition, in reading the Treaty one senses in several places the fear of the consequences which might arise from it, and simultaneously one tries to insist on possibilities of escape from this principle. Since the tight spiritual link is lacking, the practical application of the Treaty will be decisively important, and not least the filling of the decisive positions, in order to arrive at a clear and decisive course.

Even if, as a result of my objections to the so-called 'social harmonization', a looser but no clearer version were achieved, I am afraid that with it a highly dangerous principle would be made legitimate and legalized. Not that I should not want every country to render maximum social support according to its productivity. But how does it look in practice? The tendency to inflation in individual countries (with fixed exchange rates) can largely be traced back to granting social benefits which put too great a strain on the abilities of the national economies. But since politically the adjustment of benefit payments never takes place downwards but always upwards, even those national economies which hitherto had managed to preserve a balanced order will either be pushed into this disastrous trend, or else will have to pay for the fault of others by suffering the use of protective clauses applied by their partners.

No Return to the Ideology of Big Blocs

If the 'Common Market' does not adopt a clearly liberal trade policy towards other economic areas, we are threatened with a return to other ideological conceptions of a truly unhappy past, viz., the splitting of the world into so-called big blocs which breathe the selfish spirit of economic inbreeding and which will sharpen the conflicts within the free world. Those who realize the dangers must not remain silent, and they cannot comfort themselves with the political pretext that everything will be well once the form has been cast which will force the partners together. Nothing has manifested itself more strongly in the past 30 or 40 years than the spirit of national selfishness and protectionism, and I would have wished that this evil could have been countered more decisively. Thus it is in the future form of European collaboration that my third anxiety lies.

Though my idea of the urgent need to return to freely convertible currencies has already been made sufficiently clear in these pages, I must yet once more mention the unhappy situation arising from a renunciation of good inter-governmental order. It is an illusion to believe that this form of freedom could automatically be realized of its own accord. On the contrary, it presupposes a conscious desire, and even more a definite attitude by national governments, and above all the evil idea that it can be left to the individual economies to pursue this or that economic or financial policy must be ended. Though the application of the best means can and, even perhaps must, be different from country to country, yet the main aim should be the responsibility of preserving a balanced order.

In view of this it still today seems at times as if individual countries held the magic belief that it was only necessary to abandon the basis of a good order to achieve better deeds. These mistaken ideas have brought us to the point where ideological political conceptions contrast with a responsible economic policy and even more with theoretical knowledge, and that falsely understood ideas of national sovereignty and of the primacy of politics come more and more to paralyse the energies and the will for order.

If knowledge forces us to move out of national isolation to progress to further integration, if governmental life in the narrow economic confines can only be pursued at the price of progress and social security, then above all the conclusion must be drawn that in the future national economies must be prevented from pursuing economic and trade policies which might disturb or disrupt relations between Governments. I should have liked therefore to have seen this special obligation put more clearly in the Treaty of the Common Market.

The picture presented today of extreme debtor and creditor positions in the European Payments Union should be sufficient warning against allowing the economic contradiction expressed by the completely different price trends with fixed exchange rates to continue. When further developments might lead to an even greater gap between national price levels, then in the long run no politician can disregard the theoretical knowledge that at that stage increasingly far-reaching measures will undermine freedom, and will necessarily lead to a return of the horrible forms of *dirigisme* of the past. So long as the people wish to remain on a basis of relations of free economic exchanges, every individual country is concerned with the behaviour of his partners. In particular it would in the long run prove impossible to integrate national economies if these cannot decide on uniform actions and attitudes.

So the good and the bad are closely linked in the Common Market. Either the spirit of freedom will triumph, and we shall then experience a happy, progressive and strong Europe, or else we shall try to link different systems by manipulations, when we shall miss the big chance of a true integration. A Europe which is dirigistically manipulated will itself paralyse the powers of resistance against the spirit of collectivism and allow the feeling for the benefits of freedom to perish.

Convertibility on the Widest Plane

Since the usefulness and fruitfulness of freely convertible currencies increase with the size of the area and the number of the participating economies, this problem, in the first place, cannot be solved on the plane of a Common Market; rather it will be necessary to act in concert and on the broadest possible terms with the United States, Great Britain and other European countries. It must be stated again and again that opposition from the sector of the national economy is almost invariably based on the use of the current economic factors as a yardstick to judge the venture, without allowing some imagination or intuition to point out that simply with changes in the currency system completely new factors will be brought into play.

This touches on my fourth anxiety, which is based on the conviction that the best national order and discipline no longer suffice to secure inner stability.

Freedom and Responsibility

I wrote above of the disastrous tendency towards planned economic *dirigisme* and the fear of competition: the same applies to some tendencies in the Federal Republic itself. Here I should like to point to earlier chapters of this book. The pressure for organizations, for collective plans and order can only succeed if the individual is prepared to cease speaking for himself and to forgo personal responsibility. It cannot be doubted that this serious development receives encouragement from politicians and even more from party politics. I do not allow myself any speculative reflections on whether it would be possible to arrive at a more balanced synthesis. To me only one thing seems to be certain: that in individual man the feeling for freedom cannot be separated from the consciousness of responsibility, while by agglomerating social-economic decisions less and less can be sensed of this link.

If, for example, I point to the demand for rendering a 'national income account',[10] I do not wish to deny that no useful ideas or valuable knowledge can be gained from it. Naturally economic policy has always taken such data into account. But the idea of a national economic account smacks of the unfailing fulfilment of a plan, and thus all too easily becomes not just a piece of knowledge but the basis of calculation for a fixed economic plan. For the rest we must not base ourselves on the belief that the economic power groups in their political role would tend to recognize results which would be uncomfortable for them.

Is the Second Industrial Revolution Coming?

My fifth anxiety, that we are being pushed from the right path by political forces, has a very real background in the way in which the socialist Opposition speculates about the increase in automation in industrial techniques. Even if I leave on one side the Jules Verne-like fantasies, it does not seem proper to speak of a 'second industrial revolution'. For one thing we are dealing here not with a definite event, but with a process without time-limit, and for another the social-political situation which favours this development is not marked by a surplus but on the contrary by a shortage of labour which will become even more acute. Though in some sectors a revolution of a technical kind is taking place, which will confine human performance to adjusting and supervising machinery, certainly no industrial revolution, which clearly awakens tragic memories of the social difficulties connected with the first establishment of machinery, will take place.

Nevertheless, far-reaching consequences will follow from the increasing demand for a technically skilled labour force. But this does not inevitably lead to revolutionary change; on the contrary in using modern techniques at least an enrichment of material human existence is to be expected. In theory the concepts of automation and mechanization should not be thrown indiscriminately into one pot. Automation (in so far as anything exact can be understood by it) will one day complete the progressive process of mechanization. Certainly this will bring difficult problems in its train as the chances and possibilities of automation vary for the different parts of any national economy. The differences in potential increases in productivity will thus become greater than they are today, and correspondingly the social problem of the working man's wages will gain in political importance.

Nor must it be forgotten that in the course of their industrial progress the less developed countries will jump certain stages of industrial techniques and will want to use modern machinery. But finally all will depend—if the countries of the Western world avail themselves of the opportunity—on the fact that their intellectual level provides them not only with the chance of using automatic machinery but also with the ability to invent it. We may have confidence that even in future not electronic brains but simply brains will determine the fate of man and peoples. If then automation favours a progressive integration of the national economies, since the use of this modern technique presupposes large areas with large masses of consumers, then this can greatly help towards satisfaction throughout the world.

The decisive question, however, is the use that can be made of this trend. The socialists who speak in one breath of atom technology, mechanization and automation, believe that the private sector of our economic order is unsuited or even useless for mastering the new problems on the technical as well as on the financial front. Already there reappears, according to the individual point of view, the patent nostrum, or the rattling skeleton of a State-directed economy. It cannot be disputed that the increasing amount of mechanization in the direction of automation will need an appreciable amount of capital. But the acceptance of this truth can rarely be seen in a political discussion about the sensible division of national income into consumption or capital investment.

Here the need for the State to take a hand, or for the State to take over, cannot be argued, for when neither the income of the private economy nor the private savings of all citizens prove sufficient to finance those investments regarded as necessary, the State also cannot find a way—unless, of course, it goes in for inflationary creation of credit, or uses taxation for the purposes of State investment and capital creation. But both these forms of capital creation mean dispossessing the citizen without compensation, and must therefore be firmly opposed. On this question, too, I have come to the conclusion that human freedom, initiative and enterprise promise more than State *dirigisme*.

Though at the beginning of these final reflections I have written of confidence and anxiety, I have given more space to the latter. This, however, does not mean that the anxieties which threaten our future can extinguish my confidence. This confidence can certainly not be pinned down as concrete plans or objectives, but is rooted in a spiritual attitude. Just as I could not pre-calculate the transition from the State-controlled economy to the social market economy, or predict what would happen in all its stages, and yet was immovably convinced of the propriety of this path, so too I have confidence that freedom, as the strongest human force and as its highest value, will conquer and triumph. Perhaps we should once again become conscious of the danger of losing it, in order to awaken new forces to save our most precious possession. It is my hope that those who realize the dangers that I have emphasized in this, the last chapter of my book, will be encouraged to think and act according to their convictions. They may then fight and resist, when it becomes a question of defending the market economic order which, against all attempts to undermine it, we regained in 1948. If so, this book will have served its purpose.

NOTES

[1] *Wirtschaft ohne Wunder*, 1953, Eugen-Rentsch Verlag, Erlenbach/Zurich.

[2] 'Government Appropriations for Relief in Occupied Areas', which provided some 'first-aid', as Germany was, of course, not covered by UNNRA.

[3] On the day of the announcement of currency reform all banking and savings accounts were frozen, to be re-opened only several weeks later. The result, briefly, was to wipe out 90% of all savings, since every RM 100 in the old account became DM 10 in the new when accounts were finally freed.

[4] While all accounts remained frozen, German Food Offices issued DM 60 per head of population on two separate occasions. This was done to enable people to pay for the necessities of life until the currency operation was completed.

[5] Bills of exchange of the 'Metallurgische Forschungsanstalt' were introduced by Dr. Schacht, who used them to finance German rearmament.

[6] *Mitbestimmung*, or joint management, is a method of giving workers a share in management at several levels. Originally first put forward in the Works Council Law of 1920, it went into cold storage under Hitler, to be revived and developed under Allied Occupation after 1945. Legislation which made detailed stipulation about joint management was passed by the German Parliament in 1951 and 1952. Joint management is fully effective only in the coal and steel industries, where one-half (but one-third only in other industries) of the Supervisory Board is elected by the Works Council (itself elected by the workers). The Works Council also elects one of the three members—the Labour Director—of the Board of Management.

[7] The law was based on the old German 'Guild Statutes' of each individual trade which, in modified form, have survived into the present time from the Middle Ages.

[8] The German Council of the Trades Union formulated a law which would have protected trade occupational designations. For example, no one could have called himself a carpenter without having passed an approved apprenticeship and otherwise conforming to an established standard.

[9] New legislation concerning insurance was passed early in 1957 by the German Parliament. One of its important provisions is that all social payments are adjustable with variations in the cost of living.

[10] This would correspond to something like Britain's National Income and Expenditure Account which has been issued as a Government publication annually since the war.

Table I

INDICES OF INDUSTRIAL NET PRODUCTION						
Basis: 1936=100						*Per working day*
Time			*Total Industry*	*Raw Materials and Producers' goods Industries*	*Capital goods Industries*	*Consumer goods Industries*
1948	1	Half year	50·2[2]	43·8	45·0	42·4
	2	,,	69·1[2]	64·1	67·2	60·8
1949	1	,,	82·9	78·5	84·2	78·2
	2	,,	94·0	83·7	87·4	92·6
1950	1	,,	99·7	93·1	98·8	103·4
	2	,,	121·7	113·5	126·5	123·1
1951	1	,,	127·7	120·9	144·6	129·1
	2	,,	134·3	122·3	149·9	128·3
1952	1	,,	133·4	122·8	161·5	120·3
	2	,,	145·3	129·9	167·2	139·9
1953	1	,,	145·6	132·3	167·6	142·2
	2	,,	161·5	141·2	178·4	161·5
1954	1	quarter	153·4	137·1	182·3	154·5
	2	,,	171·2	158·2	205·6	161·3
	3	,,	171·4	162·5	200·5	162·8
	4	,,	191·0	166·6	230·1	183·9
1955	1	,,	178·5	163·7	230·0	170·6
	2	,,	197·8	185·1	255·0	177·7
	3	,,	197·1	185·7	248·1	180·3
	4	,,	216·6	188·0	274·6	207·4
1956	1	,,	197·2	176·1	263·2	187·5
	2	,,	216·9	202·0	285·7	195·6
	3	,,	211·8	199·3	266·4	195·2
	4	,,	225·9[1]	197·0	280·5	219·0
1957	1	,,	212·9	195·2	275·1	206·1
	2	,,	230·3	211·1	298·0	209·5

[1] not final

[2] without main building trade

TABLE II

THE RECONSTRUCTION OF THE CAPITAL MARKET					
Sales (in Mill. DM.)					
Time	*Fixed interest-bearing securities*		*Shares*		*Fixed interest-bearing securities and shares since currency reform*
	annually	*since currency reform*	*annually*	*since currency reform*	
1948 21.6—31.12	18·6	18·6	0·5	0·5	19·1
1949	770·1	788·7	41·3	41·8	830·5
1950	676·5	1,465·2	51·2	93·0	1,558·2
1951	747·4	2,212·6	164·7	257·7	2,470·3
1952	1,557·7	3,770·3	259·3	517·0	4,287·3
1953	2,901·9	6,672·2	268·7	785·7	7,457·9
1954	4,691·0	11,363·2	453·0	1,238·7	12,601·9
1955	3,680·7	15,043·9	1,554·8	2,793·5	17,837·4
1956	2,564·2	17,608·1	1,837·5	4,631·0	22,239·1

TABLE III

THE THREE MOST IMPORTANT PRICE INDICES				
		Cost of living of medium consumer groups 1950=100	*Cost prices of industrial products 1950=100*	*Cost prices of agricultural products 1950/51=100*
July	1948	102	103	104
January	1949	110	106	121
July	1949	106	102	118
January	1950	102	100	107
July	1950	99	98	101
January	1951	102	111	103
July	1951	108	118	113
January	1952	112	123	120
July	1952	109	121	118
January	1953	110	120	114
July	1953	108	118	114
January	1954	107	116	115
July	1954	108	116	124
January	1955	110	118	120
July	1955	111	119	122
January	1956	112	120	124
July	1956	113	120	127
December	1956	114	124	126
July	1957	116	124	138